CHRISTMASTIDE

PRAYERS FOR ADVENT
THROUGH EPIPHANY
FROM *THE DIVINE HOURS*™

Ephesians 5:19 and 20:
Sing psalms and hymns and inspired songs among yourselves,
singing and chanting to the Lord in your hearts, always and everywhere giving
thanks to God who is our Father in the name of our Lord Jesus Christ.

CHRISTMASTIDE

PRAYERS FOR ADVENT
THROUGH EPIPHANY
FROM *THE DIVINE HOURS*™

Compiled and with a Preface by
Phyllis Tickle

Galilee

New York London Toronto Sydney Auckland

A GALILEE BOOK
PUBLISHED BY DOUBLEDAY
a division of Random House, Inc.

GALILEE and DOUBLEDAY are registered trademarks of Random House, Inc., and the portrayal
of a ship with a cross above a book is a trademark of Random House, Inc.

First Galilee edition published November 2003

Excerpted material contained herein previously appeared in *The Divine Hours: Prayers for
Autumn and Wintertime*, published by Doubleday in 2000.

The Library of Congress has cataloged the hardcover edition of *The Divine Hours* as follows:
Divine hours: prayers for autumn and wintertime / compiled and with a preface by
Phyllis Tickle.—1st ed.
p.   cm.
Includes index.
1. Prayers.   2. Winter—Prayer-books and devotions—English.
I. Tickle, Phyllis
BV135.W56D58 2000
264'.15—dc21   99-046160

ISBN 978-0-385-51026-4

PRINTED IN THE UNITED STATES OF AMERICA

Contents

"Whoever sings, prays twice."

—ST. AUGUSTINE

An Introduction to
This Manual

Despite its title, the book you are holding in your hands is not a book of prayers in the usual sense of that term. That is, while this is indeed a collection of prayers and while the ancient words it contains are intended for use during the four weeks of Advent and the twelve days of Christmas, it is neither a random collection of Psalms, hymns, scripture, and prayers, nor is it arranged for random or casual use. Rather, this is a manual—a manual for doing fixed-hour prayer during the holy weeks of wintertime.

Sometimes called "keeping the daily offices" or "observing the divine hours," fixed-hour prayer, together with the hallowing of the Sabbath and the celebration of Communion, is the oldest and most authentic form of Christian spiritual practice. Like Sabbath observance and participation in the communal Passover meal, it comes to us out of ancient Judaism and by way of the devout, practicing Jews who were first Jesus' disciples and then, after the resurrection, His evangelists and missionaries. Through them and through the early regimens of the Church, all three practices—Sabbath, Communion, and fixed-hour prayer—were passed to us and have remained with us as central, though adapted, parts of Christian discipline and Christian worship.

For me, and based on my own years of "praying the hours," fixed-hour prayer is best understood as a kind of free, widely windowed, and open passageway between two places—one very physical and the other very virtual. Put more concretely, observing the divine hours allows our human awareness or mental focus to move back and forth on a daily basis and in a disciplined way from attending to the necessary bustle of each day of our lives to attending to the eternal timelessness and magnificence of divine life.

By the time of Our Lord, the hours for such praying had become "fixed" into a regimen almost identical to that followed by the Christian Communion today. The hours of six and nine in the morning, noon, three in the afternoon, sunset, retirement, and sometimes midnight were, as they still are, the ones when the faithful—either alone or together—stopped what they were doing, invoked the presence of God, praised him with the beloved hymns of two or three appointed Psalms, meditated on a piece of holy scripture, sang another hymn, and returned to the workaday world aware of the God to Whom they belonged and of the privilege of worship that had just been granted them.

While we do not have in the Gospels any record of Our Lord's keeping fixed-hour prayer, we must assume that as a devout Jew, He did. We certainly know that the disciples did. Thus, the Spirit fell as tongues of fire upon them on Pentecost while, as we are told in Acts, they were gathered for prayer "at the third hour of the day"—that is, at nine o'clock in the morning. Christianity spread beyond the confines of Judaism primarily because of a vision granted Peter early in the faith's history. That vision involved a sheet filled with unclean or forbidden, but edible, creatures and a heavenly voice instructing Peter to kill and eat. Three times Peter refused, saying that he had never broken halakah or Jewish dietary law in his life; and three times the voice answered by saying, "What God has called holy, humankind must not call profane." Just as the sheet and voice withdrew for the third time, there came a knock at the door below. A Gentile, the servant of a Gentile, was there to beg Peter "to come over into Macedonia" and instruct them in this new way of salvation. It is a story we all remember. What we often forget to remember is that the knock of Cornelius's servant came from downstairs only because Peter was upstairs. That is, the story says, he had gone up to the rooftop at twelve o'clock for what? For noonday prayers. In the same way, of course, the first healing miracle after Jesus' Ascension occurred on the steps of the Temple as Peter and John, on their way to ninth hour (three o'clock) prayers, passed and took pity upon a cripple begging there.

Because the words and hymns of the divine hours are ancient and because they are the hallowed verbal heritage of our faith, their use is not subject to much modification and/or license. Because they are words, however, and because the words appointed for each fixed hour vary not only from one another but also in accordance with the place of their observance in each day in the Church's calendar (thus, Advent's offices differ in content from one another and from those of Christmas), they require a degree of literacy. One must be able to read at some more or less fundamental level in order to follow the changing course of each fixed hour.

As Rome grew increasingly weaker, eventually falling into disrepair, and as the known world spun down into the Dark Ages, so too did literacy retreat from the citizenry of Europe, becoming instead the often rote possession of certain communities of monks. Thus, while the peasant faithful could observe the Sabbath without reading and could attend the Mass without being literate, they could no longer "pray" the divine hours. The observation of the offices passed, along with literacy, into the monasteries. Up until fairly recently, many American Christians, especially Protestant ones, thought of the daily offices almost entirely as something that monks did and that involved rote, albeit glorious, Gregorian chant. Even Protestants whose faith resonated with that of the praying couple in Jean-François Millet's popular painting *The Angelus* failed to perceive any identity between themselves and the artist's subject, between their own history and that vestigial and humble fragment of what had once been part of the office of sundown.

During the last decades of the twentieth century, however, that sense of alienation began to diminish, and lay Christians of every persuasion started to reclaim the divine hours as the third and missing piece in original Christian practice. This manual, like the larger ones from which it is abstracted, was born out of the urgency of that return. Using it requires no instruction beyond that printed on each page itself, save for three things.

First, many Christians—especially Protestant ones who are accustomed to singing the fixed words of their worship—find themselves more comfortable singing both the time-honored and fixed words of the Psalter and the beloved hymns of the vesper office. There is, in the midst of each line of the Psalms, a small asterisk that was originally set there as pointing in the Jewish psalter. On the last syllable before this asterisk, the singer will want to raise his or her monotonal pitch by a single note, just as the last syllable before the end of a line is lowered a note. Your ear will carry you from there to some of the nuisances that lie beyond this primary rule.

Second, a wise rabbi once told me that it is not how many prayers we don't say that matters to God, but rather how many we do. That is important for all of us, but especially for beginners. If this is your first attempt to return to this most ancient of Christian practices, it is wise to remember that you are entering into a discipline and, like all disciplines, this one sits hard and heavy upon one at times. There are hours you will miss and/or some that you can't even begin to figure out how to observe. That is all right, for either the joy will carry you into greater joy and transmute the discipline into privilege, or you will find yourself simply the wiser and the richer for such experience as you have had. As the rabbi said, that is what matters ultimately.

And last as well as most central, perhaps, is this: Though most contemporary Christians of necessity will observe many offices alone—that is, without the participation in real place and time of other Christians—there are always those fortunate ones of us and/or those blessed occasions in our daily lives when the office can be kept in company with others. When that happens, the pronouns may, and should, be changed from singular to plural. Many of us make that change at all times, however, because (and this is perhaps the most obvious gift of the divine hours) when one prays the hours, one is using the exact words, phrases, and petitions that have informed our faith for centuries. In addition, we are also using the exact words, phrases, and petitions that were offered just an hour earlier by our fellow Christians in the prior time zone and that, in an hour, will be picked up and offered again by our fellow believers in the next time zone. The result is a constant cascade before the throne of God of the "unceasing prayer" to which St. Paul urged us. The result also is the communion of the saints fully realized in words both horizontally through the ages and vertically within this day and hour.

Even so, come, Lord Jesus.

The Symbols and Conventions Used in This Manual

NJB: New Jerusalem Bible

KJV: King James Bible

BCP: Book of Common Prayer †

❖:   a medley or hymning of the canonical Psalms as assembled by Dr. Fred
        Bassett

§:   from the work of St. Augustine

†:   adapted from the Book of Common Prayer

*:   indicate the poetic breaks in the original Hebrew

CHRISTMASTIDE

PRAYERS FOR ADVENT
THROUGH EPIPHANY
FROM *THE DIVINE HOURS*™

Ephesians 5:19 and 20:
Sing psalms and hymns and inspired songs among yourselves,
singing and chanting to the Lord in your hearts, always and everywhere giving
thanks to God who is our Father in the name of our Lord Jesus Christ.

The season of Advent, which contains four Sundays, begins, in the Western church, on the Sunday nearest to November 30. The first Sunday of Advent is also the first day of the new liturgical, or church, year.

The Lord's Prayer
Our Father, who art in heaven, hallowed be your Name.
May your kingdom come, and your will be done, on earth as in heaven.
Give us today our daily bread.
Forgive us our sins as we forgive those who sin against us.
Lead us not into temptation, but deliver us from evil;
for yours are the kingdom and the power and the glory
forever and ever. *Amen.*

Compline Prayers for Advent Are Located on Page 127.

The Following Holy Days Occur in Advent:
The Feast of St. Thomas, the Apostle: *December 21*

Advent

The Morning Office   **To Be Observed on the Hour or Half Hour**
                                     Between 6 and 9 a.m.

The Call to Prayer
Hallelujah! I will give thanks to the LORD with my whole heart,* in the assembly of
    the upright, in the congregation.

Psalm 111:1

The Request for Presence
Let them know that you, whose Name is YAHWEH,* you alone are the Most High
    over all the earth.

Psalm 83:18

The Greeting
I shall always wait in patience,* and shall praise you more and more.

Psalm 71:14

The Refrain for the Morning Lessons
The same stone which the builders rejected* has become the chief cornerstone.

Psalm 118:22

A Reading   *During Advent the Church celebrates the messianic works of the
                         Hebrew prophets, especially that of the prophet Isaiah. Advent
                         emphasizes as well the promise of the second coming of the
                         Messiah in kingly triumph.*

Jesus taught us, saying: "As it was in Noah's day, so will it be when the Son of
    man comes. For in those days before the Flood people were eating, drinking,
    taking wives, taking husbands, right up to the day Noah went into the ark, and
    they suspected nothing till the Flood came and swept them away. This is what
    it will be like when the Son of man comes."

Matthew 24:37–39

The Refrain
The same stone which the builders rejected* has become the chief cornerstone.

The Morning Psalm   *In His Time Shall the Righteous Flourish*
Give the King your justice, O God,* and your righteousness to the King's Son;
That he may rule your people righteously* and the poor with justice;
That the mountains may bring prosperity to the people,* and the little hills bring
    righteousness.
He shall defend the needy among the people;* he shall rescue the poor and crush
    the oppressor.
He shall live as long as the sun and moon endure,* from one generation to another.
He shall come down like rain upon the mown field,* like showers that water the
    earth.

In his time shall the righteous flourish;* there shall be abundance of peace till the
  moon shall be no more.
He shall rule from sea to sea,* and from the River to the ends of the earth.

Psalm 72:1–8

The Refrain
The same stone which the builders rejected* has become the chief cornerstone.

The Cry of the Church
Even so, come, Lord Jesus!

The Lord's Prayer

The Prayer Appointed for the Week
Almighty God, give all of us grace to cast away the works of darkness, and put on
  the armor of light, now in the time of this mortal life in which your Son Jesus
  Christ came to visit us in great humility; that in the last day, when he shall
  come again in his glorious majesty to judge both the living and the dead, we
  may rise to the life immortal; through him who lives and reigns with you and
  the Holy Spirit, one God, now and for ever. *Amen.*†

The Concluding Prayer of the Church
Lord God, almighty and everlasting Father, you have brought me in safety to this
  new day: Preserve me with your mighty power, that I may not fall into sin, nor
  be overcome by adversity; and in all I do direct me to the fulfilling of your purpose; through Jesus Christ my Lord. *Amen.*†

The Midday Office   To Be Observed on the Hour or Half Hour
                                          Between 11 a.m. and 2 p.m.

The Call to Prayer
God is the Lord; he has shined upon us;* form a procession with branches up to
  the horns of the altar.

Psalm 118:27

The Request for Presence
Open my lips, O Lord,* and my mouth shall proclaim your praise.

Psalm 51:16

The Greeting
Let all who seek you rejoice and be glad in you;* let those who love your salvation
  say for ever, "Great is the Lord!"

Psalm 70:4

The Refrain for the Midday Lessons
The words of the Lord are tried in the fire;* he is a shield to all who trust in him.

Psalm 18:31

A Reading

The vision of Isaiah son of Amoz, concerning Judah and Jerusalem: It will happen in the final days that the mountain of YAHWEH's house will rise higher than the mountains and tower above the heights. Then all the nations will stream to it, many peoples will come to it and say, 'Come, let us go up to the mountain of YAHWEH, to the house of the God of Jacob that he may teach us his ways so that we may walk in his paths.' For the Law will issue from Zion and the word of YAHWEH from Jerusalem. Then he will judge between the nations and arbitrate between many peoples. They will hammer their swords into plowshares and their spears into sickles. Nation will not lift sword against nation, no longer will they learn to make war. House of Jacob, come, let us walk in YAHWEH's light.

Isaiah 2:1–5

The Refrain

The words of the LORD are tried in the fire;* he is a shield to all who trust in him.

The Midday Psalm   *There Are the Thrones of the House of David*

I was glad when they said to me,* "Let us go to the house of the LORD."
Now our feet are standing* within your gates, O Jerusalem.
Jerusalem is built as a city* that is at unity with itself;
To which the tribes go up, the tribes of the LORD,* the assembly of Israel, to praise the Name of the LORD.
For there are the thrones of judgment,* the thrones of the house of David.
Pray for the peace of Jerusalem:* "May they prosper who love you.
Peace be within your walls* and quietness within your towers.
For my brethren and companions' sake,* I pray for your prosperity.
Because of the house of the LORD our God,* I will seek to do you good."

Psalm 122

The Refrain

The words of the LORD are tried in the fire;* he is a shield to all who trust in him.

The Small Verse

Blessed be the Lord God of Israel for he has visited and delivered us. Alleluia, alleluia, alleluia.

Traditional

The Lord's Prayer

The Prayer Appointed for the Week

Almighty God, give all of us grace to cast away the works of darkness, and put on the armor of light, now in the time of this mortal life in which your Son Jesus Christ came to visit us in great humility; that in the last day, when he shall come again in his glorious majesty to judge both the living and the dead, we may rise to the life immortal; through him who lives and reigns with you and the Holy Spirit, one God, now and for ever. *Amen.*†

The Concluding Prayer of the Church

O God, you make me glad with the weekly remembrance of the glorious resurrection of your Son my Lord: Give me this day such blessing through my worship of you, that the week to come may be spent in your favor; through Jesus Christ our Lord. *Amen.*†

The Vespers Office   **To Be Observed on the Hour or Half Hour Between 5 and 8 p.m.**

The Call to Prayer

Enter his gates with thanksgiving; go into his courts with praise;* give thanks to him and call upon his Name.

Psalm 100:3

The Request for Presence

May God give us his blessing,* and may all the ends of the earth stand in awe of him.

Psalm 67:7

The Greeting

We give you thanks, O God, we give you thanks,* calling upon your Name and declaring all your wonderful deeds.

Psalm 75:1

The Hymn   *Come, Thou Long Expected Jesus*

Come, thou long expected Jesus,	Born your people to deliver,
Born to set your people free;	Born a child, and yet a king,
From our fears and sins release us,	Born to reign in us for ever,
Let us find our rest in thee.	Now your gracious kingdom bring.
Israel's strength and consolation,	By your own eternal spirit
Hope of all the earth thou art:	Rule in all our hearts alone;
Dear desire of every nation,	By your all sufficient merit
Joy of every longing heart.	Raise us to your glorious throne.

Charles Wesley

The Refrain for the Vespers Lessons

I will fulfill my vows to the LORD* in the presence of all his people.

Psalm 116:16

The Vespers Psalm   *Restore Us, O God of Hosts*

Hear, O Shepherd of Israel, leading Joseph like a flock;* shine forth, you that are enthroned upon the cherubim.

In the presence of Ephraim, Benjamin, and Manasseh,* stir up your strength and come to help us.

Restore us, O God of hosts;* show the light of your countenance, and we shall be saved.

O LORD God of hosts,* how long will you be angered despite the prayers of your people?

You have fed them with the bread of tears;* you have given them bowls of tears to drink.

You have made us the derision of our neighbors,* and our enemies laugh us to scorn.

Restore us, O God of hosts;* show the light of your countenance, and we shall be saved.

Psalm 80:1–7

The Refrain
I will fulfill my vows to the LORD* in the presence of all his people.

The Cry of the Church
Even so, come, Lord Jesus!

The Lord's Prayer

The Prayer Appointed for the Week
Almighty God, give all of us grace to cast away the works of darkness, and put on the armor of light, now in the time of this mortal life in which your Son Jesus Christ came to visit us in great humility; that in the last day, when he shall come again in his glorious majesty to judge both the living and the dead, we may rise to the life immortal; through him who lives and reigns with you and the Holy Spirit, one God, now and for ever. *Amen.*†

The Concluding Prayer of the Church
Lord God, whose Son our Savior Jesus Christ, triumphed over the powers of death and prepared for us our place in the new Jerusalem: Grant that I, who have this day given thanks for his resurrection, may praise you in the City of which he is the light, and where he lives and reigns for ever and ever. *Amen.*†

The Morning Office **To Be Observed on the Hour or Half Hour Between 6 and 9 a.m.**

The Call to Prayer
Let my mouth be full of your praise* and your glory all the day long.
Psalm 71:8

The Request for Presence
Your word is a lantern to my feet* and a light upon my path.
Psalm 119:105

The Greeting
O God, you have taught me since I was young,* and to this day I tell of your wonderful works.

Psalm 71:17

The Refrain for the Morning Lessons
This is the LORD's doing,* and it is marvelous in our eyes.

Psalm 118:23

A Reading
And he went on to tell his parable, 'A man planted a vineyard and leased it to tenants and went abroad for a long while. When the right time came, he sent a servant to the tenant to get his share of the produce of the vineyard. But the tenants thrashed him, and sent him away empty-handed. But he went on to send a second servant; they thrashed him too and treated him shamefully and sent him away empty-handed. He still went on to send a third; they wounded this one too, and threw him out. Then the owner of the vineyard thought, "What am I to do? I will send them my own beloved son. Perhaps they will respect him." But when the tenants saw him they put their heads together saying, "This is the heir, let us kill him so that the inheritance will be ours." So they threw him out of the vineyard and killed him.
'Now what will the owner of the vineyard do to them? He will come and make an end of these tenants and give the vineyard to others.' Hearing this they said, 'God forbid!' But he looked hard at them and said, 'Then what does this text in scripture mean: *The stone which the builders rejected has become the chief cornerstone?* Anyone who falls on that stone will be dashed to pieces; anyone it falls on will be crushed.'

Luke 20:9–18

The Refrain
This is the LORD's doing,* and it is marvelous in our eyes.

The Morning Psalm   *Early in the Morning I Make My Appeal*
Give ear to my words, O LORD;* consider my meditation.
Hearken to my cry for help, my King and my God,* for I make my prayer to you.
In the morning, LORD, you hear my voice;* early in the morning I make my appeal
    and watch for you.
For you are not a God who takes pleasure in wickedness,* and evil cannot dwell
    with you.
Braggarts cannot stand in your sight;* you hate all those who work wickedness.
You destroy those who speak lies;* the bloodthirsty and deceitful, O LORD, you
    abhor.
But as for me, through the greatness of your mercy I go into your house;* I will
    bow down toward your holy temple in awe of you.

Psalm 5:1–7

The Refrain
This is the LORD's doing,* and it is marvelous in our eyes.

The Cry of the Church
Even so, come, Lord Jesus!

The Lord's Prayer

The Prayer Appointed for the Week

Almighty God, give all of us grace to cast away the works of darkness, and put on the armor of light, now in the time of this mortal life in which your Son Jesus Christ came to visit us in great humility; that in the last day, when he shall come again in his glorious majesty to judge both the living and the dead, we may rise to the life immortal; through him who lives and reigns with you and the Holy Spirit, one God, now and for ever. *Amen.*✝

The Concluding Prayer of the Church

Lord God, almighty and everlasting Father, you have brought me in safety to this new day: Preserve me with your mighty power, that I may not fall into sin, nor be overcome by adversity; and in all I do direct me to the fulfilling of your purpose; through Jesus Christ my Lord. *Amen.*✝

The Midday Office   To Be Observed on the Hour or Half Hour Between 11 a.m. and 2 p.m.

The Call to Prayer

Blessed be the LORD, the God of Israel, from everlasting and to everlasting;* and let all the people say, "Amen!" Hallelujah!

Psalm 106:48

The Request for Presence

Turn to me and have mercy upon me;* give your strength to your servant; and save the child of your handmaid.

Psalm 86:16

The Greeting

O LORD, your love endures for ever;* do not abandon the works of your hands.

Psalm 138:9

The Refrain for the Midday Lessons

The fear of the LORD is the beginning of wisdom;* those who act accordingly have a good understanding; his praise endures for ever.

Psalm 111:10

A Reading

Listen now, House of David: are you not satisfied with trying human patience that you should try God's patience too? The Lord will give you a sign in any case: It is this: the young woman is with child and will give birth to a son whom she will call Immanuel. On curds and honey will he feed until he knows how to refuse the bad and choose the good.

Isaiah 7:13–15

The Refrain

The fear of the LORD is the beginning of wisdom;* those who act accordingly have a good understanding; his praise endures for ever.

The Midday Psalm   *The LORD Has Pleasure in Those Who Fear Him*

Hallelujah! How good it is to sing praises to our God!* how pleasant it is to honor
 him with praise!

The LORD rebuilds Jerusalem;* he gathers the exiles of Israel.

He heals the brokenhearted* and binds up their wounds.

He counts the number of the stars* and calls them all by their names.

Great is our LORD and mighty in power;* there is no limit to his wisdom.

The LORD lifts up the lowly,* but casts the wicked to the ground.

Sing to the LORD with thanksgiving;* make music to our God upon the harp.

He is not impressed by the might of a horse;* he has no pleasure in the strength of
 a man;

But the LORD has pleasure in those who fear him,* in those who await his gracious
 favor.

Psalm 147:1–7, 11–12

The Refrain

The fear of the LORD is the beginning of wisdom;* those who act accordingly have
 a good understanding; his praise endures for ever.

The Small Verse

The Lord is my shepherd and nothing is wanting to me. In green pastures He hath
 settled me.

THE SHORT BREVIARY

The Lord's Prayer

The Prayer Appointed for the Week

Almighty God, give all of us grace to cast away the works of darkness, and put on
 the armor of light, now in the time of this mortal life in which your Son Jesus
 Christ came to visit us in great humility; that in the last day, when he shall
 come again in his glorious majesty to judge both the living and the dead, we
 may rise to the life immortal; through him who lives and reigns with you and
 the Holy Spirit, one God, now and for ever. *Amen.†*

The Concluding Prayer of the Church

Heavenly Father, you have promised to hear what we ask in the Name of your
 Son: Accept and fulfill my petitions, I pray, not as I ask in my ignorance, nor as
 I deserve in my sinfulness, but as you know and love me in your Son Jesus
 Christ our Lord. *Amen.†*

The Vespers Office   **To Be Observed on the Hour or Half Hour
 Between 5 and 8 p.m.**

The Call to Prayer

Sing to the LORD a new song;* sing to the LORD, all the whole earth.

For great is the LORD and greatly to be praised;* he is more to be feared than all
 gods.

Psalm 96:1, 4

The Request for Presence
Give ear, O LORD, to my prayer,* and attend to the voice of my supplications.

Psalm 86:6

The Greeting
Your way, O God, is holy;* who is so great a god as our God?

Psalm 77:13

The Hymn   *Rejoice, Rejoice, Believers!*
Rejoice! Rejoice, believers, and let your lights appear!
The evening is advancing, and darker night is near.
The Bridegroom is arising, and soon he will draw nigh;
Up, watch in expectation! At midnight comes the cry.

See that your lamps are burning, replenish them with oil;
Look now for your salvation, the end of sin and toil.
The marriage feast is waiting, the gates wide open stand;
Rise up, you heirs of glory, the Bridegroom is at hand!

Our hope and expectation, O Jesus, now appear;
Arise, you Sun so longed for, above this darkened sphere!
With hearts and hands uplifted, we plead, O Lord, to see
The day of earth's redemption, and ever be with thee!

Laurentis Laurenti

The Refrain for the Vespers Lessons
He will judge the world with righteousness* and the peoples with his truth.

Psalm 96:13

The Vespers Psalm   *Light Shines in the Darkness for the Upright*
Light shines in the darkness for the upright;* the righteous are merciful and full of
   compassion.
It is good for them to be generous in lending* and to manage their affairs with
   justice.
For they will never be shaken;* the righteous will be kept in everlasting
   remembrance.
They will not be afraid of any evil rumors;* their heart is right; they put their trust
   in the Lord.
Their heart is established and will not shrink,* until they see their desire upon
   their enemies.
They have given freely to the poor,* and their righteousness stands fast for ever;
   they will hold up their head with honor.
The wicked will see it and be angry; they will gnash their teeth and pine away;*
   the desires of the wicked will perish.

Psalm 112:4–10

The Refrain
He will judge the world with righteousness* and the peoples with his truth.

The Small Verse
Come forth, O Christ, and help me. For your name's sake deliver me.

The Lord's Prayer

The Prayer Appointed for the Week
Almighty God, give all of us grace to cast away the works of darkness, and put on
   the armor of light, now in the time of this mortal life in which your Son Jesus
   Christ came to visit us in great humility; that in the last day, when he shall
   come again in his glorious majesty to judge both the living and the dead, we
   may rise to the life immortal; through him who lives and reigns with you and
   the Holy Spirit, one God, now and for ever. *Amen.*†

The Concluding Prayer of the Church
O God of unchangeable power and eternal light: Look favorably on your whole
   Church, that wonderful and sacred mystery; by the effectual working of your
   providence, carry out in tranquility the plan of salvation; let the whole world
   see and know that things which are cast down are being raised up, and things
   which had grown old are being made new, and that all things are being
   brought to their perfection by him though whom all things were made, your
   Son Jesus Christ our Lord; who lives and reigns with you, in the unity of the
   Holy Spirit, one God, for ever and ever. *Amen.*†

The Morning Office   **To Be Observed on the Hour or Half Hour**
Between 6 and 9 a.m.

The Call to Prayer
Come, let us sing to the LORD;* let us shout for joy to the Rock of our salvation.
Let us come before his presence with thanksgiving* and raise a loud shout to him
   with psalms.

Psalm 95:1-2

The Request for Presence
Show us the light of your countenance, O God,* and come to us.

based on Psalm 67:1

The Greeting
To you I lift up my eyes,* to you enthroned in the heavens.
As the eyes of servants look to the hand of their masters,* and the eyes of a maid to
   the hand of her mistress,
So our eyes look to the LORD our God,* until he shows us his mercy.

Psalm 123:1-3

The Refrain for the Morning Lessons
I will bear witness that the LORD is righteous;* I will praise the Name of the LORD
   Most High.

Psalm 7:18

A Reading

Jesus said: "For this is how God loved the world: he gave his only Son, so that everyone who believes in him may not perish but may have eternal life. For God sent his Son into the world not to judge the world, but so that through him the world might be saved. No one who believes in him will be judged; but whoever does not believe is judged already, because that person does not believe in the Name of God's only Son."

John 3:16–18

The Refrain

I will bear witness that the LORD is righteous;* I will praise the Name of the LORD Most High.

The Morning Psalm   *The LORD Is a Shield About Me*

LORD, how many adversaries I have!* how many there are who rise up against me!
How many there are who say of me,* "There is no help for him in his God."
But you, O LORD, are a shield about me;* you are my glory, the one who lifts up my head.
I call aloud upon the LORD,* and he answers me from his holy hill;
I lie down and go to sleep;* I wake again, because the LORD sustains me.

Psalm 3:1–5

The Refrain

I will bear witness that the LORD is righteous;* I will praise the Name of the LORD Most High.

The Small Verse

Keep me, Lord, as the apple of your eye and carry me under the shadow of your wings.

Traditional

The Lord's Prayer

The Prayer Appointed for the Week

Almighty God, give all of us grace to cast away the works of darkness, and put on the armor of light, now in the time of this mortal life in which your Son Jesus Christ came to visit us in great humility; that in the last day, when he shall come again in his glorious majesty to judge both the living and the dead, we may rise to the life immortal; through him who lives and reigns with you and the Holy Spirit, one God, now and for ever. *Amen.*†

The Concluding Prayer of the Church

Lord God, almighty and everlasting Father, you have brought me in safety to this new day: Preserve me with your mighty power, that I may not fall into sin, nor be overcome by adversity; and in all I do direct me to the fulfilling of your purpose; through Jesus Christ my Lord. *Amen.*†

The Midday Office   **To Be Observed on the Hour or Half Hour**
                                          Between 11 a.m. and 2 p.m.

The Call to Prayer
Open my lips, O Lord,* and my mouth shall proclaim your praise.

Psalm 51:16

The Request for Presence
You are my helper and my deliverer;* do not tarry, O my God.

Psalm 40:19

The Greeting
Hosanna, LORD, hosanna!* LORD, send us now success.
Blessed is he who comes in the name of the Lord;* we bless you from the house of
    the LORD.

Psalm 118:25–26

The Refrain for the Midday Lessons
Whom have I in heaven but you?* and having you I desire nothing upon earth.

Psalm 73:25

A Reading
The days are coming—declares YAHWEH—when the plowman will tread on the
    heels of the reaper and the treader of grapes on the heels of the sower of seed,
    and the mountains will run with new wine and the hills all flow with it. I shall
    restore the fortunes of my people Israel; they will rebuild the ruined cities and
    live in them, they will plant vineyards and drink their wine, they will lay out
    gardens and eat their produce. And I shall plant them in their own soil and
    they will never be uprooted again from the country which I have given them,
    declares YAHWEH, your God.

Amos 9:13–15

The Refrain
Whom have I in heaven but you?* and having you I desire nothing upon earth.

The Midday Psalm   *Give Praise You Servants of the LORD*
Hallelujah! Give praise, you servants of the LORD;* praise the Name of the LORD.
Let the Name of the LORD be blessed,* from this time forth for evermore.
From the rising of the sun to its going down* let the Name of the LORD be praised.
The LORD is high above all nations,* and his glory above the heavens.

Psalm 113:1–4

The Refrain
Whom have I in heaven but you?* and having you I desire nothing upon earth.

The Small Verse
My help is in the Name of the Lord who made the heavens and the earth. What
    then shall I fear, of what shall I be afraid?

Traditional

The Lord's Prayer

The Prayer Appointed for the Week
Almighty God, give all of us grace to cast away the works of darkness, and put on the armor of light, now in the time of this mortal life in which your Son Jesus Christ came to visit us in great humility; that in the last day, when he shall come again in his glorious majesty to judge both the living and the dead, we may rise to the life immortal; through him who lives and reigns with you and the Holy Spirit, one God, now and for ever. *Amen.*✝

The Concluding Prayer of the Church
Direct me, O Lord, in all my doings with your most gracious favor, and further me with your continual help; that in all my work begun, continued, and ended in you, I may glorify your holy name, and finally, by your mercy, obtain everlasting life; through Jesus Christ my Lord. *Amen.*

The Vespers Office   **To Be Observed on the Hour or Half Hour**
                                                          Between 5 and 8 p.m.

The Call to Prayer
Open my lips, O Lord,* and my mouth shall proclaim your praise.
Had you desired it, I would have offered sacrifice,* but you take no delight in burnt-offerings.
The sacrifice of God is a troubled spirit;* a broken and contrite heart, O God, you will not despise.

Psalm 51:16–18

The Request for Presence
Out of the depths have I called to you, O LORD; LORD, hear my voice;* let your ears consider well the voice of my supplication.

Psalm 130:1

The Greeting
You have put gladness in my heart,* more than when grain and wine and oil increase.
I lie down in peace; at once I fall asleep;* for only you, LORD, make me dwell in safety.

Psalm 4:7–8

The Hymn

O God, creation's secret force,
Yourself unmoved, yet motion's source,
Who from the morn till evening's ray
Through every change does guide the day:

Grant us, when this short life is past,
The glorious evening that will last;
That, by a holy death attained
Eternal glory may be gained.

Grant this, O Father ever one
With Jesus Christ Your only Son
And Holy Ghost, whom all adore,
Reigning and blessed forevermore.

adapted from THE SHORT BREVIARY

The Refrain for the Vespers Lessons

The LORD has sworn an oath to David;* in truth, he will not break it:
"A son, the fruit of your body* will I set upon your throne."

Psalm 132:11–12

The Vespers Psalm   *My Heart, Therefore, Is Glad*

O LORD, you are my portion and my cup;* it is you who uphold my lot.
My boundaries enclose a pleasant land;* indeed, I have a goodly heritage.
I will bless the LORD who gives me counsel;* my heart teaches me, night after night.
I have set the LORD always before me;* because he is at my right hand I shall not fall.
My heart, therefore, is glad, and my spirit rejoices;* my body also shall rest in
    hope.
For you will not abandon me to the grave,* nor let your holy one see the Pit.
You will show me the path of life;* in your presence there is fullness of joy, and in
    your right hand are pleasures for evermore.

Psalm 16:5–11

The Refrain

The LORD has sworn an oath to David;* in truth, he will not break it:
"A son, the fruit of your body* will I set upon your throne."

The Cry of the Church

Even so, come, Lord Jesus!

The Lord's Prayer

The Prayer Appointed for the Week

Almighty God, give all of us grace to cast away the works of darkness, and put on
    the armor of light, now in the time of this mortal life in which your Son Jesus
    Christ came to visit us in great humility; that in the last day, when he shall
    come again in his glorious majesty to judge both the living and the dead, we
    may rise to the life immortal; through him who lives and reigns with you and
    the Holy Spirit, one God, now and for ever. *Amen.*†

The Concluding Prayer of the Church

Stir up Your power, we beseech You, O Lord, and come, that by Your protection
    we may deserve to be rescued from the threatening dangers of our sins and
    saved by Your deliverance. Who lives and reigns with God the Father in the
    unity of the Holy Ghost, God, world without end. *Amen.*

adapted from THE SHORT BREVIARY

The Morning Office   **To Be Observed on the Hour or Half Hour**
Between 6 and 9 a.m.

The Call to Prayer

Let us make a vow to the LORD our God and keep it;* let all around him bring gifts
    to him who is worthy to be feared.

Psalm 76:11

The Request for Presence
Let my cry come before you, O LORD;* give me understanding, according to your
     word.
Let my supplication come before you;* deliver me, according to your promise.
Psalm 119:169–170

The Greeting
I will offer you a freewill sacrifice* and praise your Name, O LORD, for it is good.
Psalm 54:6

The Refrain for the Morning Lessons
With my whole heart I seek you;* let me not stray from your commandments.
Psalm 119:10

A Reading
Jesus taught us, saying: "In truth I tell you, all human sins will be forgiven, and all
     the blasphemies ever uttered; but anyone who blasphemes against the Holy
     Spirit will never be forgiven, but is guilty of an eternal sin."
Mark 3:28–29

The Refrain
With my whole heart I seek you;* let me not stray from your commandments.

The Morning Psalm   *Only You, LORD, Make Me Dwell in Safety*
Answer me when I call, O God, defender of my cause;* you set me free when I am
     hard-pressed; have mercy on me and hear my prayer.
"You mortals, how long will you dishonor my glory;* how long will you worship
     dumb idols and run after false gods?"
Know that the LORD does wonders for the faithful;* when I call upon the LORD, he
     will hear me.
Tremble, then, and do not sin;* speak to your heart in silence upon your bed.
Offer the appointed sacrifices* and put your trust in the LORD.
Many are saying, "Oh, that we might see better times!"* Lift up the light of your
     countenance upon us, O LORD.
You have put gladness in my heart,* more than when grain and wine and oil increase.
I lie down in peace; at once I fall asleep;* for only you, LORD, make me dwell in safety.
Psalm 4

The Refrain
With my whole heart I seek you;* let me not stray from your commandments.

The Cry of the Church
O God, come to my assistance! O Lord, make haste to help me!

The Lord's Prayer

The Prayer Appointed for the Week
Almighty God, give all of us grace to cast away the works of darkness, and put on
     the armor of light, now in the time of this mortal life in which your Son Jesus

Christ came to visit us in great humility; that in the last day, when he shall come again in his glorious majesty to judge both the living and the dead, we may rise to the life immortal; through him who lives and reigns with you and the Holy Spirit, one God, now and for ever. *Amen.*†

The Concluding Prayer of the Church

Lord God, almighty and everlasting Father, you have brought me in safety to this new day: Preserve me with your mighty power, that I may not fall into sin, nor be overcome by adversity; and in all I do direct me to the fulfilling of your purpose; through Jesus Christ my Lord. *Amen.*†

The Midday Office   To Be Observed on the Hour or Half Hour
Between 11 a.m. and 2 p.m.

The Call to Prayer

"Come now, let us reason together," says the Lord.

Isaiah 1:18 (KJV)

The Request for Presence

O LORD, I call to you; come to me quickly;* hear my voice when I cry to you.

Psalm 141:1

The Greeting

In you, O LORD, have I taken refuge;* let me never be ashamed.

Psalm 71:1

The Refrain for the Midday Lessons

Happy are they all who fear the LORD,* and who follow in his ways!

Psalm 128:1

A Reading

"What are your endless sacrifices to me?" says YAHWEH. "I am sick of burnt offerings of rams and the fat of calves. I take no pleasure in the blood of bulls and lambs and goats. When you come and present yourselves before me, who asked you to trample through my courts? Bring no more futile cereal offerings, the smoke from them fills me with disgust. Take your wrong-doing out of my sight. Cease doing evil. Learn to do good, search for justice, discipline the violent, be just to the orphan, plead for the widow."

Isaiah 1:11–13a, 16b–17

The Refrain

Happy are they all who fear the LORD,* and who follow in his ways!

The Midday Psalm   *Happy Are They Who Delight in the LORD*

Happy are they who have not walked in the counsel of the wicked,* nor lingered in the way of sinners, nor sat in the seats of the scornful!

Their delight is in the law of the LORD,* and they meditate on his law day and night.

They are like trees planted by streams of water, bearing fruit in due season, with leaves that do not wither;* everything they do shall prosper.

It is not so with the wicked;* they are like chaff which the wind blows away.

Therefore the wicked shall not stand upright when judgment comes,* nor the sinner in the council of the righteous.

For the LORD knows the way of the righteous,* but the way of the wicked is doomed.

Psalm 1

The Refrain
Happy are they all who fear the LORD,* and who follow in his ways!

The Cry of the Church
Be, Lord, my helper and forsake me not. Do not despise me, O God, my savior.

THE SHORT BREVIARY

The Lord's Prayer

The Prayer Appointed for the Week
Almighty God, give all of us grace to cast away the works of darkness, and put on the armor of light, now in the time of this mortal life in which your Son Jesus Christ came to visit us in great humility; that in the last day, when he shall come again in his glorious majesty to judge both the living and the dead, we may rise to the life immortal; through him who lives and reigns with you and the Holy Spirit, one God, now and for ever. *Amen.*†

The Concluding Prayer of the Church
Direct me, O Lord, in all my doings with your most gracious favor, and further me with your continual help; that in all my work begun, continued, and ended in you, I may glorify your holy name, and finally, by your mercy, obtain everlasting life; through Jesus Christ our Lord. *Amen.*†

The Vespers Office   To Be Observed on the Hour or Half Hour
Between 5 and 8 p.m.

The Call to Prayer
Come, let us sing to the LORD;* let us shout for joy to the Rock of our salvation.

Let us come before his presence with thanksgiving* and raise a loud shout to him with psalms.

For the LORD is a great God,* and a great King above all gods.

In his hand are the caverns of the earth,* and the heights of the hills are his also.

The sea is his, for he made it,* and his hands have molded the dry land.

Psalm 95:1–5

The Request for Presence
May God be merciful to us and bless us,* show us the light of his countenance and come to us.

Psalm 67:1

The Greeting
Exalt yourself above the heavens, O God,* and your glory over all the earth.

Psalm 57:6

The Hymn
Comfort, comfort you my people, speak you peace, so says our God;
Comfort those who sit in darkness mourning beneath their sorrow's load.
Speak you to Jerusalem of the peace that waits for them;
Tell her that her sins I cover, and her warfare now is over.

Hark, the voice of one that cries out in the desert far and near,
Calling us to new repentance since the kingdom now is here.
Oh, the warning cry obey! Now prepare for God a way;
Let the valleys rise to meet him and the hills bow down to greet him.

Make you straight what long was crooked, make the rougher places plain;
Let your hearts be true and humble, as befits his holy reign.
For the glory of the Lord now over earth is shed abroad;
And the flesh will see the token that his word is never broken.

Johann Olearius

The Refrain for the Vespers Lessons
Those who trust in the Lord are like Mount Zion,* which cannot be moved, but
stands fast for ever.

Psalm 125:1

The Vespers Psalm   The Words of the LORD Are Pure Words
"Because the needy are oppressed, and the poor cry out in misery,* I will rise up,"
says the LORD, "and give them the help they long for."
The words of the LORD are pure words,* like silver refined from ore and purified
seven times in the fire.
O LORD, watch over us* and save us from this generation for ever.
The wicked prowl on every side,* and that which is worthless is highly prized by
everyone.

Psalm 12:5–8

The Refrain
Those who trust in the Lord are like Mount Zion,* which cannot be moved, but
stands fast for ever.

The Cry of the Church
Even so, come, Lord Jesus!

The Lord's Prayer

The Prayer Appointed for the Week
Almighty God, give all of us grace to cast away the works of darkness, and put on
the armor of light, now in the time of this mortal life in which your Son Jesus

Christ came to visit us in great humility; that in the last day, when he shall come again in his glorious majesty to judge both the living and the dead, we may rise to the life immortal; through him who lives and reigns with you and the Holy Spirit, one God, now and for ever. *Amen.*†

The Concluding Prayer of the Church

Protect us, Lord, as we stay awake; watch over us as we sleep, that awake we may watch with Christ, and asleep, rest in peace. *Amen.*

The Morning Office	To Be Observed on the Hour or Half Hour Between 6 and 9 a.m.

The Call to Prayer

Know this: The LORD himself is God;* he himself has made us, and we are his; we are his people and the sheep of his pasture.

Psalm 100:2

The Request for Presence

For God alone my soul in silence waits;* truly, my hope is in him.

Psalm 62:6

The Greeting

Your testimonies are very sure,* and holiness adorns your house, O LORD, for ever and for evermore.

Psalm 93:6

The Refrain for the Morning Lessons

Blessed is he who comes in the name of the Lord;* we bless you from the house of the LORD.

Psalm 118:26

A Reading

In the sixth month the angel Gabriel was sent by God to a town in Galilee called Nazareth, to a virgin betrothed to a man called Joseph, of the House of David; and the virgin's name was Mary. He went in and said to her, 'Rejoice, you who enjoy God's favor! The Lord is with you.' She was deeply disturbed by these words and asked herself what this greeting could mean, but the angel said to her, 'Mary, do not be afraid; you have won God's favor.'

Luke 1:26–31

The Refrain

Blessed is he who comes in the name of the Lord;* we bless you from the house of the LORD.

The Morning Psalm   *Your Garments Are Fragrant with Myrrh, Aloes, and Cassia*

My heart is stirring with a noble song; let me recite what I have fashioned for the king;* my tongue shall be the pen of a skilled writer.

You are the fairest of men;* grace flows from your lips, because God has blessed
you for ever.

Strap your sword upon your thigh, O mighty warrior,* in your pride and in your
majesty.

Ride out and conquer in the cause of truth* and for the sake of justice.

Your right hand will show you marvelous things;* your arrows are very sharp,
O mighty warrior.

The peoples are falling at your feet,* and the king's enemies are losing heart.

Your throne, O God, endures for ever and ever,* a scepter of righteousness is the
scepter of your kingdom; you love righteousness and hate iniquity.

Therefore God, your God, has anointed you* with the oil of gladness above your
fellows.

All your garments are fragrant with myrrh, aloes, and cassia,* and the music of
strings from ivory palaces makes you glad.

Kings' daughters stand among the ladies of the court;* on your right hand is the
queen, adorned with the gold of Ophir.

"Hear, O daughter; consider and listen closely;* forget your people and your
father's house.

The king will have pleasure in your beauty;* he is your master; therefore do him
honor."

Psalm 45:1–12

The Refrain
Blessed is he who comes in the name of the Lord;* we bless you from the house of
the LORD.

The Cry of the Church
O God, come to my assistance! O Lord, make haste to help me!

The Lord's Prayer

The Prayer Appointed for the Week
Almighty God, give all of us grace to cast away the works of darkness, and put on
the armor of light, now in the time of this mortal life in which your Son Jesus
Christ came to visit us in great humility; that in the last day, when he shall
come again in his glorious majesty to judge both the living and the dead, we
may rise to the life immortal; through him who lives and reigns with you and
the Holy Spirit, one God, now and for ever. *Amen.*†

The Concluding Prayer of the Church
Lord God, almighty and everlasting Father, you have brought me in safety to this
new day: Preserve me with your mighty power, that I may not fall into sin, nor
be overcome by adversity; and in all I do direct me to the fulfilling of your purpose; through Jesus Christ my Lord. *Amen.*†

The Midday Office   **To Be Observed on the Hour or Half Hour**
       Between 11 a.m. and 2 p.m.

The Call to Prayer

Praise God from whom all blessings flow; praise him, all creatures here below;
    praise him, you heavenly hosts; praise Father, Son and Holy Ghost.

Traditional

The Request for Presence

Hear my prayer, O LORD,* and give ear to my cry; . . .
For I am but a sojourner with you,* a wayfarer, as all my forebears were.

Psalm 39:13–14

The Greeting

With my whole heart I seek you;* let me not stray from your commandments.

Psalm 119:10

The Refrain for the Midday Lessons

The LORD loves those who hate evil; he preserves the lives of his saints* and delivers them from the hand of the wicked.

Psalm 97:10

A Reading

First of all, do not forget that in the final days there will come sarcastic scoffers
whose life is ruled by their passions. 'What has happened to the promise of his
coming?' they will say, 'Since our Fathers died everything has gone on just as it
has since the beginning of creation!' They deliberately ignore the fact that long
ago there were the heavens and the earth, formed out of water and through
water by the Word of God, and that it was through these same factors that the
world of those days was destroyed by floodwaters. . . . But there is one thing,
my dear friends, that you must never forget: . . . The Day of the Lord will come
like a thief, and then with a roar the sky will vanish, the elements will catch fire
and melt away, the earth and all that it contains will be burned up.

2 Peter 3:3ff

The Refrain

The LORD loves those who hate evil; he preserves the lives of his saints* and delivers them from the hand of the wicked.

The Midday Psalm   *The Fool Has Said in His Heart, "There Is No God."*

The fool has said in his heart, "There is no God."* All are corrupt and commit
abominable acts; there is none who does any good.
The LORD looks down from heaven upon us all,* to see if there is any who is wise,
if there is one who seeks after God.
Every one has proved faithless; all alike have turned bad;* there is none who does
good; no, not one.
Have they no knowledge, all those evildoers* who eat up my people like bread
and do not call upon the LORD?

See how they tremble with fear,* because God is in the company of the righteous.
Their aim is to confound the plans of the afflicted,* but the LORD is their refuge.
Oh, that Israel's deliverance would come out of Zion!* when the LORD restores the
fortunes of his people, Jacob will rejoice and Israel be glad.

Psalm 14

The Refrain
The LORD loves those who hate evil; he preserves the lives of his saints* and delivers them from the hand of the wicked.

The Cry of the Church
O God, come to my assistance! O Lord, make haste to help me!

The Lord's Prayer

The Prayer Appointed for the Week
Almighty God, give all of us grace to cast away the works of darkness, and put on
the armor of light, now in the time of this mortal life in which your Son Jesus
Christ came to visit us in great humility; that in the last day, when he shall
come again in his glorious majesty to judge both the living and the dead, we
may rise to the life immortal; through him who lives and reigns with you and
the Holy Spirit, one God, now and for ever. *Amen.*†

The Concluding Prayer of the Church
Almighty and everlasting God, by whose Spirit the whole body of your faithful is
governed and sanctified: Receive my supplications and prayers which I offer
before you for all members of your holy Church, that in our vocation and ministry we all may truly serve you through our Lord and Savior Jesus Christ.
Amen.†

The Vespers Office   **To Be Observed on the Hour or Half Hour**
Between 5 and 8 p.m.

The Call to Prayer
Come now and see the works of God,* how wonderful he is in his doing toward
all people.
In his might he rules for ever; his eyes keep watch over the nations;* let no rebel
rise up against him.

Psalm 66:4, 6

The Request for Presence
Show us your mercy, O LORD,* and grant us your salvation.

Psalm 85:7

The Greeting
Praise God from whom all blessings flow; praise Him all creatures here below;
praise Him above, you heavenly hosts; praise Father, Son, and Holy Ghost.

Traditional Doxology

The Hymn
> Let all mortal flesh keep silence, and with fear and trembling stand;
> Ponder nothing earthly minded, for with blessing in his hand
> Christ our God to earth descended, our full homage to demand.
>
> Rank on rank the host of heaven spreads its vanguard on the way,
> As the light of light descending from the realm of endless day,
> That the powers of hell may vanish as the darkness clears away.
>
> At his feet the six-winged seraph; cherubim with sleepless eye,
> Veil their faces to the Presence, as with ceaseless voice they cry,
> "Alleluia, Alleluia! Alleluia, Lord Most High!"

Liturgy of St. James

The Refrain for the Vespers Lessons
Our sins are stronger than we are,* but you will blot them out.

Psalm 65:3

The Vespers Psalm   *Be Seated on Your Lofty Throne, O Most High*
Awake, O my God, decree justice;* let the assembly of the peoples gather round
> you.
Be seated on your lofty throne, O Most High;* O LORD, judge the nations.
Let the malice of the wicked come to an end, but establish the righteous;* for you
> test the mind and heart, O righteous God.
God is my shield and defense;* he is the savior of the true in heart.
God is a righteous judge;* God sits in judgment every day.

Psalm 7:7-8, 10-12

The Refrain
Our sins are stronger than we are,* but you will blot them out.

The Small Verse
The Lord is my shepherd and nothing is wanting to me. In green pastures He hath
> settled me.

THE SHORT BREVIARY

The Lord's Prayer

The Prayer Appointed for the Week
Almighty God, give all of us grace to cast away the works of darkness, and put on
> the armor of light, now in the time of this mortal life in which your Son Jesus
> Christ came to visit us in great humility; that in the last day, when he shall
> come again in his glorious majesty to judge both the living and the dead, we
> may rise to the life immortal; through him who lives and reigns with you and
> the Holy Spirit, one God, now and for ever. *Amen.*†

The Concluding Prayer of the Church

Help each one of us, gracious Father, to live in such magnanimity and restraint that the Head of the Church may never have cause to say to any one of us, This is my body, broken by you.

Prayer from China

The Morning Office   **To Be Observed on the Hour or Half Hour**
Between 6 and 9 a.m.

The Call to Prayer

Come now and see the works of God,* how wonderful he is in his doing toward all people.

Psalm 66:4

The Request for Presence

Show me your marvelous loving-kindness,* O Savior of those who take refuge at your right hand from those who rise up against them.

Keep me as the apple of your eye;* hide me under the shadow of your wings.

Psalm 17:7–8

The Greeting

Hosanna, LORD, hosanna! . . . Blessed is he who comes in the name of the LORD;* we bless you from the house of the LORD.

Psalm 118:25–26

The Refrain for the Morning Lessons

For God, who commanded the light to shine out of darkness, hath shined in our hearts, to give the light of the knowledge of the glory of God in the face of Jesus Christ.

2 Corinthians 4:6 (KJV)

A Reading

Jesus taught the people, saying: "The children of this world take wives and husbands, but those who are judged worthy of a place in the other world and in the resurrection from the dead do not marry because they can no longer die, for they are the same as the angels, and being children of the resurrection they are children of God. And Moses himself implies that the dead rise again, in the passage about the bush where he calls the Lord *the God of Abraham, the God of Isaac and the God of Jacob.* Now he is God, not of the dead, but of the living; for to him everyone is alive."

Luke 20:35–38

The Refrain

For God, who commanded the light to shine out of darkness, hath shined in our hearts, to give the light of the knowledge of the glory of God in the face of Jesus Christ.

The Morning Psalm   *What Is Man That You Should Be Mindful of Him?*

O LORD our Governor,* how exalted is your Name in all the world!

Out of the mouths of infants and children* your majesty is praised above the
    heavens.

When I consider your heavens, the work of your fingers,* the moon and the stars
    you have set in their courses,

What is man that you should be mindful of him?* the son of man that you should
    seek him out?

You have made him but little lower than the angels;* you adorn him with glory
    and honor;

You give him mastery over the works of your hands;* you put all things under his
    feet:

All sheep and oxen,* even the wild beasts of the field,

The birds of the air, the fish of the sea,* and whatsoever walks in the paths of the sea.

O LORD our Governor,* how exalted is your Name in all the world!

Psalm 8:1–2, 4–10

The Refrain

For God, who commanded the light to shine out of darkness, hath shined in our
    hearts, to give the light of the knowledge of the glory of God in the face of
    Jesus Christ.

The Cry of the Church

Even so, come, Lord Jesus!

The Lord's Prayer

The Prayer Appointed for the Week

Almighty God, give all of us grace to cast away the works of darkness, and put on
    the armor of light, now in the time of this mortal life in which your Son Jesus
    Christ came to visit us in great humility; that in the last day, when he shall
    come again in his glorious majesty to judge both the living and the dead, we
    may rise to the life immortal; through him who lives and reigns with you and
    the Holy Spirit, one God, now and for ever. *Amen.*†

The Concluding Prayer of the Church

Lord God, almighty and everlasting Father, you have brought me in safety to this
    new day: Preserve me with your mighty power, that I may not fall into sin, nor
    be overcome by adversity; and in all I do direct me to the fulfilling of your pur-
    pose; through Jesus Christ my Lord. *Amen.*†

The Midday Office   **To Be Observed on the Hour or Half Hour**
Between 11 a.m. and 2 p.m.

The Call to Prayer

Give thanks to the LORD, for he is good;* his mercy endures for ever.

Psalm 118:29

The Request for Presence
You are the LORD; do not withhold your compassion from me;* let your love and your faithfulness keep me safe for ever.

Psalm 40:12

The Greeting
There is forgiveness with you;* therefore you shall be feared.

Psalm 130:3

The Refrain for the Midday Lessons
For you, O LORD, are good and forgiving,* and great is your love toward all who call upon you.

Psalm 86:5

A Reading
And, that day, you will say: 'I praise you, YAHWEH, you have been angry with me but your anger is now appeased and you have comforted me. Look, he is the God of my salvation: I shall have faith and not be afraid, for YAHWEH is my strength and my song, he has been my salvation.' Joyfully you will draw water from the springs of salvation and, that day, you will say, 'Praise YAHWEH, invoke his name. Proclaim his deeds to the people, declare his name sublime.'

Isaiah 12:1–4

The Refrain
For you, O LORD, are good and forgiving,* and great is your love toward all who call upon you.

The Midday Psalm   *We Will Call Upon the Name of the LORD Our God*
May the LORD answer you in the day of trouble,* the Name of the God of Jacob defend you;

Send you help from his holy place* and strengthen you out of Zion;

Remember all your offerings* and accept your burnt sacrifice;

Grant you your heart's desire* and prosper all your plans.

We will shout for joy at your victory and triumph in the Name of our God;* may the LORD grant all your requests.

Now I know that the LORD gives victory to his anointed;* he will answer him out of his holy heaven, with the victorious strength of his right hand.

Some put their trust in chariots and some in horses,* but we will call upon the Name of the LORD our God.

They collapse and fall down,* but we will arise and stand upright.

O LORD, give victory to the king* and answer us when we call.

Psalm 20

The Refrain
For you, O LORD, are good and forgiving,* and great is your love toward all who call upon you.

The Cry of the Church
In the evening, in the morning, and at noonday, I will complain and lament,* and
he will hear my voice.

Psalm 55:18

The Lord's Prayer

The Prayer Appointed for the Week
Almighty God, give all of us grace to cast away the works of darkness, and put on
the armor of light, now in the time of this mortal life in which your Son Jesus
Christ came to visit us in great humility; that in the last day, when he shall
come again in his glorious majesty to judge both the living and the dead, we
may rise to the life immortal; through him who lives and reigns with you and
the Holy Spirit, one God, now and for ever. *Amen.†*

The Concluding Prayer of the Church
Lord Jesus Christ, by your death you took away the sting of death: Grant me to so
follow in faith where you have led the way, that I may at length fall asleep
peacefully in you and wake in your likeness; for your tender mercies' sake.
Amen.†

The Vespers Office   **To Be Observed on the Hour or Half Hour
Between 5 and 8 p.m.**

The Call to Prayer
Behold now, bless the LORD, all you servants of the LORD,* you that stand by night
in the house of the LORD.
Lift up your hands in the holy place and bless the LORD;* the LORD who made
heaven and earth bless you out of Zion.

Psalm 134

The Request for Presence
Look upon me and answer me, O LORD my God;* give light to my eyes, lest I sleep
in death.

Psalm 13:3

The Greeting
O LORD, I am not proud;* I have no haughty looks.
I do not occupy myself with great matters,* or with things that are too hard for me.
But I still my soul and make it quiet, like a child upon its mother's breast;* my soul
is quieted within me.

Psalm 131:1–3

The Hymn

Lo, how a rose e'er blooming	Isaiah 'twas foretold it,
From tender stem has sprung!	The Rose I have in mind;
Of Jesse's lineage coming,	With Mary we behold it,
As those of old have sung.	The Virgin Mother kind.
It came a floweret bright,	To show God's love aright,
Amid the cold of winter,	She bore to us a Savior,
When half spent was the night.	When half spent was the night.

German, 15th Century

The Refrain for the Vespers Lessons

Those who are planted in the house of the LORD* shall flourish in the courts of our God.

Psalm 92:12

The Vespers Psalm   *Let Me Announce the Decree of the LORD*

Why are the nations in an uproar?* Why do the peoples mutter empty threats?

Why do the kings of the earth rise up in revolt, and the princes plot together,* against the LORD and against his Anointed?

"Let us break their yoke," they say;* "let us cast off their bonds from us."

He whose throne is in heaven is laughing;* the Lord has them in derision.

Then he speaks to them in his wrath,* and his rage fills them with terror.

"I myself have set my king* upon my holy hill of Zion."

Let me announce the decree of the LORD:* he said to me, "You are my Son; this day have I begotten you.

Ask of me, and I will give you the nations for your inheritance* and the ends of the earth for your possession.

You shall crush them with an iron rod* and shatter them like a piece of pottery."

And now, you kings, be wise;* be warned, you rulers of the earth.

Submit to the LORD with fear,* and with trembling bow before him;

Lest he be angry and you perish;* for his wrath is quickly kindled.

Happy are they all* who take refuge in him!

Psalm 2

The Refrain

Those who are planted in the house of the LORD* shall flourish in the courts of our God.

The Cry of the Church

Even so, come, Lord Jesus!

The Lord's Prayer

The Prayer Appointed for the Week

Almighty God, give all of us grace to cast away the works of darkness, and put on the armor of light, now in the time of this mortal life in which your Son Jesus Christ came to visit us in great humility; that in the last day, when he shall come again in his glorious majesty to judge both the living and the dead, we may rise to the life immortal; through him who lives and reigns with you and the Holy Spirit, one God, now and for ever. *Amen.*†

Concluding Prayers of the Church

Almighty God, who has promised to hear the petitions of those who ask in your Son's Name: I beseech you mercifully to incline your ear to me who have made my prayers and supplications to you; and grant that those things which I have faithfully asked according to your will, I may effectually obtain, to the relief of my necessity, and to the setting forth of your glory; through Jesus Christ my Lord. *Amen.*†

May the souls of the faithful departed, through the mercy of God, rest in eternal peace. *Amen.*

The Morning Office

To Be Observed on the Hour or Half Hour
Between 6 and 9 a.m.

The Call to Prayer

Come now and look upon the works of the LORD,* what awesome things he has done on earth.

Psalm 46:9

The Request for Presence

O LORD . . . answer us when we call.

Psalm 20:9

The Greeting

My eyes are fixed on you, O my Strength;* for you, O God, are my stronghold.

Psalm 59:10

The Refrain for the Morning Lessons

As a father cares for his children,* so does the LORD care for those who fear him.

Psalm 103:13

A Reading

The gospeler wrote, saying: "Now all this took place to fulfill what the Lord had spoken through the prophet: *Look! The virgin is with child and will give birth to a son whom they will call Immanuel,* a name which means 'God-is-with-us.' "

Matthew 1:22–23

The Refrain

As a father cares for his children,* so does the LORD care for those who fear him.

The Morning Psalm   *Who May Abide on Your Holy Hill*

LORD, who may dwell in your tabernacle?* who may abide upon your holy hill?
Whoever leads a blameless life and does what is right,* who speaks the truth from his heart.

There is no guile upon his tongue; he does no evil to his friend;* he does not heap
   contempt upon his neighbor.
In his sight the wicked is rejected,* but he honors those who fear the LORD.
He has sworn to do no wrong* and does not take back his word.
He does not give his money in hope of gain,* nor does he take a bribe against the
   innocent.
Whoever does these things* shall never be overthrown.

Psalm 15

The Refrain
As a father cares for his children,* so does the LORD care for those who fear him.

The Cry of the Church
Lord, have mercy on us. Christ, have mercy on us. Lord, have mercy on us.

The Lord's Prayer

The Prayer Appointed for the Week
Almighty God, give all of us grace to cast away the works of darkness, and put on
   the armor of light, now in the time of this mortal life in which your Son Jesus
   Christ came to visit us in great humility; that in the last day, when he shall
   come again in his glorious majesty to judge both the living and the dead, we
   may rise to the life immortal; through him who lives and reigns with you and
   the Holy Spirit, one God, now and for ever. *Amen.*†

The Concluding Prayer of the Church
Lord God, almighty and everlasting Father, you have brought me in safety to this
   new day: Preserve me with your mighty power, that I may not fall into sin, nor
   be overcome by adversity; and in all I do direct me to the fulfilling of your purpose; through Jesus Christ my Lord. *Amen.*†

The Midday Office

**To Be Observed on the Hour or Half Hour
Between 11 a.m. and 2 p.m.**

The Call to Prayer
Be strong and let your heart take courage,* all you who wait for the LORD.

Psalm 31:24

The Request for Presence
Give ear to my words, O LORD;* consider my meditation.
Hearken to my cry for help, my King and my God,* for I make my prayer to you.

Psalm 5:1–2

The Greeting
You are God; we praise you;
You are the Lord: we acclaim you;
You are the eternal Father:
All creation worships you.

To you all angels, all powers of heaven,
Cherubim and Seraphim, sing in endless praise:
> Holy, holy, holy Lord, God of power and might,
> heaven and earth are full of your glory.

Te Deum

The Refrain for the Midday Lessons
Great peace have they who love your law;* for them there is no stumbling block.

Psalm 119:165

A Reading
Yes, I know what plans I have in mind for you, YAHWEH declares, plans for peace,
not for disaster, to give you a future and a hope. When you call to me and come
and pray to me, I shall listen to you. When you search for me, you will find me;
when you search wholeheartedly for me, I shall let you find me . . .

Jeremiah 29:11–14a

The Refrain
Great peace have they who love your law;* for them there is no stumbling block.

The Midday Psalm   *We Will Sing Out Our Joy For Ever*
But all who take refuge in you will be glad;* they will sing out their joy for ever.
You will shelter them,* so that those who love your Name may exult in you.
For you, O LORD, will bless the righteous;* you will defend them with your favor
as with a shield.

Psalm 5:13–15

The Refrain
Great peace have they who love your law;* for them there is no stumbling block.

The Cry of the Church
O Lord, hear my prayer and let my cry come unto you. Thanks be to God.

THE SHORT BREVIARY

The Lord's Prayer

The Prayer Appointed for the Week
Almighty God, give all of us grace to cast away the works of darkness, and put on
the armor of light, now in the time of this mortal life in which your Son Jesus
Christ came to visit us in great humility; that in the last day, when he shall
come again in his glorious majesty to judge both the living and the dead, we
may rise to the life immortal; through him who lives and reigns with you and
the Holy Spirit, one God, now and for ever. *Amen.*†

The Concluding Prayer of the Church
O God, the source of eternal light: Shed forth your unending day upon all of us
who watch for you, that our lips may praise you, our lives may bless you, and
our worship may give you glory; through Jesus Christ our Lord. *Amen.*†

The Vespers Office   **To Be Observed on the Hour or Half Hour**
                                          Between 5 and 8 p.m.

The Call to Prayer
Bless our God, you peoples;* make the voice of his praise to be heard;
Who holds our souls in life,* and will not allow our feet to slip.

Psalm 66:7–8

The Request for Presence
O God of hosts;* show us the light of your countenance, and we shall be saved.

Psalm 80:7

The Greeting
As the eyes of servants look to the hand of their masters,* and the eyes of a maid to
    the hand of her mistress,
So my eyes look to you, O LORD my God.

based on Psalm 123:2–3

The Hymn

I sing the mighty power of God,
That made the mountains rise;
That spread the flowing seas abroad,
And built the lofty skies.
I sing the wisdom that ordained
The sun to rule the day;
The moon shines full at his command,
And all the stars obey.

I sing the goodness of the Lord,
That filled the earth with food;
He formed the creatures with his word,
And then pronounced them good.
Lord, how your wonders are displayed,
Wherever I turn my eye:
If I survey the ground I tread,
Or gaze upon the sky!

There's not a plant or flower below,
But makes your glories known;
And clouds arise, and tempests blow,
By order of your throne;
While all that borrows life from you
Is ever in your care,
And everywhere that man can be,
You, God, are present there.

Isaac Watts

The Refrain for the Vespers Lessons
And now, what is my hope?* O Lord, my hope is in you.

Psalm 39:8

The Vespers Psalm   ***Proclaim to the Peoples the Things He Has Done***
I will give thanks to you, O LORD, with my whole heart;* I will tell of all your
    marvelous works.
I will be glad and rejoice in you;* I will sing to your Name, O Most High.
But the LORD is enthroned for ever;* he has set up his throne for judgment.
It is he who rules the world with righteousness;* he judges the peoples with
    equity.

The Lord will be a refuge for the oppressed,* a refuge in time of trouble.
Those who know your Name will put their trust in you,* for you never forsake
those who seek you, O Lord.
Sing praise to the Lord who dwells in Zion;* proclaim to the peoples the things he
has done.

Psalm 9:1–2, 7–11

The Refrain
And now, what is my hope?* O Lord, my hope is in you.

The Cry of the Church
Even so, come, Lord Jesus!

The Lord's Prayer

The Prayer Appointed for the Week
Almighty God, give all of us grace to cast away the works of darkness, and put on
the armor of light, now in the time of this mortal life in which your Son Jesus
Christ came to visit us in great humility; that in the last day, when he shall
come again in his glorious majesty to judge both the living and the dead, we
may rise to the life immortal; through him who lives and reigns with you and
the Holy Spirit, one God, now and for ever. *Amen.*†

The Concluding Prayer of the Church
Almighty God, who after the creation of the world rested from all your works
and sanctified a day of rest for all your creatures: Grant that I, putting away all
earthly anxieties, may be duly prepared for the service of public worship, and
grant as well that my Sabbath upon earth may be a preparation for the eternal
rest promised to your people in heaven; through Jesus Christ our Lord.
Amen.†

The Morning Office

**To Be Observed on the Hour or Half Hour
Between 6 and 9 a.m.**

The Call to Prayer
I will sing of mercy and justice;* to you, O Lord, will I sing praises.

Psalm 101:1

The Request for Presence
But as for me, O Lord, I cry to you for help;* in the morning my prayer comes
before you.

Psalm 88:14

Faithful

Jesus is the Way

The Greeting

Your testimonies are very sure,* and holiness adorns your house, O LORD, for ever
and for evermore.

Psalm 93:6

The Refrain for the Morning Lessons

This is the LORD's doing,* and it is marvelous in our eyes.

Psalm 118:23

A Reading   *During Advent, the Church remembers with thanksgiving the life
and ministry of John the Baptizer, cousin of Our Lord and the
promised messenger of His first coming.*

Jesus began to talk to the people about John: "What did you go into the desert
to see? A reed swaying in the breeze? No! Then what did you go out to see?
A man dressed in fine clothes? Look, those who go in magnificent clothes
and live luxuriously are to be found at royal courts! Then what did you go to
see? A prophet? Yes, I tell you, and much more than a prophet: he is the one
of whom scripture says: *Look I am going to send my messenger in front of you to
prepare your way before you.* I tell you, of all the children born to women, there
is no one greater than John; yet the least in the kingdom of God is greater
than he."

Luke 7:25–28

The Refrain

This is the LORD's doing,* and it is marvelous in our eyes.

The Morning Psalm   *Sing to the LORD a New Song*

Hallelujah! Sing to the LORD a new song;* sing his praise in the congregation of the
faithful.

Let Israel rejoice in his Maker;* let the children of Zion be joyful in their King.

Let them praise his Name in the dance;* let them sing praise to him with timbrel
and harp.

For the LORD takes pleasure in his people* and adorns the poor with victory.

Let the faithful rejoice in triumph;* let them be joyful on their beds.

Let the praises of God be in their throat* and a two-edged sword in their hand;

To wreak vengeance on the nations* and punishment on the peoples;

To bind their kings in chains* and their nobles with links of iron;

To inflict on them the judgment decreed;* this is glory for all his faithful people.
Hallelujah!

Psalm 149

The Refrain

This is the LORD's doing,* and it is marvelous in our eyes.

The Cry of the Church

Even so, come, Lord Jesus!

The Lord's Prayer

The Prayer Appointed for the Week

Merciful God, who sent your messengers the prophets to preach repentance and
   prepare the way for our salvation: Grant us grace to heed their warnings and
   forsake our sins, that we may greet with joy the coming of Jesus Christ our
   Redeemer; who lives and reigns with you and the Holy Spirit, one God, now
   and for ever. *Amen.*†

The Concluding Prayer of the Church

Lord God, almighty and everlasting Father, you have brought me in safety to this
   new day: Preserve me with your mighty power, that I may not fall into sin, nor
   be overcome by adversity; and in all I do direct me to the fulfilling of your purpose; through Jesus Christ my Lord. *Amen.*†

The Midday Office   To Be Observed on the Hour or Half Hour
Between 11 a.m. and 2 p.m.

The Call to Prayer

Hallelujah! Praise the Name of the LORD;* give praise, you servants of the LORD,
You who stand in the house of the LORD,* in the courts of the house of our God.
Praise the LORD, for the LORD is good;* sing praises to his Name, for it is lovely.

Psalm 135:1–3

The Request for Presence

Let them know that you, whose Name is YAHWEH,* you alone are the Most High
   over all the earth.

Psalm 83:18

The Greeting

. . . My heart sings to you without ceasing;* O LORD my God, I will give you
   thanks for ever.

Psalm 30:13

The Refrain for the Midday Lessons

When I called, you answered me;* you increased my strength within me.

Psalm 138:4

A Reading

A shoot will spring from the stock of Jesse, a new shoot will grow from his roots.
   On him will rest the spirit of YAHWEH, the spirit of wisdom and insight, the spirit
   of counsel and power, the spirit of knowledge and fear of YAHWEH: his inspira-
   tion will lie in fearing YAHWEH. His judgment will not be by appearances, his
   verdict not given on hearsay. He will judge the weak with integrity and give fair
   sentence for the humblest in the land. He will strike the country with the rod of
   his mouth and with the breath of his lips bring death to the wicked. Uprightness
   will be a belt around his waist, and constancy the belt about his hips.

Isaiah 11:1–5

The Refrain
When I called, you answered me;* you increased my strength within me.

The Midday Psalm   *My Foot Stands on Level Ground*
Give judgment for me, O LORD, for I have lived with integrity;* I have trusted in
    the Lord and have not faltered.
Test me, O LORD, and try me;* examine my heart and my mind.
For your love is before my eyes;* I have walked faithfully with you.
I have not sat with the worthless,* nor do I consort with the deceitful.
I have hated the company of evildoers;* I will not sit down with the wicked.
I will wash my hands in innocence, O LORD,* that I may go in procession round
    your altar,
Singing aloud a song of thanksgiving* and recounting all your wonderful deeds.
LORD, I love the house in which you dwell* and the place where your glory abides.
Do not sweep me away with sinners,* nor my life with those who thirst for blood,
Whose hands are full of evil plots,* and their right hand full of bribes.
As for me, I will live with integrity;* redeem me, O LORD, and have pity on me.
My foot stands on level ground;* in the full assembly I will bless the LORD.

Psalm 26

The Refrain
When I called, you answered me;* you increased my strength within me.

The Cry of the Church
Even so, come, Lord Jesus!

The Lord's Prayer

The Prayer Appointed for the Week
Merciful God, who sent your messengers the prophets to preach repentance and
    prepare the way for our salvation: Grant us grace to heed their warnings and
    forsake our sins, that we may greet with joy the coming of Jesus Christ our
    Redeemer; who lives and reigns with you and the Holy Spirit, one God, now
    and for ever. *Amen.*†

The Concluding Prayer of the Church
O God, you make me glad with the weekly remembrance of the glorious resurrec-
    tion of your Son my Lord: Give me this day such blessing through my worship
    of you, that the week to come may be spent in your favor; through Jesus Christ
    our Lord. *Amen.*†

The Vespers Office   **To Be Observed on the Hour or Half Hour**
Between 5 and 8 p.m.

The Call to Prayer
Open my lips, O LORD,* and my mouth shall proclaim your praise.

Psalm 51:16

The Request for Presence

Be my strong rock, a castle to keep me safe,* for you are my crag and my stronghold; for the sake of your Name, lead me and guide me.

Psalm 31:3

The Greeting

O gracious Light, pure brightness of the everlasting Father in heaven, O Jesus
Christ, holy and blessed! Now as we come to the setting of the sun, and our
eyes behold the vesper light, we sing your praises O God: Father, Son and Holy
Spirit. You are worthy at all times to be praised by happy voices, O Son of God,
O giver of life, and to be glorified through all the worlds.

Phos Hilaron

The Hymn   *Lift Up Your Heads, You Mighty Gates*

Lift up your heads, you mighty gates;   Redeemer, come, with us abide;
Behold, the King of glory waits;   Our hearts to you we open wide;
The King of kings is drawing near;   Let us your inner presence feel;
The Savior of the world is here!   Your grace and love in us reveal.

Fling wide the portals of your heart;   Your Holy Spirit lead us on
Make it a temple, set apart   Until our glorious goal is won;
From earthly use for heaven's employ,   Eternal praise, eternal fame
Adorned with prayer and love and joy.   Be offered, Savior, to your name!

George Weissel

The Refrain for the Vespers Lessons

For you have rescued my soul from death and my feet from stumbling,* that I may
walk before God in the light of the living.

Psalm 56:12

The Vespers Psalm   *Tremble at the Presence of the LORD*

Hallelujah! When Israel came out of Egypt,* the house of Jacob from a people of
strange speech,
Judah became God's sanctuary* and Israel his dominion.
The sea beheld it and fled;* Jordan turned and went back.
The mountains skipped like rams,* and the little hills like young sheep.
What ailed you, O sea, that you fled?* O Jordan, that you turned back?
You mountains, that you skipped like rams?* you little hills like young sheep?
Tremble, O earth, at the presence of the Lord,* at the presence of the God of Jacob,
Who turned the hard rock into a pool of water* and flint-stone into a flowing
spring.

Psalm 114

The Refrain

For you have rescued my soul from death and my feet from stumbling,* that I may
walk before God in the light of the living.

The Small Verse

Into your hands I commend my spirit for you have redeemed me, O God of my life. Glory be to the Father, and to the Son and to the comforting Spirit.

Traditional

The Lord's Prayer

The Prayer Appointed for the Week

Merciful God, who sent your messengers the prophets to preach repentance and prepare the way for our salvation: Grant us grace to heed their warnings and forsake our sins, that we may greet with joy the coming of Jesus Christ our Redeemer; who lives and reigns with you and the Holy Spirit, one God, now and for ever. *Amen.*†

The Concluding Prayer of the Church

O God, you have brought me near to an innumerable company of angels, and to the spirits of just men made perfect: Grant me during my earthly pilgrimage to abide in their fellowship, and in your heavenly country to become partakers of their joy; through Jesus Christ our Lord, who lives and reigns with you and the Holy Spirit, one God, now and for ever. *Amen.*†

The Morning Office	**To Be Observed on the Hour or Half Hour Between 6 and 9 a.m.**

The Call to Prayer

Open my lips, O Lord,* and my mouth shall proclaim your praise.

Psalm 51:16

The Request for Presence

Open my eyes, that I may see* the wonders of your law.

Psalm 119:18

The Greeting

I will thank you, O Lord my God, with all my heart,* and glorify your Name for evermore.

Psalm 86:12

The Refrain for the Morning Lessons

For who is God, but the Lord?* who is the Rock, except our God?

Psalm 18:32

A Reading

As he was returning to the city in the early morning, he felt hungry. Seeing a fig tree by the road, he went up to it and found nothing on it but leaves. And he said to it 'May you never bear fruit again,' and instantly the fig tree withered. The disciples were amazed when they saw it and said, 'How is it that the fig tree withered instantly?' Jesus answered, 'In truth I tell you, if you have faith and do not doubt at all, not only will you do what I have done to the fig tree, but even if you say to this mountain, "Be pulled up and thrown into the sea," it will be done. And if you have faith, everything you ask for in prayer, you will receive.'

Matthew 21:18–22

The Refrain
For who is God, but the LORD?* who is the Rock, except our God?

The Morning Psalm   *He Sends Redemption to His People*
Great are the deeds of the LORD!* they are studied by all who delight in them.
His work is full of majesty and splendor,* and his righteousness endures for ever.
He makes his marvelous works to be remembered;* the LORD is gracious and full of compassion.
He gives food to those who fear him;* he is ever mindful of his covenant.
He has shown his people the power of his works* in giving them the lands of the nations.
The works of his hands are faithfulness and justice;* all his commandments are sure.
They stand fast for ever and ever,* because they are done in truth and equity.
He sent redemption to his people; he commanded his covenant for ever;* holy and awesome is his Name.

Psalm 111:2–9

The Refrain
For who is God, but the LORD?* who is the Rock, except our God?

The Cry of the Church
Even so, come, Lord Jesus!

The Lord's Prayer

The Prayer Appointed for the Week
Merciful God, who sent your messengers the prophets to preach repentance and prepare the way for our salvation: Grant us grace to heed their warnings and forsake our sins, that we may greet with joy the coming of Jesus Christ our Redeemer; who lives and reigns with you and the Holy Spirit, one God, now and for ever. *Amen.*†

The Concluding Prayer of the Church
Lord God, almighty and everlasting Father, you have brought me in safety to this new day: Preserve me with your mighty power, that I may not fall into sin, nor be overcome by adversity; and in all I do direct me to the fulfilling of your purpose; through Jesus Christ my Lord. *Amen.*†

The Midday Office   **To Be Observed on the Hour or Half Hour Between 11 a.m. and 2 p.m.**

The Call to Prayer
Be glad, you righteous, and rejoice in the LORD;* shout for joy, all who are true of heart.

Psalm 32:12

The Request for Presence

LORD, hear my prayer, and let my cry come before you;* hide not your face from me in the day of my trouble.

Psalm 102:1

The Greeting

Into your hands I commend my spirit,* for you have redeemed me, O LORD, O God of truth.

Psalm 31:5

The Refrain for the Midday Lessons

My help comes from the LORD,* the maker of heaven and earth.

Psalm 121:2

A Reading

Listen and you will live. I shall make an everlasting covenant with you in fulfill-ment of the favors promised to David. Look, I have made him a witness to the peoples, a leader and lawgiver to the peoples. Look, you will summon a nation unknown to you, a nation unknown to you will hurry to you for the sake of YAHWEH your God, because the Holy One of Israel has glorified you.

Isaiah 55:3b–5

The Refrain

My help comes from the LORD,* the maker of heaven and earth.

The Midday Psalm   *Let Everything That Has Breath Praise the LORD*

Hallelujah! Praise God in his holy temple;* praise him in the firmament of his power.
Praise him for his mighty acts;* praise him for his excellent greatness.
Praise him with the blast of the ram's-horn;* praise him with lyre and harp.
Praise him with timbrel and dance;* praise him with strings and pipe.
Praise him with resounding cymbals;* praise him with loud-clanging cymbals.
Let everything that has breath* praise the LORD. Hallelujah!

Psalm 150

The Refrain

My help comes from the LORD,* the maker of heaven and earth.

The Cry of the Church

O God, come to my assistance! O Lord, make haste to help me!

The Lord's Prayer

The Prayer Appointed for the Week

Merciful God, who sent your messengers the prophets to preach repentance and prepare the way for our salvation: Grant us grace to heed their warnings and forsake our sins, that we may greet with joy the coming of Jesus Christ our Redeemer; who lives and reigns with you and the Holy Spirit, one God, now and for ever. *Amen.*†

The Concluding Prayer of the Church

O God, the King eternal, whose light divides the day and the night and turns the shadow of death into the morning: Drive far from me all wrong desires, incline my heart to keep your law, and guide my feet into the way of peace; that, having done your will with cheerfulness during the day, I may, when night comes, rejoice to give you thanks; through Jesus Christ my Lord. *Amen.*†

The Vespers Office **To Be Observed on the Hour or Half Hour Between 5 and 8 p.m.**

The Call to Prayer

Come now and look upon the works of the LORD,* what awesome things he has done on earth.

Psalm 46:9

The Request for Presence

May God be merciful to us and bless us,* show us the light of his countenance and come to us.

Let your ways be known upon earth,* your saving health among all nations.

Psalm 67:1–2

The Greeting

O LORD of hosts,* happy are they who put their trust in you!

Psalm 84:12

The Hymn

Once he came in blessing, all our ills redressing;
Came in likeness lowly, Son of God most holy;
Bore the cross to save us, hope and freedom gave us.

Still he comes within us, still his voice would win us
From the sins that hurt us, would to Truth convert us:
Not in torment hold us, but in love enfold us.

Thus, if you can but name him, not ashamed to claim him,
But will trust him boldly not to love him coldly,
He will then receive you, heal you, and forgive you.

One who can endure, a bright reward secures.
Come, then, O Lord Jesus, from our sins release us;
Let us here confess you till in heaven we bless you.

Jan Roh

The Refrain for the Vespers Lessons

Bless the LORD, you angels of his, you mighty ones who do his bidding,* and hearken to the voice of his word.

Psalm 103:20

The Vespers Psalm   *Praise the LORD from the Heavens*

Hallelujah! Praise the LORD from the heavens;* praise him in the heights.

Praise him, all you angels of his;* praise him, all his host.

Praise him, sun and moon;* praise him, all you shining stars.

Praise him, heaven of heavens,* and you waters above the heavens.

Let them praise the Name of the LORD;* for he commanded, and they were
    created.

He made them stand fast for ever and ever;* he gave them a law which shall not
    pass away.

Psalm 148:1–6

The Refrain

Bless the LORD, you angels of his, you mighty ones who do his bidding,* and hear-
    ken to the voice of his word.

The Small Verse

In the sight of the Angels I praise You. I adore at Your holy temple and give praise
    to Your Name.

adapted from THE SHORT BREVIARY

The Lord's Prayer

The Prayer Appointed for the Week

Merciful God, who sent your messengers the prophets to preach repentance and
    prepare the way for our salvation: Grant us grace to heed their warnings and
    forsake our sins, that we may greet with joy the coming of Jesus Christ our
    Redeemer; who lives and reigns with you and the Holy Spirit, one God, now
    and for ever. *Amen.*†

The Concluding Prayer of the Church

O God, who in Your ineffable providence has deigned to send Your holy Angels to
    watch over us, grant to Your suppliants always to find safety in their protection
    and in eternity to share their happiness. Through our Lord.

THE SHORT BREVIARY

The Morning Office   **To Be Observed on the Hour or Half Hour**
                                      Between 6 and 9 a.m.

The Call to Prayer

Bless God in the congregation;* bless the LORD, you that are of the fountain of
    Israel.

Psalm 68:26

The Request for Presence

Look upon your covenant;* the dark places of the earth are haunts of violence.

Psalm 74:19

The Greeting
Deliver me, O LORD, by your hand* from those whose portion in life is this world.
Psalm 17:14

The Refrain for the Morning Lessons
. . . when God restores the fortunes of his people Jacob will rejoice and Israel be
glad.

[handwritten: John the Baptist showed the Way]

Psalm 53:6b

A Reading
Concerning the birth of John the Baptizer, scripture says: "The time came for
Elizabeth to have her child, and she gave birth to a son; and when her neighbors and relations heard that the Lord had lavished on her his faithful love,
they shared her joy. Now it happened that on the eighth day they came to cir-
cumcise the child; they were going to call him Zechariah after his father, but his
mother spoke up. 'No,' she said, 'he is to be called John.' They said to her, 'But
no one in your family has that name,' and made signs to his father to find out
what he wanted him called. The father asked for a writing tablet and wrote,
'His name is John.' And they were all astonished. At that instant his power of
speech returned and he spoke and praised God. All their neighbors were filled
with awe and the whole affair was talked about throughout the hill country of
Judaea. All those who heard of it treasured it in their hearts. 'What will this
child turn out to be?' they wondered. And indeed the hand of the Lord was
with him. . . . Meanwhile the child grew up and his spirit grew strong. And he
lived in the desert until the day he appeared openly to Israel."
Luke 1:57–66, 80

The Refrain
. . . when God restores the fortunes of his people Jacob will rejoice and Israel be
glad.

The Morning Psalm *Joy Comes in the Morning*
I will exalt you, O LORD, because you have lifted me up* and have not let my
enemies triumph over me.
O LORD my God, I cried out to you,* and you restored me to health.
You brought me up, O LORD, from the dead;* you restored my life as I was going
down to the grave.
Sing to the LORD, you servants of his;* give thanks for the remembrance of his
holiness.
For his wrath endures but the twinkling of an eye,* his favor for a lifetime.
Weeping may spend the night,* but joy comes in the morning.
Psalm 30:1–6

The Refrain
. . . when God restores the fortunes of his people Jacob will rejoice and Israel be
glad.

The Small Verse
Keep me, Lord, as the apple of your eye and carry me under the shadow of your
    wings.

Traditional

The Lord's Prayer

The Prayer Appointed for the Week
Merciful God, who sent your messengers the prophets to preach repentance and
    prepare the way for our salvation: Grant us grace to heed their warnings and
    forsake our sins, that we may greet with joy the coming of Jesus Christ our
    Redeemer; who lives and reigns with you and the Holy Spirit, one God, now
    and for ever. *Amen.*†

The Concluding Prayer of the Church
Lord God, almighty and everlasting Father, you have brought me in safety to this
    new day: Preserve me with your mighty power, that I may not fall into sin, nor
    be overcome by adversity; and in all I do direct me to the fulfilling of your pur-
    pose; through Jesus Christ my Lord. *Amen.*†

The Midday Office　　　　　**To Be Observed on the Hour or Half Hour**
Between 11 a.m. and 2 p.m.

The Call to Prayer
Open my lips, O LORD,* and my mouth shall proclaim your praise.

Psalm 51:16

The Request for Presence
Let my cry come before you, O LORD;* give me understanding, according to your
    word.
Let my supplication come before you;* deliver me, according to your promise.

Psalm 119:169–170

The Greeting
How priceless is your love, O God!* your people take refuge under the shadow of
    your wings.
They feast upon the abundance of your house;* you give them drink from the
    river of your delights.
For with you is the well of life,* and in your light we see light.

Psalm 36:7–9

The Refrain for the Midday Lessons
Mercy and truth have met together;* righteousness and peace have kissed each
    other.

Psalm 85:10

A Reading

. . . do not judge anything before the due time, until the Lord comes; he will bring to light everything that is hidden in darkness and reveal the designs of all hearts. Then everyone will receive from God the appropriate commendation.

1 Corinthians 4:5

The Refrain

Mercy and truth have met together;* righteousness and peace have kissed each other.

The Midday Psalm   All the Paths of the LORD Are Love and Faithfulness

Gracious and upright is the LORD;* therefore he teaches sinners in his way.

He guides the humble in doing right* and teaches his way to the lowly.

All the paths of the LORD are love and faithfulness* to those who keep his covenant and his testimonies.

Who are they who fear the LORD?* he will teach them the way that they should choose.

They shall dwell in prosperity,* and their offspring shall inherit the land.

The LORD is a friend to those who fear him* and will show them his covenant.

My eyes are ever looking to the LORD,* for he shall pluck my feet out of the net.

Psalm 25:7–9, 11–14

The Refrain

Mercy and truth have met together;* righteousness and peace have kissed each other.

The Small Verse

Lord, be merciful to me, a sinner. Christ, be merciful to me, a sinner. Father, be merciful to me, a sinner. Spirit, be merciful to me, a sinner. Lord, be merciful to me, a sinner.

Traditional

The Lord's Prayer

The Prayer Appointed for the Week

Merciful God, who sent your messengers the prophets to preach repentance and prepare the way for our salvation: Grant us grace to heed their warnings and forsake our sins, that we may greet with joy the coming of Jesus Christ our Redeemer; who lives and reigns with you and the Holy Spirit, one God, now and for ever. *Amen.*†

The Concluding Prayer of the Church

Let us bless the Lord God living and true! Let us always render him praise, glory, honor, blessing, and all good things! Amen. Amen. So be it! So be it!

St. Francis of Assisi

The Vespers Office   **To Be Observed on the Hour or Half Hour**
                                          Between 5 and 8 p.m.

The Call to Prayer
Sing to the LORD with thanksgiving;* make music to our God upon the harp.

Psalm 147:7

The Request for Presence
Let your countenance shine upon your servant* and teach me your statutes.

Psalm 119:135

The Greeting
How glorious you are!* more splendid than the everlasting mountains!

Psalm 76:4

The Hymn

Hark! The glad sound! The Savior comes,
the Savior promised long:
let every heart prepare a throne,
and every voice a song.

He comes, the broken heart to bind,
the bleeding soul to cure;
and with the treasures of his grace
to enrich the humble poor.

He comes, the prisoners to release
in Satan's bondage held;
the gates of brass before him burst,
the iron fetters yield.

Our glad hosannas, Prince of Peace,
your welcome shall proclaim;
and heaven's eternal arches ring
with your beloved Name.

Phillip Doddridge

The Refrain for the Vespers Lessons
Your love, O LORD, for ever will I sing;* from age to age my mouth will proclaim
your faithfulness.

Psalm 89:1

The Vespers Psalm   *Send Out Your Light and Your Truth*
Send out your light and your truth, that they may lead me,* and bring me to your
holy hill and to your dwelling;
That I may go to the altar of God, to the God of my joy and gladness;* and on the
harp I will give thanks to you, O God my God.
Why are you so full of heaviness, O my soul?* and why are you so disquieted
within me?
Put your trust in God;* for I will yet give thanks to him, who is the help of my
countenance, and my God.

Psalm 43:3–6

The Refrain
Your love, O LORD, for ever will I sing;* from age to age my mouth will proclaim
your faithfulness.

The Cry of the Church
Even so, come, Lord Jesus!

The Lord's Prayer

The Prayer Appointed for the Week

Merciful God, who sent your messengers the prophets to preach repentance and
    prepare the way for our salvation: Grant us grace to heed their warnings and
    forsake our sins, that we may greet with joy the coming of Jesus Christ our
    Redeemer; who lives and reigns with you and the Holy Spirit, one God, now
    and for ever. *Amen.*†

The Concluding Prayer of the Church

Lord Jesus Christ, you have prepared a quiet place for us in your Father's eternal
    home. Watch over our welfare on this perilous journey, shade us from the
    burning heat of day, and keep our lives free of evil until the end. *Amen.*

THE LITURGY OF THE HOURS, VOL. III

The Morning Office   **To Be Observed on the Hour or Half Hour**
Between 6 and 9 a.m.

The Call to Prayer

Rejoice in the LORD, you righteous,* and give thanks to his holy Name.

Psalm 97:12

The Request for Presence

Bow down your ear, O LORD, and answer me,* for I am poor and in misery.
Keep watch over my life, for I am faithful;* save your servant who puts his trust in
    you.

Psalm 86:1–2

The Greeting

Blessed is the LORD!* for he has heard the voice of my prayer.

Psalm 28:7

The Refrain for the Morning Lessons

Blessed are they which do hunger and thirst after righteousness: for they shall be
    filled.

Matthew 5:6 (KJV)

A Reading

In due course John the Baptist appeared; he proclaimed this message in the desert
    of Judaea, 'Repent, for the kingdom of Heaven is close at hand.' This was the
    man spoken of by the prophet Isaiah when he said: *A voice of one that cries in the
    desert, 'Prepare a way for the Lord, make his paths straight.'* This man John wore a
    garment made of camel-hair with a leather loin-cloth round his waist, and his
    food was locusts and wild honey. Then Jerusalem and all Judaea and the whole
    Jordan district made their way to him, and as they were baptized by him in the
    river Jordan they confessed their sins.

Matthew 3:1–6

The Refrain

Blessed are they which do hunger and thirst after righteousness: for they shall be filled.

The Morning Psalm   *My Soul Longs for You*

As the deer longs for the water-brooks,* so longs my soul for you, O God.

My soul is athirst for God, athirst for the living God;* when shall I come to appear before the presence of God?

My tears have been my food day and night, while all day long they say to me,* "Where now is your God?"

I pour out my soul when I think on these things:* how I went with the multitude and led them into the house of God,

With the voice of praise and thanksgiving,* among those who keep holy-day.

Why are you so full of heaviness, O my soul?* and why are you so disquieted within me?

Put your trust in God;* for I will yet give thanks to him, who is the help of my countenance, and my God.

Psalm 42:1–7

The Refrain

Blessed are they which do hunger and thirst after righteousness: for they shall be filled.

The Small Verse

My soul thirsts for the strong, living God and all that is within me cries out to him.

Traditional

The Lord's Prayer

The Prayer Appointed for the Week

Merciful God, who sent your messengers the prophets to preach repentance and prepare the way for our salvation: Grant us grace to heed their warnings and forsake our sins, that we may greet with joy the coming of Jesus Christ our Redeemer; who lives and reigns with you and the Holy Spirit, one God, now and for ever. *Amen.*†

The Concluding Prayer of the Church

Lord God, almighty and everlasting Father, you have brought me in safety to this new day: Preserve me with your mighty power, that I may not fall into sin, nor be overcome by adversity; and in all I do direct me to the fulfilling of your purpose; through Jesus Christ my Lord. *Amen.*†

The Midday Office   **To Be Observed on the Hour or Half Hour**
                                          Between 11 a.m. and 2 p.m.

The Call to Prayer

Come, let us sing to the LORD;* let us shout for joy to the Rock of our salvation.

Let us come before his presence with thanksgiving* and raise a loud shout to him with psalms.

For the LORD is a great God,* and a great King above all gods.
In his hand are the caverns of the earth,* and the heights of the hills are his also.
The sea is his, for he made it,* and his hands have molded the dry land.

Psalm 95:1–5

The Request for Presence
Remember not our past sins;* let your compassion be swift to meet us.

Psalm 79:8

The Greeting
Zion hears and is glad, and the cities of Judah rejoice,* because of your judgments,
O LORD.

Psalm 97:8

The Refrain for the Midday Lessons
I will listen to what the LORD God is saying,* for he is speaking peace to his faithful
people and to those who turn their hearts to him.

Psalm 85:8

A Reading
"Look, the days are coming, YAHWEH declares, when I shall fulfill the promise of
happiness I made to the House of Israel and the House of Judah: In those days
and at that time, I shall make an upright Branch grow for David, who will do
what is just and upright in the country. In those days Judah will triumph and
Israel live in safety. And this is the name the city will be called: Yahweh-is-our-
Saving-Justice."

Jeremiah 33:14–16

The Refrain
I will listen to what the LORD God is saying,* for he is speaking peace to his faithful
people and to those who turn their hearts to him.

The Midday Psalm   *Let Your Heart Take Courage*
How great is your goodness, O LORD! which you have laid up for those who fear
you;* which you have done in the sight of all for those who put their trust in
you.
You hide them in the covert of your presence from those who slander them;* you
keep them in your shelter from the strife of tongues.
Blessed be the LORD!* for he has shown me the wonders of his love in a besieged
city.
Love the LORD, all you who worship him;* the LORD protects the faithful, but
repays to the full those who act haughtily.
Be strong and let your heart take courage,* all you who wait for the LORD.

Psalm 31:19–21, 23–24

The Refrain
I will listen to what the LORD God is saying,* for he is speaking peace to his faithful
people and to those who turn their hearts to him.

The Cry of the Church
Even so, come, Lord Jesus!

The Lord's Prayer

The Prayer Appointed for the Week
Merciful God, who sent your messengers the prophets to preach repentance and
    prepare the way for our salvation: Grant us grace to heed their warnings and
    forsake our sins, that we may greet with joy the coming of Jesus Christ our
    Redeemer; who lives and reigns with you and the Holy Spirit, one God, now
    and for ever. *Amen.†*

The Concluding Prayer of the Church
Direct me, O Lord, on all my doings with your most gracious favor, and further
    me with your continual help; that in all my work begun, continued, and ended
    in you, I may glorify your holy name, and finally, by your mercy, obtain ever-
    lasting life; through Jesus Christ my Lord. *Amen.†*

The Vespers Office   **To Be Observed on the Hour or Half Hour
Between 5 and 8 p.m.**

The Call to Prayer
Come, let us sing to the LORD;* let us shout for joy to the Rock of our salvation.
Psalm 95:1

The Request for Presence
May the glory of the LORD endure for ever;* may the LORD rejoice in all his works.
Psalm 104:32

The Greeting
How great is your goodness, O LORD! which you have laid up for those who fear
    you;* which you have done in the sight of all for those who put their trust in you.
Psalm 31:19

The Hymn

The setting sun now dies away,	To God the Father, God the Son,
And darkness comes at close of day;	And Holy Spirit, Three in One,
Your brightest beams, dear Lord impart,	Trinity blessed whom we adore,
And let them shine within our heart.	Be praise and glory evermore.

Geoffrey Laylock

We praise your name with joy this night;
Please watch and guide us till the light;
Joining the music of the blessed,
O Lord, we sing ourselves to rest.

The Refrain for the Vespers Lessons
I am small and of little account,* yet I do not forget your commandments.
Psalm 119:141

The Vespers Psalm   *How Priceless Is Your Love, O God*

Your love, O LORD, reaches to the heavens;* and your faithfulness to the clouds.

Your righteousness is like the strong mountains, your justice like the great deep;*
    you save both man and beast, O LORD.

How priceless is your love, O God!* your people take refuge under the shadow of
    your wings.

They feast upon the abundance of your house;* you give them drink from the
    river of your delights.

For with you is the well of life,* and in your light we see light.

Continue your loving-kindness to those who know you,* and your favor to those
    who are true of heart.

Psalm 36:5–10

The Refrain

I am small and of little account,* yet I do not forget your commandments.

The Small Verse

Those who sowed with tears* will reap with songs of joy.

Those who go out weeping, carrying the seed,* will come again with joy, shoul-
    dering their sheaves.

Psalm 126:6–7

The Lord's Prayer

The Prayer Appointed for the Week

Merciful God, who sent your messengers the prophets to preach repentance and
    prepare the way for our salvation: Grant us grace to heed their warnings and
    forsake our sins, that we may greet with joy the coming of Jesus Christ our
    Redeemer; who lives and reigns with you and the Holy Spirit, one God, now
    and for ever. *Amen.†*

The Concluding Prayer of the Church

Almighty God, to whom our needs are known before we even ask, Help me to ask
    only what accords with your will; and those good things which I dare not, or in
    my blindness I cannot ask, grant for the sake of your Son Jesus Christ our Lord.
    Amen.†

The Morning Office   **To Be Observed on the Hour or Half Hour**
                                                   Between 6 and 9 a.m.

The Call to Prayer

Worship the LORD in the beauty of holiness;* let the whole earth tremble before him.

Psalm 96:9

The Request for Presence

Show us the light of your countenance, O God,* and come to us.

based on Psalm 67:1

The Greeting
Seven times a day do I praise you,* because of your righteous judgments.

Psalm 119:164

The Refrain for the Morning Lessons
Let integrity and uprightness preserve me,* for my hope has been in you.

Psalm 25:20

A Reading
Now it happened that one day while he was teaching the people in the Temple and proclaiming the good news, the chief priests and the scribes came up, together with the elders, and spoke to him. 'Tell us,' they said, 'what authority have you for acting like this? Or who gives you this authority?' In reply he said to them, 'And I will ask you a question, just one. Tell me: John's baptism: what was its origin, heavenly or human?' And they debated this way among themselves, 'If we say heavenly, he will retort, "why did you refuse to believe him?"; and if we say human, the whole people will stone us, for they are convinced that John was a prophet.' So their reply was that they did not know where it came from. And Jesus said to them, 'Nor will I tell you my authority for acting like this.'

Luke 20:1–8

The Refrain
Let integrity and uprightness preserve me,* for my hope has been in you.

The Morning Psalm   *Take Delight in the LORD*
Do not fret yourself because of evildoers;* do not be jealous of those who do wrong.
For they shall soon wither like the grass,* and like the green grass fade away.
Put your trust in the LORD and do good;* dwell in the land and feed on its riches.
Take delight in the LORD,* and he shall give you your heart's desire.
Commit your way to the LORD and put your trust in him,* and he will bring it to pass.
He will make your righteousness as clear as the light* and your just dealing as the noonday.
Be still before the LORD* and wait patiently for him.

Psalm 37:1–7

The Refrain
Let integrity and uprightness preserve me,* for my hope has been in you.

The Cry of the Church
O Lamb of God, that takes away the sins of the world, have mercy upon me.
O Lamb of God, that takes away the sins of the world, have mercy upon me.
O Lamb of God, that takes away the sins of the world, grant me your peace.

The Lord's Prayer

The Prayer Appointed for the Week
Merciful God, who sent your messengers the prophets to preach repentance and
    prepare the way for our salvation: Grant us grace to heed their warnings and
    forsake our sins, that we may greet with joy the coming of Jesus Christ our
    Redeemer; who lives and reigns with you and the Holy Spirit, one God, now
    and for ever. *Amen.*†

The Concluding Prayer of the Church
Lord God, almighty and everlasting Father, you have brought me in safety to this
    new day: Preserve me with your mighty power, that I may not fall into sin, nor
    be overcome by adversity; and in all I do direct me to the fulfilling of your pur-
    pose; through Jesus Christ my Lord. *Amen.*†

The Midday Office   To Be Observed on the Hour or Half Hour
                                   Between 11 a.m. and 2 p.m.

The Call to Prayer
Glory in his holy Name;* let the hearts of those who seek the LORD rejoice.

Psalm 105:3

The Request for Presence
Let your compassion come to me, that I may live,* for your law is my delight.

Psalm 119:77

The Greeting
Your righteousness, O God, reaches to the heavens;* you have done great things;
    who is like you, O God?

Psalm 71:19

The Refrain for the Midday Lessons
"I will instruct you and teach you in the way that you should go;* I will guide you
    with my eye.
Do not be like horse or mule, which have no understanding;* who must be fitted
    with bit and bridle, or else they will not stay near you."

Psalm 32:9–10

A Reading
Once the oppression is past, and the devastation has stopped and those now tram-
    pling on the country have gone away, the throne will be made secure in faithful
    love, and on it will sit in constancy within the tent of David a judge seeking fair
    judgment and pursuing uprightness.

Isaiah 16:4b–5

The Refrain
"I will instruct you and teach you in the way that you should go;* I will guide you
    with my eye.
Do not be like horse or mule, which have no understanding;* who must be fitted
    with bit and bridle, or else they will not stay near you."

The Midday Psalm   *Never Have I Seen the Righteous Forsaken*

Our steps are directed by the LORD;* he strengthens those in whose way he
    delights.
If they stumble, they shall not fall headlong,* for the LORD holds them by the hand.
I have been young and now I am old,* but never have I seen the righteous
    forsaken, . . .

Psalm 37:24–26

The Refrain

"I will instruct you and teach you in the way that you should go;* I will guide you
    with my eye.
Do not be like horse or mule, which have no understanding;* who must be fitted
    with bit and bridle, or else they will not stay near you."

The Cry of the Church

Lord, have mercy on us. Christ, have mercy on us. Lord, have mercy on us.

The Lord's Prayer

The Prayer Appointed for the Week

Merciful God, who sent your messengers the prophets to preach repentance and
    prepare the way for our salvation: Grant us grace to heed their warnings and
    forsake our sins, that we may greet with joy the coming of Jesus Christ our
    Redeemer; who lives and reigns with you and the Holy Spirit, one God, now
    and for ever. *Amen.*†

The Concluding Prayer of the Church

Open, Lord, my eyes that I may see.
Open, Lord, my ears that I may hear.
Open, Lord, my heart and my mind that I may understand.
So shall I turn to you and be healed.

Traditional

The Vespers Office   **To Be Observed on the Hour or Half Hour**
                                          Between 5 and 8 p.m.

The Call to Prayer

God is the LORD; he has shined upon us;* form a procession with branches up to
    the horns of the altar.

Psalm 118:27

The Request for Presence

Hear the voice of my prayer when I cry out to you,* when I lift up my hands to
    your holy of holies.

Psalm 28:2

The Greeting

All your works praise you, O LORD,* and your faithful servants bless you.
They make known the glory of your kingdom and speak of your power . . . * and
　　the glorious splendor of your kingdom.

Psalm 145:10–12

The Hymn

　　Of the Father's love begotten, ere the winds began to be,
　　He is Alpha and Omega, he the source, the ending he
　　Of the things that are, that have been and that future years shall see.

　　O you heights of heaven adore him; angel hosts, his praises sing;
　　Powers, dominions, bow before him, and extol our God and King;
　　Let no tongue on earth be silent, every voice in concert ring.

　　Christ, to you with God the Father, and O Holy Ghost, to thee,
　　Hymn and chant and high thanksgiving, and unwearied praises be:
　　Honor, glory and dominion, and eternal victory.

Aurelius Clemens Prudentius

The Refrain for the Vespers Lessons

Those who trust in the LORD are like Mount Zion,* which cannot be moved, but
　　stands fast for ever.

Psalm 125:1

The Vespers Psalm　　　　　　　　　　*Let Your Ways Be Known Upon Earth*

May God be merciful to us and bless us,* show us the light of his countenance and
　　come to us.
Let your ways be known upon earth,* your saving health among all nations.
Let the peoples praise you, O God;* let all the peoples praise you.
Let the nations be glad and sing for joy,* for you judge the peoples with equity and
　　guide all the nations upon earth.
Let the peoples praise you, O God;* let all the peoples praise you.

Psalm 67:1–5

The Refrain

Those who trust in the LORD are like Mount Zion,* which cannot be moved, but
　　stands fast for ever.

The Small Verse

The earth is the Lord's and all the fullness thereof, the world and we who dwell
　　within. Thanks be to God.

Traditional

The Lord's Prayer

The Prayer Appointed for the Week

Merciful God, who sent your messengers the prophets to preach repentance and
　　prepare the way for our salvation: Grant us grace to heed their warnings and

forsake our sins, that we may greet with joy the coming of Jesus Christ our Redeemer; who lives and reigns with you and the Holy Spirit, one God, now and for ever. *Amen.*†

The Concluding Prayer of the Church

May God himself order my days and make them acceptable in his sight. Blessed is the Lord always, my strength and my redeemer.

Traditional

The Morning Office
To Be Observed on the Hour or Half Hour Between 6 and 9 a.m.

The Call to Prayer

Know this: The LORD himself is God;* he himself has made us, and we are his; we are his people and the sheep of his pasture.

Psalm 100:2

The Request for Presence

Lead me, O LORD, in your righteousness, . . . * make your way straight before me.

Psalm 5:8

The Greeting

Hosannah, LORD, hosannah!* LORD, send us now success.

Blessed is he who comes in the name of the Lord;* we bless you from the house of the LORD.

God is the LORD; he has shined upon us;* form a procession with branches up to the horns of the altar.

Psalm 118:25–27

The Refrain for the Morning Lessons

Let not those who hope in you be put to shame through me, Lord GOD of hosts;* let not those who seek you be disgraced because of me, O God of Israel.

Psalm 69:7

A Reading

Of the Baptizer, scripture says: "A feeling of expectancy had grown among the people, who were beginning to wonder whether John might be the Christ, so John declared before them all, 'I baptize you with water, but someone is coming, someone who is more powerful than me, and I am not fit to undo the strap of his sandals; he will baptize you with the Holy Spirit and fire. His winnowing-fan is in his hand, to clear his threshing floor and to gather the wheat into his barn; but the chaff he will burn in a fire that will never go out.' And he proclaimed the good news to the people with many other exhortations too."

Luke 3:15–18

The Refrain

Let not those who hope in you be put to shame through me, Lord GOD of hosts;* let not those who seek you be disgraced because of me, O God of Israel.

The Morning Psalm   *Shepherd Your Inheritance, O* LORD

Blessed is the LORD!* for he has heard the voice of my prayer.

The LORD is my strength and my shield;* my heart trusts in him, and I have been
    helped;

Therefore my heart dances for joy,* and in my song will I praise him.

The LORD is the strength of his people,* a safe refuge for his anointed.

Save your people and bless your inheritance;* shepherd them and carry them for
    ever.

Psalm 28:7–11

The Refrain

Let not those who hope in you be put to shame through me, Lord GOD of hosts;*
    let not those who seek you be disgraced because of me, O God of Israel.

The Cry of the Church

O God, come to my assistance! O Lord, make haste to help me!

The Lord's Prayer

The Prayer Appointed for the Week

Merciful God, who sent your messengers the prophets to preach repentance and
    prepare the way for our salvation: Grant us grace to heed their warnings and
    forsake our sins, that we may greet with joy the coming of Jesus Christ our
    Redeemer; who lives and reigns with you and the Holy Spirit, one God, now
    and for ever. *Amen.*†

The Concluding Prayer of the Church

Lord God, almighty and everlasting Father, you have brought me in safety to this
    new day: Preserve me with your mighty power, that I may not fall into sin, nor
    be overcome by adversity; and in all I do direct me to the fulfilling of your pur-
    pose; through Jesus Christ my Lord. *Amen.*†

The Midday Office   **To Be Observed on the Hour or Half Hour**
                                 Between 11 a.m. and 2 p.m.

The Call to Prayer

Bless God in the congregation;* bless the LORD, you that are of the fountain of
    Israel.

Psalm 68:26

The Request for Presence

Be my strong rock, a castle to keep me safe;* you are my crag and my stronghold.

Psalm 71:3

The Greeting

Your way, O God, is holy;* who is so great a god as our God?

Psalm 77:13

The Refrain for the Midday Lessons
He who dwells in the shelter of the Most High,* abides under the shadow of the
Almighty.

Psalm 91:1

A Reading
For YAHWEH Sabaoth says this: A little while now, and I shall shake the heavens and
the earth, the sea and the dry land. I shall shake all the nations, and the treasure
of all the nations will flow in, and I shall fill this Temple with glory, says YAHWEH
Sabaoth ... The glory of this new Temple will surpass that of the old, says
YAHWEH Sabaoth, and in this place I shall give peace—YAHWEH Sabaoth declares.

Haggai 2:6–7, 9

The Refrain
He who dwells in the shelter of the Most High,* abides under the shadow of the
Almighty.

The Midday Psalm   *O Israel, Trust in the LORD*
O Israel, trust in the LORD;* he is their help and their shield.
O house of Aaron, trust in the LORD;* he is their help and their shield.
You who fear the LORD, trust in the LORD;* he is their help and their shield.
The LORD has been mindful of us, and he will bless us;* he will bless the house of
    Israel; he will bless the house of Aaron;
He will bless those who fear the LORD,* both small and great together.
May the LORD increase you more and more,* you and your children after you.
May you be blessed by the LORD,* the maker of heaven and earth.
The heaven of heavens is the LORD's,* but he entrusted the earth to its peoples.
But we will bless the LORD,* from this time forth for evermore. Hallelujah!

Psalm 115:9–16, 18

The Refrain
He who dwells in the shelter of the Most High,* abides under the shadow of the
Almighty.

Cry of the Church
O Lamb of God, that takes away the sins of the world, have mercy upon me.
O Lamb of God, that takes away the sins of the world, have mercy upon me.
O Lamb of God, that takes away the sins of the world, grant me your peace.

The Lord's Prayer

The Prayer Appointed for the Week
Merciful God, who sent your messengers the prophets to preach repentance and
    prepare the way for our salvation: Grant us grace to heed their warnings and
    forsake our sins, that we may greet with joy the coming of Jesus Christ our
    Redeemer; who lives and reigns with you and the Holy Spirit, one God, now
    and for ever. *Amen.*†

The Concluding Prayer of the Church
Lord Jesus Christ, by your death you took away the sting of death: Grant me to so
follow in faith where you have led the way, that I may at length fall asleep
peacefully in you and wake in your likeness; for your tender mercies' sake.
Amen.†

The Vespers Office   **To Be Observed on the Hour or Half Hour**
                                          Between 5 and 8 p.m.

The Call to Prayer
Taste and see that the LORD is good;* happy are they who trust in him!

Psalm 34:8

The Request for Presence
Turn to me and have pity on me . . .
The sorrows of my heart have increased . . .
Look upon my adversity and misery* and forgive me all my sin.

Psalm 25:15–17

The Greeting
It is a good thing to give thanks to the LORD,* and to sing praises to your Name,
O Most High;
To tell of your loving-kindness early in the morning* and of your faithfulness in
the night season.

Psalm 92:1–2

The Hymn
The King shall come when morning dawns and light triumphant breaks;
When beauty gilds the eastern hills and life to joy awakes.
Not, as of old, a little child, to bear, and fight, and die,
But crowned with glory like the sun that lights the morning sky.
The King shall come when morning dawns and earth's dark night is past;
O haste the rising of that morn, the day that shall ever last;
And let the endless bliss begin, by weary saints foretold,
When right shall triumph over wrong, and truth shall be extolled.
The King shall come when morning dawns and light and beauty brings:
Hail, Christ the Lord! Your people pray, come quickly, King of Kings.

Greek

The Refrain for the Vespers Lessons
When I was in trouble, I called to the LORD;* I called to the LORD, and he answered
me.

Psalm 120:1

The Vespers Psalm   *In You, O LORD, Have I Taken Refuge*
In you, O LORD, have I taken refuge; let me never be put to shame;* deliver me in
your righteousness.

Incline your ear to me;* make haste to deliver me.

Be my strong rock, a castle to keep me safe, for you are my crag and my stronghold;* for the sake of your Name, lead me and guide me.

Take me out of the net that they have secretly set for me,* for you are my tower of strength.

Into your hands I commend my spirit,* for you have redeemed me, O LORD, O God of truth.

Psalm 31:1-5

The Refrain
When I was in trouble, I called to the LORD;* I called to the LORD, and he answered me.

The Cry of the Church
Be, Lord, my helper and forsake me not. Do not despise me, O God, my savior.

THE SHORT BREVIARY

The Lord's Prayer

The Prayer Appointed for the Week
Merciful God, who sent your messengers the prophets to preach repentance and prepare the way for our salvation: Grant us grace to heed their warnings and forsake our sins, that we may greet with joy the coming of Jesus Christ our Redeemer; who lives and reigns with you and the Holy Spirit, one God, now and for ever. *Amen.*†

Concluding Prayers of the Church
Almighty God, who has promised to hear the petitions of those who ask in your Son's Name: I beseech you mercifully to incline your ear to me who have made my prayers and supplications to you; and grant that those things which I have faithfully asked according to your will, I may effectually obtain, to the relief of my necessity, and to the setting forth of your glory; through Jesus Christ my Lord. *Amen.*†

May the souls of the faithful departed, through the mercy of God, rest in eternal peace. *Amen.*

The Morning Office   **To Be Observed on the Hour or Half Hour Between 6 and 9 a.m.**

The Call to Prayer
Bless the LORD, you angels of his, you mighty ones who do his bidding,* and hearken to the voice of his word.

Bless the LORD, all you his hosts,* you ministers of his who do his will.

Bless the LORD, all you works of his, in all places of his dominion;* bless the LORD, O my soul.

Psalm 103:20-22

The Request for Presence
Show me the light of your countenance, O God,* and come to me.
based on Psalm 67:1

The Greeting
As the deer longs for the water-brooks,* so longs my soul for you, O God.
Psalm 42:1

The Refrain for the Morning Lessons
The same stone which the builders rejected* has become the chief cornerstone.
This is the LORD's doing,* and it is marvelous in our eyes.
Psalm 118:22–23

A Reading
Then Jesus appeared: he came from Galilee to the Jordan to be baptized by John.
John tried to dissuade him, with the words, 'It is I who need baptism from you,
and yet you come to me!' But Jesus replied, 'Leave it like this for the time
being; it is fitting that we should, in this way, do all that uprightness demands.'
Then John gave in to him. And when Jesus had been baptized he at once came
up from the water, and suddenly the heavens opened and he saw the Spirit of
God descending like a dove and coming down on him. And suddenly there
was a voice from heaven, 'This is my Son, the Beloved; my favor rests on him.'
Matthew 3:13–17

The Refrain
The same stone which the builders rejected* has become the chief cornerstone.
This is the LORD's doing,* and it is marvelous in our eyes.

The Morning Psalm   *In a Little While the Wicked Shall Be No More*
In a little while the wicked shall be no more;* you shall search out their place, but
they will not be there.
But the lowly shall possess the land;* they will delight in abundance of peace.
The wicked plot against the righteous* and gnash at them with their teeth.
The LORD laughs at the wicked,* because he sees that their day will come.
The wicked draw their sword and bend their bow to strike down the poor and
needy,* to slaughter those who are upright in their ways.
Their sword shall go through their own heart,* and their bow shall be broken.
The little that the righteous has* is better than great riches of the wicked.
For the power of the wicked shall be broken,* but the LORD upholds the righteous.
Psalm 37:11–18

The Refrain
The same stone which the builders rejected* has become the chief cornerstone.
This is the LORD's doing,* and it is marvelous in our eyes.

The Cry of the Church
Even so, come, Lord Jesus!

The Lord's Prayer

The Prayer Appointed for the Week

Merciful God, who sent your messengers the prophets to preach repentance and
prepare the way for our salvation: Grant us grace to heed their warnings and
forsake our sins, that we may greet with joy the coming of Jesus Christ our
Redeemer; who lives and reigns with you and the Holy Spirit, one God, now
and for ever. *Amen.*†

The Concluding Prayer of the Church

Lord God, almighty and everlasting Father, you have brought me in safety to this
new day: Preserve me with your mighty power, that I may not fall into sin, nor
be overcome by adversity; and in all I do direct me to the fulfilling of your purpose; through Jesus Christ my Lord. *Amen.*†

The Midday Office

**To Be Observed on the Hour or Half Hour
Between 11 a.m. and 2 p.m.**

The Call to Prayer

May these words of mine please him;* I will rejoice in the LORD.

Psalm 104:35

The Request for Presence

Set a watch before my mouth, O LORD, and guard the door of my lips;* let not my
heart incline to any evil thing.

Let me not be occupied in wickedness with evildoers,* nor eat of their choice
foods.

Let the righteous smite me in friendly rebuke;* let not the oil of the unrighteous
anoint my head.

Psalm 141:3–5

The Greeting

I long for your salvation, O LORD,* and your law is my delight.
Let me live, and I will praise you,* and let your judgments help me.

Psalm 119:174–175

The Refrain for the Midday Lessons

O God, you have taught me since I was young,* and to this day I tell of your wonderful works.

Psalm 71:17

A Reading

"For the Lord YAHWEH says this: Look, I myself shall take care of my flock and
look after it . . . I myself shall pasture my sheep, I myself shall give them rest—
declares the Lord YAHWEH. I shall look for the lost one, bring back the stray,
bandage the injured and make the sick strong. I shall watch over the fat and
healthy. I shall be a true shepherd to them."

Ezekiel 34:11, 15–16

The Refrain

O God, you have taught me since I was young,* and to this day I tell of your wonderful works.

The Midday Psalm   *The LORD Does Not Forsake His Faithful Ones*

Our steps are directed by the LORD;* he strengthens those in whose way he delights.

If they stumble, they shall not fall headlong,* for the LORD holds them by the hand.

For the LORD loves justice;* he does not forsake his faithful ones.

They shall be kept safe for ever,* but the offspring of the wicked shall be destroyed.

The righteous shall possess the land* and dwell in it for ever.

The mouth of the righteous utters wisdom,* and their tongue speaks what is right.

The law of their God is in their heart,* and their footsteps shall not falter.

Psalm 37:24–25, 29–33

The Refrain

O God, you have taught me since I was young,* and to this day I tell of your wonderful works.

The Small Verse

Into your hands I commend my spirit for you have redeemed me, O God of my life. Glory be to the Father, and to the Son and to the comforting Spirit.

Traditional

The Lord's Prayer

The Prayer Appointed for the Week

Merciful God, who sent your messengers the prophets to preach repentance and prepare the way for our salvation: Grant us grace to heed their warnings and forsake our sins, that we may greet with joy the coming of Jesus Christ our Redeemer; who lives and reigns with you and the Holy Spirit, one God, now and for ever. *Amen.*†

The Concluding Prayer of the Church

O God, the source of eternal light: Shed forth your unending day upon all of us who watch for you, that our lips may praise you, our lives may bless you, and our worship may give you glory; through Jesus Christ our Lord. *Amen.*†

The Vespers Office   **To Be Observed on the Hour or Half Hour**
Between 5 and 8 p.m.

The Call to Prayer

Come, let us sing to the LORD;* let us shout for joy to the Rock of our salvation.

Let us come before his presence with thanksgiving* and raise a loud shout to him with psalms.

For the LORD is a great God,* and a great king above all gods.

Psalm 95:1–3

The Request for Presence

Send out your light and your truth, that they may lead me,* and bring me to your
holy hill and to your dwelling.

Psalm 43:3

The Greeting

You, O Lord, are my lamp;* my God, you make my darkness bright.

Psalm 18:29

The Hymn

Holy, holy, holy! Lord God the Almighty!
Early in the morning our song shall rise to Thee;
Holy, holy, holy, merciful and mighty!
God in three Persons, blessed Trinity!

Holy, holy, holy! All the saints adore Thee,
Casting down their golden crowns around the glassy sea;
Cherubim and seraphim falling down before Thee,
Who were, and are, and evermore shall be.

Holy, holy, holy! Though the darkness hides Thee,
Though the eye of sinful man Your glory may not see;
Only You are holy; there is none beside Thee,
Perfect in power, in love, and purity.

Holy, holy, holy! Lord God Almighty!
All Your works shall praise Your name, in earth, and sky, and sea;
Holy, holy, holy; merciful and mighty!
God in three Persons, blessed Trinity!

Reginald Heber

The Refrain for the Vespers Lessons

Seven times a day do I praise you,* because of your righteous judgments.
Great peace have they who love your law;* for them there is no stumbling block.

Psalm 119:164–165

The Vespers Psalm   *You Are My Hiding Place*

You are my hiding-place; you preserve me from trouble;* you surround me with
shouts of deliverance.
"I will instruct you and teach you in the way that you should go;* I will guide you
with my eye.
Do not be like horse or mule, which have no understanding;* who must be fitted
with bit and bridle, or else they will not stay near you."
Great are the tribulations of the wicked;* but mercy embraces those who trust in
the Lord.
Be glad, you righteous, and rejoice in the Lord;* shout for joy, all who are true of
heart.

Psalm 32:8–12

The Refrain
Seven times a day do I praise you,* because of your righteous judgments.
Great peace have they who love your law;* for them there is no stumbling block.

The Cry of the Church
Even so, come, Lord Jesus!

The Lord's Prayer

The Prayer Appointed for the Week
Merciful God, who sent your messengers the prophets to preach repentance and
   prepare the way for our salvation: Grant us grace to heed their warnings and
   forsake our sins, that we may greet with joy the coming of Jesus Christ our
   Redeemer; who lives and reigns with you and the Holy Spirit, one God, now
   and for ever. *Amen.*†

The Concluding Prayer of the Church
Almighty God, who after the creation of the world rested from all your works and
   sanctified a day of rest for all your creatures: Grant that I, putting away all
   earthly anxieties, may be duly prepared for the service of public worship, and
   grant as well that my Sabbath upon earth may be a preparation for the eternal
   rest promised to your people in heaven; through Jesus Christ our Lord. *Amen.*†

The Morning Office   **To Be Observed on the Hour or Half Hour**
                                        Between 6 and 9 a.m.

The Call to Prayer
Hallelujah! Praise the LORD, O my soul!* I will praise the LORD as long as I live; I
   will sing praises to my God while I have my being.

Psalm 146:1

The Request for Presence
Set a watch before my mouth, O LORD, and guard the door of my lips;* let not my
   heart incline to any evil thing.
Let me not be occupied in wickedness with evildoers,* nor eat of their choice
   foods.
Let the righteous smite me in friendly rebuke;* let not the oil of the unrighteous
   anoint my head.

Psalm 141:3–5

The Greeting

Not to us, O Lord, not to us, but to your Name give glory;* because of your love
and because of your faithfulness.

Psalm 115:1

The Refrain for the Morning Lessons

Let the words of my mouth and the meditation of my heart be acceptable in your
sight,* O Lord, my strength and my redeemer.

Psalm 19:14

A Reading   *Traditionally the Church has used the third week of Advent as a time
for giving particular attention and adoration to the Virgin and her
role as bearer and mother of our Lord.*

As the child's father and mother were wondering at the things that were being
said about him, Simeon blessed them and said to Mary his mother, 'Look, he is
destined for the fall and for the rise of many in Israel, destined to be a sign that
is opposed—and a sword will pierce your soul too—so that the secret thoughts
of many may be laid bare.'

Luke 2:33–35

The Refrain

Let the words of my mouth and the meditation of my heart be acceptable in your
sight,* O Lord, my strength and my redeemer.

The Morning Psalm   *How Long Will You Hide Your Face from Me?*

How long, O Lord? will you forget me for ever?* how long will you hide your face
from me?

How long shall I have perplexity in my mind, and grief in my heart, day after
day?* how long shall my enemy triumph over me?

Look upon me and answer me, O Lord my God;* give light to my eyes, lest I sleep
in death;

Lest my enemy say, "I have prevailed over him,"* and my foes rejoice that I have
fallen.

But I put my trust in your mercy;* my heart is joyful because of your saving help.

I will sing to the Lord, for he has dealt with me richly;* I will praise the Name of
the Lord Most High.

Psalm 13

The Refrain

Let the words of my mouth and the meditation of my heart be acceptable in your
sight,* O Lord, my strength and my redeemer.

The Cry of the Church

O God, come to my assistance! O Lord, make haste to help me!

The Lord's Prayer

The Prayer Appointed for the Week
Stir up your power, O Lord, and with great might come among us; and, because
we are sorely hindered by our sins, let your bountiful grace and mercy speedily help and deliver us; through Jesus Christ our Lord, to whom, with you and
the Holy Spirit, be honor and glory now and for ever. *Amen.*†

The Concluding Prayer of the Church
Lord God, almighty and everlasting Father, you have brought me in safety to this
new day: Preserve me with your mighty power, that I may not fall into sin, nor
be overcome by adversity; and in all I do direct me to the fulfilling of your purpose; through Jesus Christ my Lord. *Amen.*†

The Midday Office **To Be Observed on the Hour or Half Hour**
Between 11 a.m. and 2 p.m.

The Call to Prayer
Come and listen, all you who fear God,* and I will tell you what he has done for
me.

Psalm 66:14

The Request for Presence
I call upon you, O God, for you will answer me;* incline your ear to me and hear
my words.

Psalm 17:6

The Greeting
The Lord is in his holy temple; let all the earth keep silence before him. Amen.

Traditional

The Refrain for the Midday Lessons
The LORD is my strength and my song,* and he has become my salvation.

Psalm 118:14

A Reading
What you have come to is nothing known to the senses: not a *blazing fire,* or *gloom*
or *total darkness,* or a *storm;* or *trumpet blast* or the *sound of a voice*
speaking . . . But what you have come to is Mount Zion and the city of the living
God, the heavenly Jerusalem where the millions of angels have gathered for
the festival, with the whole Church of first-born sons, enrolled as citizens of
heaven. You have come to God himself, the supreme Judge, and to the spirits of
the upright who have been made perfect; and to Jesus, the mediator of a new
covenant, and to purifying blood which pleads more insistently than Abel's.

Hebrews 12:18ff

The Refrain
The LORD is my strength and my song,* and he has become my salvation.

The Midday Psalm   *God Has Gone Up with a Shout*

Clap your hands, all you peoples;* shout to God with a cry of joy.

For the LORD Most High is to be feared;* he is the great King over all the earth.

He subdues the peoples under us,* and the nations under our feet.

He chooses our inheritance for us,* the pride of Jacob whom he loves.

God has gone up with a shout,* the LORD with the sound of the ram's-horn.

Sing praises to God, sing praises;* sing praises to our King, sing praises.

For God is King of all the earth;* sing praises with all your skill.

God reigns over the nations;* God sits upon his holy throne.

The nobles of the peoples have gathered together* with the people of the God of Abraham.

The rulers of the earth belong to God,* and he is highly exalted.

Psalm 47

The Refrain

The LORD is my strength and my song,* and he has become my salvation.

The Cry of the Church

Even so, come, Lord Jesus!

The Lord's Prayer

The Prayer Appointed for the Week

Stir up your power, O Lord, and with great might come among us; and, because we are sorely hindered by our sins, let your bountiful grace and mercy speedily help and deliver us; through Jesus Christ our Lord, to whom, with you and the Holy Spirit, be honor and glory now and for ever. *Amen.*†

The Concluding Prayer of the Church

O God, you make me glad with the weekly remembrance of the glorious resurrection of your Son my Lord: Give me this day such blessing through my worship of you, that the week to come may be spent in your favor; through Jesus Christ our Lord. *Amen.*†

The Vespers Office   **To Be Observed on the Hour or Half Hour**
Between 5 and 8 p.m.

The Call to Prayer

Hallelujah! Praise the LORD from the heavens;* praise him in the heights.

Psalm 148:1

The Request for Presence

You are my helper and my deliverer;* O LORD, do not tarry.

Psalm 70:6

The Greeting

O LORD, I am your servant;* I am your servant and the child of your handmaid; you have freed me from my bonds.

Psalm 116:14

The Hymn

When peace, like a river, attends to my way,
When sorrows like sea billows roll;
Whatever my lot, You have taught me to say,
It is well, it is well with my soul.
It is well with my soul,
It is well, it is well with my soul.

And, Lord, haste the day when faith will be sight,
The clouds be rolled back as a scroll,
The trump shall resound and the Lord shall descend,
"Even so," it is well with my soul.
It is well with my soul,
It is well, it is well with my soul.

Horatio Spafford

The Refrain for the Vespers Lessons

Turn again to your rest, O my soul,* for the LORD has treated you well.

Psalm 116:6

The Vespers Psalm   *My Soul Is Content*

O God, you are my God; eagerly I seek you;* my soul thirsts for you, my flesh
   faints for you, as in a barren and dry land where there is no water.
Therefore I have gazed upon you in your holy place,* that I might behold your
   power and your glory.
For your loving-kindness is better than life itself;* my lips shall give you praise.
So will I bless you as long as I live* and lift up my hands in your Name.
My soul is content, as with marrow and fatness,* and my mouth praises you with
   joyful lips,
When I remember you upon my bed,* and meditate on you in the night watches.
For you have been my helper,* and under the shadow of your wings I will rejoice.

Psalm 63:1–7

The Refrain

Turn again to your rest, O my soul,* for the LORD has treated you well.

The Cry of the Church

Even so, come, Lord Jesus!

The Lord's Prayer

The Prayer Appointed for the Week

Stir up your power, O Lord, and with great might come among us; and, because
   we are sorely hindered by our sins, let your bountiful grace and mercy speedily help and deliver us; through Jesus Christ our Lord, to whom, with you and
   the Holy Spirit, be honor and glory now and for ever. *Amen.*†

The Concluding Prayer of the Church

Lord God, whose Son our Savior Jesus Christ, triumphed over the powers of death
and prepared for us our place in the new Jerusalem: Grant that I, who have this
day given thanks for his resurrection, may praise you in the City of which he is
the light, and where he lives and reigns for ever and ever. *Amen.*†

The Morning Office **To Be Observed on the Hour or Half Hour
Between 6 and 9 a.m.**

The Call to Prayer

Bless the Lord, you angels of his, you mighty ones who do his bidding,* and hear-
ken to the voice of his word.
Bless the Lord, all you his hosts,* you ministers of his who do his will.
Bless the Lord, all you works of his,* in all places of his dominion . . .

Psalm 103:20–22

The Request for Presence

Be seated on your lofty throne, O Most High;* O Lord, judge the nations.

Psalm 7:8

The Greeting

Not to us, O Lord, not to us, but to your Name give glory;* because of your love
and because of your faithfulness.

Psalm 115:1

The Refrain for the Morning Lessons

On this day the Lord has acted;* we will rejoice and be glad in it.

Psalm 118:24

A Reading

Mary set out at that time and went as quickly as she could into the hill country to a
town in Judah. She went into Zechariah's house and greeted Elizabeth. Now it
happened that as soon as Elizabeth heard Mary's greeting, the child leapt in
her womb and Elizabeth was filled with the Holy Spirit. She gave a loud cry
and said, 'Of all women you are the most blessed, and blessed is the fruit of
your womb. Why should I be honored with a visit from the mother of my
Lord? Look, the moment your greeting reached my ears, the child in my womb
leapt for joy. Yes, blessed is she who believed that the promise made her by the
Lord would be fulfilled.'

Luke 1:39–45

The Refrain

On this day the Lord has acted;* we will rejoice and be glad in it.

The Morning Psalm *O Lord, I Am Your Servant*

O Lord, I am your servant;* I am your servant and the child of your handmaid;
you have freed me from my bonds.
I will offer you the sacrifice of thanksgiving* and call upon the Name of the Lord.

I will fulfill my vows to the LORD* in the presence of all his people,
In the courts of the LORD's house,* in the midst of you, O Jerusalem. Hallelujah!

Psalm 116:14–17

The Refrain
On this day the LORD has acted;* we will rejoice and be glad in it.

The Cry of the Church
Let us praise the Lord, whom the Angels are praising, whom the Cherubim and
Seraphim proclaim: Holy, holy, holy!

THE SHORT BREVIARY

The Lord's Prayer

The Prayer Appointed for the Week
Stir up your power, O Lord, and with great might come among us; and, because
we are sorely hindered by our sins, let your bountiful grace and mercy speedily help and deliver us; through Jesus Christ our Lord, to whom, with you and
the Holy Spirit, be honor and glory now and for ever. *Amen.*†

The Concluding Prayer of the Church
Lord God, almighty and everlasting Father, you have brought me in safety to this
new day: Preserve me with your mighty power, that I may not fall into sin, nor
be overcome by adversity; and in all I do direct me to the fulfilling of your purpose; through Jesus Christ my Lord. *Amen.*†

The Midday Office   **To Be Observed on the Hour or Half Hour**
Between 11 a.m. and 2 p.m.

The Call to Prayer
Bless the LORD, you angels of his, you mighty ones who do his bidding,* and hear-
ken to the voice of his word.
Bless the LORD, all you his hosts,* you ministers of his who do his will.
Bless the LORD, all you works of his, in all places of his dominion;* bless the LORD,
O my soul.

Psalm 103:20–22

The Request for Presence
I am a stranger here on earth;* do not hide your commandments from me.

Psalm 119:19

The Greeting
I am bound by the vow I made to you, O God;* I will present to you thank-
offerings;
For you have rescued my soul from death and my feet from stumbling,* that I may
walk before God in the light of the living.

Psalm 56:11–12

The Refrain for the Midday Lessons

Glory be to him whose power, working in us, can do infinitely more than we can
    ask or imagine; glory be to him from generation to generation in the Church
    and in Christ Jesus for ever and ever. Amen.

Ephesians 3:20–21

A Reading

Good faith has vanished; anyone abstaining from evil is victimized. YAHWEH saw
    this and was displeased that there was no fair judgement. He saw there was no
    one and wondered there was no one to intervene. So he made his own arm his
    mainstay, his own saving justice his support. He put on saving justice like a
    breastplate, on his head the helmet of salvation. He put on the clothes of
    vengeance like a tunic and wrapped himself in jealousy like a cloak. To each he
    repays his due, retribution to his enemies, reprisals on his foes, to the coasts
    and islands he will repay their due. From the west, YAHWEH's name will be
    feared, and from the east his glory, for he will come like a pent-up stream
    impelled by the breath of YAHWEH. Then for Zion will come a redeemer, for
    those who stop rebelling in Jacob, declares YAHWEH.

Isaiah 59:15–20

The Refrain

Glory be to him whose power, working in us, can do infinitely more than we can
    ask or imagine; glory be to him from generation to generation in the Church
    and in Christ Jesus for ever and ever. Amen.

The Midday Psalm   *He Has Made the Whole World So Sure It Cannot Be Moved*

The LORD is King; he has put on splendid apparel;* the LORD has put on his
    apparel and girded himself with strength.

He has made the whole world so sure* that it cannot be moved;

Ever since the world began, your throne has been established;* you are from
    everlasting.

The waters have lifted up, O LORD, the waters have lifted up their voice;* the
    waters have lifted up their pounding waves.

Mightier than the sound of many waters, mightier than the breakers of the sea,*
    mightier is the LORD who dwells on high.

Your testimonies are very sure,* and holiness adorns your house, O LORD, for ever
    and for evermore.

Psalm 93

The Refrain

Glory be to him whose power, working in us, can do infinitely more than we can
    ask or imagine; glory be to him from generation to generation in the Church
    and in Christ Jesus for ever and ever. Amen.

The Cry of the Church

Even so, come, Lord Jesus!

The Lord's Prayer

The Prayer Appointed for the Week

Stir up your power, O Lord, and with great might come among us; and, because
we are sorely hindered by our sins, let your bountiful grace and mercy speedily help and deliver us; through Jesus Christ our Lord, to whom, with you and
the Holy Spirit, be honor and glory now and for ever. *Amen.*†

The Concluding Prayer of the Church

O God, the King eternal, whose light divides the day from the night and turns the
shadow of death into the morning: Drive from me all wrong desires, incline my
heart to keep your law, and guide my feet into the way of peace; that, having
done your will with cheerfulness during the day, I may, when night comes,
rejoice to give you thanks; through Jesus Christ my Lord. *Amen.*†

The Vespers Office   **To Be Observed on the Hour or Half Hour**
Between 5 and 8 p.m.

The Call to Prayer

Let the Name of the LORD be blessed,* from this time forth for evermore.
From the rising of the sun to its going down* let the Name of the LORD be praised.

Psalm 113:2–3

The Request for Presence

Hear my prayer, O God;* do not hide yourself from my petition.
Listen to me and answer me . . .

Psalm 55:1–2

The Greeting

The Lord is in his holy temple; let all the earth keep silence before him.

Traditional

The Hymn

At the name of Jesus every knee will bow,
Every tongue confess him King of glory now
'Tis the Father's pleasure, we should call him Lord,
Who from the beginning was the mighty Word.

In your hearts enthrone him; there, let him subdue
All that is not holy, all that is not true;
May your voice entreat him in temptation's hour;
Let his will enfold you in its light and power.

Brothers, this Lord Jesus shall return again,
With his Father's glory, o'er the earth to reign;
He is God the Savior; He is Christ the Lord,
Ever to be worshipped, always blessed, adored.

C. NOEL

The Refrain for the Vespers Lessons

Put your trust in God;* for I will yet give thanks to him, who is the help of my
countenance, and my God.

Psalm 42:7

The Vespers Psalm   *We Will Praise Your Name For Ever*

We have heard with our ears, O God, our forefathers have told us,* the deeds you
did in their days, in the days of old.

How with your hand you drove the peoples out and planted our forefathers in the
land;* how you destroyed nations and made your people flourish.

For they did not take the land by their sword, nor did their arm win the victory for
them;* but your right hand, your arm, and the light of your countenance,
because you favored them.

You are my King and my God;* you command victories for Jacob.

Through you we pushed back our adversaries;* through your Name we trampled
on those who rose up against us.

For I do not rely on my bow,* and my sword does not give me the victory.

Surely, you gave us victory over our adversaries* and put those who hate us to
shame.

Every day we gloried in God,* and we will praise your Name for ever.

Psalm 44:1–8

The Refrain

Put your trust in God;* for I will yet give thanks to him, who is the help of my
countenance, and my God.

The Cry of the Church

O God, come to my assistance! O Lord, make haste to help me!

The Lord's Prayer

The Prayer Appointed for the Week

Stir up your power, O Lord, and with great might come among us; and, because
we are sorely hindered by our sins, let your bountiful grace and mercy speedily help and deliver us; through Jesus Christ our Lord, to whom, with you and
the Holy Spirit, be honor and glory now and for ever. *Amen.*†

The Concluding Prayer of the Church

Save me, Lord, while I am awake and keep me while I sleep, that I may wake with
Christ and rest in peace. *Amen.*

The Morning Office   **To Be Observed on the Hour or Half Hour
Between 6 and 9 a.m.**

The Call to Prayer

Come, let us sing to the Lord;* let us shout for joy to the Rock of our salvation.

Psalm 95:1

The Request for Presence
Bow your heavens, O Lord, and come down;* touch the mountains, and they shall
    smoke.

Psalm 144:5

The Greeting
My lips will sing with joy when I play to you,* and so will my soul, which you
    have redeemed.

Psalm 71:23

The Refrain for the Morning Lessons
Your love, O Lord, for ever will I sing;* from age to age my mouth will proclaim
    your faithfulness.

Psalm 89:1

A Reading
Because you have kept my commandment to persevere, I will keep you safe in the
    time of trial which is coming for the whole world, to put the people of the
    world to the test. I am coming soon: hold firmly to what you already have, and
    let no one take your victor's crown away from you. Anyone who proves victo-
    rious I will make into a pillar in the sanctuary of my God, and it will stay there
    for ever; I will inscribe on it the name of my God and the name of the city of my
    God, the new Jerusalem which is coming down from my God in heaven, and
    my own new name as well. Let anyone who can hear, listen to what the Spirit is
    saying to the churches.

Revelation 3:10–13

The Refrain
Your love, O Lord, for ever will I sing;* from age to age my mouth will proclaim
    your faithfulness.

The Morning Psalm   *His Mercy Is Great*
He has not dealt with us according to our sins,* nor rewarded us according to our
    wickedness.
For as the heavens are high above the earth,* so is his mercy great upon those who
    fear him.
As far as the east is from the west,* so far has he removed our sins from us.
As a father cares for his children,* so does the Lord care for those who fear him.
For he himself knows whereof we are made;* he remembers that we are but dust.

Psalm 103:10–13

The Refrain
Your love, O Lord, for ever will I sing;* from age to age my mouth will proclaim
    your faithfulness.

The Cry of the Church
Even so, come, Lord Jesus!

The Lord's Prayer

The Prayer Appointed for the Week

Stir up your power, O Lord, and with great might come among us; and, because
we are sorely hindered by our sins, let your bountiful grace and mercy speedily help and deliver us; through Jesus Christ our Lord, to whom, with you and
the Holy Spirit, be honor and glory now and for ever. *Amen.*†

The Concluding Prayer of the Church

Lord God, almighty and everlasting Father, you have brought me in safety to this
new day: Preserve me with your mighty power, that I may not fall into sin, nor
be overcome by adversity; and in all I do direct me to the fulfilling of your purpose; through Jesus Christ my Lord. *Amen.*†

The Midday Office　　　　　　　　**To Be Observed on the Hour or Half Hour**
Between 11 a.m. and 2 p.m.

The Call to Prayer

Praise God from whom all blessings flow; praise him, all creatures here below;
praise him above, you heavenly hosts; praise Father, Son and Holy Ghost.

Doxology

The Request for Presence

May the glory of the LORD endure for ever;* may the LORD rejoice in all his works.

Psalm 104:32

The Greeting

Hosanna, LORD, hosanna!* LORD, send us now success.
Blessed is he who comes in the name of the Lord; . . .
God is the LORD; he has shined upon us;* form a procession with branches up to
the horns of the altar.

Psalm 118:25–27

The Refrain for the Midday Lessons

I will walk in the presence of the LORD* in the land of the living.

Psalm 116:8

A Reading

Listen, my God, listen to us; open your eyes and look at our plight and at the city
that bears your name. Relying not on your upright deeds but on your great
mercy, we pour out our plea to you. Listen, Lord! Forgive, Lord! Hear, Lord,
and act! For your own sake, my God do not delay—since your city and your
people alike bear your name.

Daniel 9:18–19

The Refrain

I will walk in the presence of the LORD* in the land of the living.

The Midday Psalm   *The Works of the LORD Are Sure*

Rejoice in the LORD, you righteous;* it is good for the just to sing praises.
Praise the LORD with the harp;* play to him upon the psaltery and lyre.
Sing for him a new song;* sound a fanfare with all your skill upon the trumpet.
For the word of the LORD is right,* and all his works are sure.
He loves righteousness and justice;* the loving-kindness of the LORD fills the
    whole earth.

Psalm 33:1–5

The Refrain
I will walk in the presence of the LORD* in the land of the living.

The Cry of the Church
Even so, come, Lord Jesus!

The Lord's Prayer

The Prayer Appointed for the Week
Stir up your power, O Lord, and with great might come among us; and, because
    we are sorely hindered by our sins, let your bountiful grace and mercy speed-
    ily help and deliver us; through Jesus Christ our Lord, to whom, with you and
    the Holy Spirit, be honor and glory now and for ever. *Amen.†*

The Concluding Prayer of the Church
Almighty and eternal God, ruler of all things in heaven and earth: Mercifully
    accept the prayers of your people everywhere, and strengthen each of us to do
    your will; through Jesus Christ my Lord. *Amen.†*

The Vespers Office   **To Be Observed on the Hour or Half Hour
Between 5 and 8 p.m.**

The Call to Prayer
Praise the LORD, all you nations;* laud him, all you peoples.
For his loving-kindness toward us is great,* and the faithfulness of the LORD
    endures for ever. . . .

Psalm 117:1–2

The Request for Presence
O LORD, do not forsake me;* be not far from me, O my God.
Make haste to help me,* O Lord of my salvation.

Psalm 38:21–22

The Greeting
You are my refuge and shield;* my hope is in your word.

Psalm 119:114

The Hymn

There's a song in the air! There's a star in the sky!
There's a mother's deep prayer and a baby's low cry!
And the star rains its fire while the beautiful sing,
For the manger of Bethlehem cradles a King!

There's a tumult of joy over the wonderful birth,
For the Virgin's sweet boy is the Lord of the earth.
Ay! The star rains its fire while the beautiful sing,
For the manger of Bethlehem cradles a King!

In the light of that star lie the ages impearled;
And that song from afar has swept over the world.
Every hearth is aflame, and the beautiful sing
And we greet in His cradle our Savior and king!

Josiah Holland

The Refrain for the Vespers Lessons

. . . it is good for me to be near God;* I have made the Lord GOD my refuge.

Psalm 73:28

The Vespers Psalm   *Great Things Have You Done, O LORD My God*

I waited patiently upon the LORD;* he stooped to me and heard my cry.

He lifted me out of the desolate pit, out of the mire and clay;* he set my feet upon a
high cliff and made my footing sure.

He put a new song in my mouth, a song of praise to our God;* many shall see, and
stand in awe, and put their trust in the LORD.

Happy are they who trust in the LORD!* they do not resort to evil spirits or turn to
false gods.

Great things are they that you have done, O LORD my God! how great your
wonders and your plans for us!* there is none who can be compared with you.

Oh, that I could make them known and tell them!* but they are more than I can
count.

Psalm 40:1–6

The Refrain

. . . it is good for me to be near God;* I have made the Lord GOD my refuge.

The Cry of the Church

Lord, have mercy on us. Christ, have mercy on us. Lord, have mercy on us.

The Lord's Prayer

The Prayer Appointed for the Week

Stir up your power, O Lord, and with great might come among us; and, because
we are sorely hindered by our sins, let your bountiful grace and mercy speedily help and deliver us; through Jesus Christ our Lord, to whom, with you and
the Holy Spirit, be honor and glory now and for ever. *Amen.*†

The Concluding Prayer of the Church

Save me, O Lord, while I am awake and keep me while I sleep, that I may wake in Christ and rest in peace.

adapted from THE SHORT BREVIARY

The Morning Office

To Be Observed on the Hour or Half Hour Between 6 and 9 a.m.

The Call to Prayer

My mouth shall speak the praise of the LORD;* let all flesh bless his holy Name for ever and ever.

Psalm 145:22

The Request for Presence

O Lamb of God, that takes away the sins of the world, have mercy on me.
O Lamb of God, that takes away the sins of the world, have mercy on me.
O Lamb of God, that takes away the sins of the world, grant me your peace.

Agnus Dei

The Greeting

Your love, O LORD, reaches to the heavens,* and your faithfulness to the clouds.

Psalm 36:5

The Refrain for the Morning Lessons

I will exalt you, O God my King,* and bless your Name for ever and ever.

Psalm 145:1

A Reading

Near the cross of Jesus stood his mother and his mother's sister, Mary the wife of Clopas, and Mary of Magdela. Seeing his mother and the disciple whom he loved standing near her, Jesus said to his mother, 'Woman, this is your son.' Then to the disciple he said, 'This is your mother.' And from that hour the disciple took her into his home.

John 19:25–27

The Refrain

I will exalt you, O God my King,* and bless your Name for ever and ever.

The Morning Psalm   *The LORD Will Make Good His Purposes*

I will give thanks to you, O LORD, with my whole heart;* before the gods I will sing your praise.
I will bow down toward your holy temple and praise your Name,* because of your love and faithfulness;
For you have glorified your Name* and your word above all things.
When I called, you answered me;* you increased my strength within me.
All the kings of the earth will praise you, O LORD,* when they have heard the words of your mouth.
They will sing of the ways of the LORD,* that great is the glory of the LORD.

Though the LORD be high, he cares for the lowly;* he perceives the haughty from afar.
Though I walk in the midst of trouble, you keep me safe;* you stretch forth your
    hand against the fury of my enemies; your right hand shall save me.
The LORD will make good his purpose for me;* O LORD, your love endures for
    ever; do not abandon the works of your hands.

Psalm 138

The Refrain
I will exalt you, O God my King,* and bless your Name for ever and ever.

The Cry of the Church
O God, come to my assistance! O Lord, make haste to help me!

The Lord's Prayer

The Prayer Appointed for the Week
Stir up your power, O Lord, and with great might come among us; and, because
    we are sorely hindered by our sins, let your bountiful grace and mercy speed-
    ily help and deliver us; through Jesus Christ our Lord, to whom, with you and
    the Holy Spirit, be honor and glory now and for ever. *Amen.*†

The Concluding Prayer of the Church
Lord God, almighty and everlasting Father, you have brought me in safety to this
    new day: Preserve me with your mighty power, that I may not fall into sin, nor
    be overcome by adversity; and in all I do direct me to the fulfilling of your pur-
    pose; through Jesus Christ my Lord. *Amen.*†

The Midday Office   **To Be Observed on the Hour or Half Hour**
Between 11 a.m. and 2 p.m.

The Call to Prayer
Bless the LORD, O my soul,* and all that is within me, bless his holy Name.

Psalm 103:1

The Request for Presence
Hearken to my voice, O LORD, when I call;* have mercy on me and answer me.
You speak in my heart and say, "Seek my face."* Your face, LORD, will I seek.
Hide not your face from me,* nor turn away your servant in displeasure.

Psalm 27:10–12

The Greeting
I restrain my feet from every evil way,* that I may keep your word.

Psalm 119:101

The Refrain for the Midday Lessons
For one day in your courts is better than a thousand in my own room,* and to stand
    at the threshold of the house of my God than to dwell in the tents of the wicked.

Psalm 84:9

A Reading

As there were false prophets in the past history of our people, so you too will have your false teachers, who will insinuate their own disruptive views and, by disowning the Lord who brought them freedom, will bring upon themselves a speedy destruction. Many will copy their debauched behavior and the Way of Truth will be brought into disrepute on their account.

2 Peter 2:1–2

The Refrain

For one day in your courts is better than a thousand in my own room,* and to stand at the threshold of the house of my God than to dwell in the tents of the wicked.

The Midday Psalm *Ascribe to the LORD the Glory Due His Name*

Ascribe to the LORD, you gods,* ascribe to the LORD glory and strength.

Ascribe to the LORD the glory due his Name;* worship the LORD in the beauty of holiness.

The voice of the LORD is upon the waters; the God of glory thunders;* the LORD is upon the mighty waters.

The voice of the LORD is a powerful voice;* the voice of the LORD is a voice of splendor.

The voice of the LORD breaks the cedar trees;* the LORD breaks the cedars of Lebanon;

He makes Lebanon skip like a calf,* and Mount Hermon like a young wild ox.

The voice of the LORD splits the flames of fire; the voice of the LORD shakes the wilderness;* the LORD shakes the wilderness of Kadesh.

The voice of the LORD makes the oak trees writhe* and strips the forests bare.

And in the temple of the LORD* all are crying, "Glory!"

Psalm 29:1–9

The Refrain

For one day in your courts is better than a thousand in my own room,* and to stand at the threshold of the house of my God than to dwell in the tents of the wicked.

The Cry of the Church

O Lamb of God, that takes away the sins of the world, have mercy upon me.
O Lamb of God, that takes away the sins of the world, have mercy upon me.
O Lamb of God, that takes away the sins of the world, grant me your peace.

The Lord's Prayer

The Prayer Appointed for the Week

Stir up your power, O Lord, and with great might come among us; and, because we are sorely hindered by our sins, let your bountiful grace and mercy speedily help and deliver us; through Jesus Christ our Lord, to whom, with you and the Holy Spirit, be honor and glory now and for ever. *Amen.†*

The Concluding Prayer of the Church

God of justice, God of mercy, bless all those who are surprised with pain this day
from suffering caused by their own weakness or that of others. Let what we
suffer teach us to be merciful; let our sins teach us to forgive. This we ask
through the intercession of Jesus and all who died forgiving those who
oppressed them. *Amen.*

THE NEW COMPANION TO THE BREVIARY

The Vespers Office   **To Be Observed on the Hour or Half Hour
Between 5 and 8 p.m.**

The Call to Prayer

Praise the LORD, all you nations;* laud him, all you peoples.
For his loving-kindness toward us is great,* and the faithfulness of the LORD
endures for ever. Hallelujah!

Psalm 117

The Request for Presence

Gladden the soul of your servant,* for to you, O LORD, I lift up my soul.

Psalm 86:4

The Greeting

One generation shall praise your works to another* and shall declare your power.

Psalm 145:4

The Hymn

Sing praise to God who reigns above, the God of all creation,
The God of power, the God of love, the God of our salvation;
With healing balm my soul he fills, And every faithless murmur stills:
To God all praise and glory.

What God's almighty power has made, his gracious mercy keeps;
By morning glow or evening shade his watchful eye ne'er sleeps;
Within the kingdom of his might, Lo! All is just and all is right:
To God all praise and glory.

Then all my gladsome way along, I sing aloud your praises,
That men may hear the grateful song my voice unwearied raises;
Be joyful in the Lord, my heart, both soul and body, bear your part:
To God all praise and glory.

O you who name Christ's holy name, give God all praise and glory;
All you who own his power, proclaim aloud the wondrous story!
Cast each false idol from his throne. The Lord is God and he alone:
To God all praise and glory.

Johann Schultz

The Refrain for the Vespers Lessons
Happy are they all who fear the LORD,* and who follow in his ways!

Psalm 128:1

The Vespers Psalm   *The LORD of Hosts Is the King of Glory*
Lift up your heads, O gates; lift them high, O everlasting doors;* and the King of
    glory shall come in.
"Who is this King of glory?"* "The LORD, strong and mighty, the LORD, mighty in
    battle."
Lift up your heads, O gates; lift them high, O everlasting doors;* and the King of
    glory shall come in.
"Who is he, this King of glory?"* "The LORD of hosts, he is the King of glory."

Psalm 24:7–10

The Refrain
Happy are they all who fear the LORD,* and who follow in his ways!

The Cry of the Church
Even so, come, Lord Jesus!

The Lord's Prayer

The Prayer Appointed for the Week
Stir up your power, O Lord, and with great might come among us; and, because
    we are sorely hindered by our sins, let your bountiful grace and mercy speed-
    ily help and deliver us; through Jesus Christ our Lord, to whom, with you and
    the Holy Spirit, be honor and glory now and for ever. *Amen.*†

The Concluding Prayer of the Church
May Almighty God grant me a peaceful night and a perfect end. *Amen.*

The Morning Office   **To Be Observed on the Hour or Half Hour**
Between 6 and 9 a.m.

The Call to Prayer
Open my lips, O LORD,* and my mouth shall proclaim your praise.

Psalm 51:16

The Request for Presence
Bow down your ear, O LORD, and answer me . . .
Keep watch over my life, for I am faithful.

Psalm 86:1–2

The Greeting
Lord, you have been our refuge* from one generation to another.
Before the mountains were brought forth, or the land and the earth were born,*
    from age to age you are God.

Psalm 90:1–2

The Refrain for the Morning Lessons

Truly, his salvation is very near to those who fear him,* that his glory may dwell in our land.

Psalm 85:9

A Reading

The beginning of the gospel about Jesus Christ, the Son of God. It is written in the prophet of Isaiah: *Look, I am going to send my messenger in front of you to prepare your way before you. A voice of one that cries in the desert: Prepare a way for the Lord, make his paths straight.* John the Baptist was in the desert, proclaiming a baptism of repentance for the forgiveness of sins.

Mark 1:1–4

The Refrain

Truly, his salvation is very near to those who fear him,* that his glory may dwell in our land.

The Morning Psalm   Bless Our God, You People

Come now and see the works of God,* how wonderful he is in his doing toward all people.
In his might he rules for ever; his eyes keep watch over the nations;* let no rebel rise up against him.
Bless our God, you peoples;* make the voice of his praise to be heard;
Who holds our souls in life,* and will not allow our feet to slip.

Psalm 66:4, 6–8

The Refrain

Truly, his salvation is very near to those who fear him,* that his glory may dwell in our land.

The Cry of the Church

Be, Lord, my helper and forsake me not. Do not despise me, O God, my savior.

THE SHORT BREVIARY

The Lord's Prayer

The Prayer Appointed for the Week

Stir up your power, O Lord, and with great might come among us; and, because we are sorely hindered by our sins, let your bountiful grace and mercy speedily help and deliver us; through Jesus Christ our Lord, to whom, with you and the Holy Spirit, be honor and glory now and for ever. *Amen.*†

The Concluding Prayer of the Church

Lord God, almighty and everlasting Father, you have brought me in safety to this new day: Preserve me with your mighty power, that I may not fall into sin, nor be overcome by adversity; and in all I do direct me to the fulfilling of your purpose; through Jesus Christ my Lord. *Amen.*†

The Midday Office   To Be Observed on the Hour or Half Hour
                                     Between 11 a.m. and 2 p.m.

The Call to Prayer
Sing to God, O kingdoms of the earth;* sing praises to the Lord.
He rides in the heavens, the ancient heavens;* he sends forth his voice, his mighty
    voice.

Psalm 68:33–34

The Request for Presence
For God alone my soul in silence waits;* from him comes my salvation.

Psalm 62:1

The Greeting
Awesome things will you show us in your righteousness,* O God of our salvation,
    O Hope of all the ends of the earth . . .

Psalm 65:5

The Refrain for the Midday Lessons
Happy are they who trust in the LORD!

Psalm 40:4

A Reading
Go up on a high mountain, messenger of Zion. Shout as loud as you can, messen-
    ger of Jerusalem! Shout fearlessly, say to the towns of Judah, 'Here is your
    God.' Here is Lord YAHWEH coming with power, his arm maintains his author-
    ity, his reward is with him and his prize precedes him. He is like a shepherd
    feeding his flock, gathering lambs in his arms, holding them against his breast
    and leading to their rest the mother ewes.

Isaiah 40:9–11

The Refrain
Happy are they who trust in the LORD!

The Midday Psalm   *Light Shines in the Darkness for the Upright*
Hallelujah! Happy are they who fear the Lord* and have great delight in his
    commandments!
Their descendants will be mighty in the land;* the generation of the upright will
    be blessed.
Wealth and riches will be in their house,* and their righteousness will last for ever.
Light shines in the darkness for the upright;* the righteous are merciful and full of
    compassion.
It is good for them to be generous in lending* and to manage their affairs with
    justice.
For they will never be shaken;* the righteous will be kept in everlasting
    remembrance.
They will not be afraid of any evil rumors;* their heart is right; they put their trust
    in the Lord.

Their heart is established and will not shrink,* until they see their desire upon their enemies.

They have given freely to the poor,* and their righteousness stands fast for ever; they will hold up their head with honor.

The wicked will see it and be angry; they will gnash their teeth and pine away;* the desires of the wicked will perish.

Psalm 112

The Refrain
Happy are they who trust in the LORD!

The Cry of the Church
Be, Lord, my helper and forsake me not. Do not despise me, O God, my savior.

THE SHORT BREVIARY

The Lord's Prayer

The Prayer Appointed for the Week
Stir up your power, O Lord, and with great might come among us; and, because we are sorely hindered by our sins, let your bountiful grace and mercy speedily help and deliver us; through Jesus Christ our Lord, to whom, with you and the Holy Spirit, be honor and glory now and for ever. *Amen.*†

The Concluding Prayer of the Church
May God have mercy on me, forgive me my sins and bring me to life everlasting. In Jesus' name. *Amen.*

The Vespers Office **To Be Observed on the Hour or Half Hour Between 5 and 8 p.m.**

The Call to Prayer
Let us come before his presence with thanksgiving* and raise a loud shout to him with psalms.

Psalm 95:2

The Request for Presence
Remember not our past sins; let your compassion be swift to meet us;* for we have been brought very low.

Help us, O God our Savior, for the glory of your Name;* deliver us and forgive us our sins, for your Name's sake.

Psalm 79:8–9

The Greeting
Exalt yourself above the heavens, O God,* and your glory over all the earth.

Psalm 57:11

The Hymn

Celestial Word, proceeding from
The Eternal Father's breast,
And in the wend of ages come
To aid a world distressed:

Enlighten, Lord, and set on fire
Our Spirits with Your love,
That dead to earth they may aspire
And live to joys above.

To God the Father, God the Son
And Holy Ghost to Thee
As heretofore, when time is done
Unending glory be.

adapted from THE SHORT BREVIARY

The Refrain for the Vespers Lessons

. . . when the LORD restores the fortunes of his people, Jacob will rejoice and Israel
be glad.

Psalm 14:7b

The Vespers Psalm   The Eyes of All Wait Upon You, O LORD

The LORD is faithful in all his words* and merciful in all his deeds.
The LORD upholds all those who fall;* he lifts up those who are bowed down.
The eyes of all wait upon you, O LORD,* and you give them their food in due
season.
You open wide your hand* and satisfy the needs of every living creature.
The LORD is righteous in all his ways* and loving in all his works.

Psalm 145:14–18

The Refrain

. . . when the LORD restores the fortunes of his people, Jacob will rejoice and Israel
be glad.

The Cry of the Church

Even so, come, Lord Jesus!

The Lord's Prayer

The Prayer Appointed for the Week

Stir up your power, O Lord, and with great might come among us; and, because
we are sorely hindered by our sins, let your bountiful grace and mercy speedily help and deliver us; through Jesus Christ our Lord, to whom, with you and
the Holy Spirit, be honor and glory now and for ever. *Amen.*†

The Concluding Prayer of the Church

Blessed be the Lord God of Israel for he has visited and delivered us. Alleluia,
alleluia, alleluia.

Traditional

The Morning Office   To Be Observed on the Hour or Half Hour
                                                         Between 6 and 9 a.m.

The Call to Prayer
I will call upon God,* and the LORD will deliver me.
In the evening, in the morning, and at noonday, I will complain and lament,* and
       he will hear my voice.
He will bring me safely back . . . * God, who is enthroned of old, will hear me.
                                                                 Psalm 55:17ff

The Request for Presence
Be pleased, O God, to deliver me;* O LORD, make haste to help me.
                                                                 Psalm 70:1

The Greeting
Happy are they whom you choose and draw to your courts to dwell there!* they
       will be satisfied by the beauty of your house, by the holiness of your temple.
                                                                 Psalm 65:4

The Refrain for the Morning Lessons
Our soul waits for the LORD;* he is our help and our shield.
                                                                 Psalm 33:20

A Reading
Now his mother and his brothers arrived, and standing outside, sent in a message
       asking for him. A crowd was sitting round him at the time the message was
       passed to him, 'Look, your mother and brothers and sisters are outside asking
       for you.' He replied, 'Who are my mother and my brothers? Anyone who does
       the will of God, that person is my brother and sister and mother.'
                                                                 Mark 3:31–35

The Refrain
Our soul waits for the LORD;* he is our help and our shield.

The Morning Psalm   *For God Alone My Soul in Silence Waits*
For God alone my soul in silence waits;* truly, my hope is in him.
He alone is my rock and my salvation,* my stronghold, so that I shall not be
       shaken.
In God is my safety and my honor;* God is my strong rock and my refuge.
Put your trust in him always, O people,* pour out your hearts before him, for God
       is our refuge.
Those of high degree are but a fleeting breath,* even those of low estate cannot be
       trusted.
On the scales they are lighter than a breath,* all of them together.
Put no trust in extortion; in robbery take no empty pride;* though wealth increase,
       set not your heart upon it.

God has spoken once, twice have I heard it,* that power belongs to God.
Steadfast love is yours, O Lord,* for you repay everyone according to his deeds.

Psalm 62:6–14

The Refrain
Our soul waits for the LORD;* he is our help and our shield.

The Cry of the Church
O God, come to my assistance! O Lord, make haste to help me!

The Lord's Prayer

The Prayer Appointed for the Week
Stir up your power, O Lord, and with great might come among us; and, because
we are sorely hindered by our sins, let your bountiful grace and mercy speedily help and deliver us; through Jesus Christ our Lord, to whom, with you and
the Holy Spirit, be honor and glory now and for ever. *Amen.*†

The Concluding Prayer of the Church
Lord God, almighty and everlasting Father, you have brought me in safety to this
new day: Preserve me with your mighty power, that I may not fall into sin, nor
be overcome by adversity; and in all I do direct me to the fulfilling of your purpose; through Jesus Christ my Lord. *Amen.*†

The Midday Office

**To Be Observed on the Hour or Half Hour
Between 11 a.m. and 2 p.m.**

The Call to Prayer
Sing to the LORD with thanksgiving;* make music to our God upon the harp.

Psalm 147:7

The Request for Presence
Hear, O Shepherd of Israel, leading Joseph like a flock;* shine forth, you that are
enthroned upon the cherubim.

Psalm 80:1

The Greeting
Exalt yourself above the heavens, O God,* and your glory over all the earth.

Psalm 57:6

The Refrain for the Midday Lessons
The LORD has sworn and he will not recant:* "You are a priest for ever after the
order of Melchizedek."

Psalm 110:4

A Reading
Whoever believes that Jesus is the Christ is a child of God, and whoever loves the
father loves the son. In this way we know that we love God's children, when
we love God and keep his commandments. This is what the love of God is:

keeping his commandments. Nor are his commandments burdensome, because every child of God overcomes the world. And this is the victory that has overcome the world—our faith.

1 John 5:1-4

The Refrain
The LORD has sworn and he will not recant:* "You are a priest for ever after the order of Melchizedek."

The Midday Psalm   *All Kings Shall Bow Down Before Him*
All kings shall bow down before him,* and all the nations do him service.
For he shall deliver the poor who cries out in distress,* and the oppressed who has no helper.
He shall have pity on the lowly and poor;* he shall preserve the lives of the needy.
He shall redeem their lives from oppression and violence,* and dear shall their blood be in his sight.
Long may he live! and may there be given to him gold from Arabia;* may prayer be made for him always, and may they bless him all the day long.
May there be abundance of grain on the earth, growing thick even on the hilltops;* may its fruit flourish like Lebanon, and its grain like grass upon the earth.
May his Name remain for ever and be established as long as the sun endures;* may all the nations bless themselves in him and call him blessed.
Blessed be the Lord GOD, the God of Israel,* who alone does wondrous deeds!
And blessed be his glorious Name for ever!* and may all the earth be filled with his glory. Amen. Amen.

Psalm 72:11-19

The Refrain
The LORD has sworn and he will not recant:* "You are a priest for ever after the order of Melchizedek."

The Cry of the Church
Even so, come, Lord Jesus!

The Lord's Prayer

The Prayer Appointed for the Week
Stir up your power, O Lord, and with great might come among us; and, because we are sorely hindered by our sins, let your bountiful grace and mercy speedily help and deliver us; through Jesus Christ our Lord, to whom, with you and the Holy Spirit, be honor and glory now and for ever. *Amen.†*

The Concluding Prayer of the Church
Lord Jesus Christ, by your death you took away the sting of death: Grant me to so follow in faith where you have led the way, that I may at length fall asleep peacefully in you and wake in your likeness; for your tender mercies' sake. *Amen.†*

The Vespers Office   **To Be Observed on the Hour or Half Hour**
                                          Between 5 and 8 p.m.

The Call to Prayer
I will call upon the LORD,* and so shall I be saved from my enemies.
Psalm 18:3

The Request for Presence
I have said to the Lord, "You are my God;* Listen, O Lord, to my supplication."
Psalm 140:6

The Greeting
But you, O Lord my GOD, oh, deal with me according to your Name;* for your tender mercy's sake, deliver me.
For I am poor and needy,* and my heart is wounded within me.
Psalm 109:20–21

The Hymn
Hail to the Lord's Anointed, great David's greater Son!
Hail in the time appointed, his reign on earth begun!
He comes to break oppression, to set the captive free;
To take away transgression, and rule in equity.

He comes with succor speedy to those who suffer wrong;
To help the poor and needy, and bid the weak be strong;
To give them songs for sighing, their darkness turn to light,
Whose souls condemned and dying, are precious in his sight.

He shall come down like showers upon the fruitful earth;
Love, joy, and hope like flowers, spring in his path to birth.
Before him, on the mountains, shall peace, the herald, go,
And righteousness, in fountains, from hill and valley flow.

To him shall prayer unceasing and daily vows ascend;
His kingdom still increasing, a kingdom without end.
The tide of time shall never his covenant remove;
His name shall stand forever; that name to us is love.
James Montgomery

The Refrain for the Vespers Lessons
For the LORD has heard the sound of my weeping.
The LORD has heard my supplication;* the LORD accepts my prayer.
Psalm 6:8–9

The Vespers Psalm   *The God of Gods Will Reveal Himself in Zion*
How dear to me is your dwelling, O LORD of hosts!* My soul has a desire and
    longing for the courts of the LORD; my heart and my flesh rejoice in the living God.
The sparrow has found her a house and the swallow a nest where she may lay her
    young;* by the side of your altars, O LORD of hosts, my King and my God.

Happy are they who dwell in your house!* they will always be praising you.
Happy are the people whose strength is in you!* whose hearts are set on the
pilgrims' way.
Those who go through the desolate valley will find it a place of springs,* for the
early rains have covered it with pools of water.
They will climb from height to height,* and the God of gods will reveal himself in
Zion.

Psalm 84:1–6

The Refrain
For the LORD has heard the sound of my weeping.
The LORD has heard my supplication;* the LORD accepts my prayer.

The Cry of the Church
Be, Lord, my helper and forsake me not. Do not despise me, O God, my savior.

THE SHORT BREVIARY

The Lord's Prayer

The Prayer Appointed for the Week
Stir up your power, O Lord, and with great might come among us; and, because
we are sorely hindered by our sins, let your bountiful grace and mercy speedily help and deliver us; through Jesus Christ our Lord, to whom, with you and
the Holy Spirit, be honor and glory now and for ever. *Amen.†*

Concluding Prayers of the Church
Almighty God, who has promised to hear the petitions of those who ask in your
Son's Name: I beseech you mercifully to incline your ear to me who have made
my prayers and supplications to you; and grant that those things which I have
faithfully asked according to your will, I may effectually obtain, to the relief of
my necessity, and to the setting forth of your glory; through Jesus Christ my
Lord. *Amen.†*

May the souls of the faithful departed, through the mercy of God, rest in eternal
peace. *Amen.*

The Morning Office
**To Be Observed on the Hour or Half Hour
Between 6 and 9 a.m.**

The Call to Prayer
Proclaim with me the greatness of the LORD;* let us exalt his Name together.

Psalm 34:3

The Request for Presence
Open my eyes, that I may see* the wonders of your law.

Psalm 119:18

The Greeting
I will confess you among the peoples, O LORD;* I will sing praise to you among the
nations.

For your loving-kindness is greater than the heavens,* and your faithfulness
reaches to the clouds.

Psalm 57:9–10

The Refrain for the Morning Lessons
Let the sorrowful sighing of the prisoners come before you,* and by your great
might spare those who are condemned to die.

Psalm 79:11

A Reading
Zechariah, the father of John the Baptizer, being filled with the Holy Spirit, spoke
this prophecy about his son, saying: "And you, little child, you shall be called
Prophet of the Most High, for you will go before *the Lord to prepare a way for him,*
to give his people knowledge of salvation through forgiveness of their sins,
because of the faithful love of our God in which the rising Sun has come from
on high to visit us, to give light to *those who live in darkness and the shadow dark as
death,* and to guide our feet into *the way of peace."*

Luke 1:76–79

The Refrain
Let the sorrowful sighing of the prisoners come before you,* and by your great
might spare those who are condemned to die.

The Morning Psalm   *Arise, O God, and Rule the Earth*
God takes his stand in the council of heaven;* he gives judgment in the midst of
the gods:
"How long will you judge unjustly,* and show favor to the wicked?
Save the weak and the orphan;* defend the humble and needy;
Rescue the weak and the poor;* deliver them from the power of the wicked.
They do not know, neither do they understand;* they go about in darkness; all the
foundations of the earth are shaken.
Now I say to you, 'You are gods,* and all of you children of the Most High;
Nevertheless, you shall die like mortals,* and fall like any prince.' "
Arise, O God, and rule the earth,* for you shall take all nations for your own.

Psalm 82

The Refrain
Let the sorrowful sighing of the prisoners come before you,* and by your great
might spare those who are condemned to die.

The Cry of the Church
Even so, come, Lord Jesus!

The Lord's Prayer

The Prayer Appointed for the Week
Stir up your power, O Lord, and with great might come among us; and, because
we are sorely hindered by our sins, let your bountiful grace and mercy speed-

ily help and deliver us; through Jesus Christ our Lord, to whom, with you and the Holy Spirit, be honor and glory now and for ever. *Amen.*†

The Concluding Prayer of the Church

Lord God, almighty and everlasting Father, you have brought me in safety to this new day: Preserve me with your mighty power, that I may not fall into sin, nor be overcome by adversity; and in all I do direct me to the fulfilling of your purpose; through Jesus Christ my Lord. *Amen.*†

The Midday Office

To Be Observed on the Hour or Half Hour Between 11 a.m. and 2 p.m.

The Call to Prayer

'Come, we will go up to YAHWEH's mountain, to the Temple of the God of Jacob so that he may teach us his ways and we may walk in his paths.'

Micah 4:2

The Request for Presence

Hear, O Shepherd of Israel, leading Joseph like a flock;* shine forth, you that are enthroned upon the cherubim.

Psalm 80:1

The Greeting

The LORD lives! Blessed is my Rock!* Exalted is the God of my salvation!

Psalm 18:46

The Refrain for the Midday Lessons

"I will appoint a time," says God;* "I will judge with equity. . . ."

Psalm 75:2

A Reading

But you (Bethlehem) Ephrathah, the least of the clans of Judah, from you will come for me a future ruler of Israel whose origins go back to the distant past, to the days of old. Hence YAHWEH will abandon them only until she who is in labor gives birth, and then those who survive of his race will be reunited to the Israelites. He will take his stand and he will shepherd them with the power of YAHWEH, with the majesty of the name of his God, and they will be secure, for his greatness will extend henceforth to the most distant parts of the country.

Micah 5:1-3

The Refrain

"I will appoint a time," says God;* "I will judge with equity. . . ."

The Midday Psalm

Your Dominion Endures Throughout the Ages

I will exalt you, O God my King,* and bless your Name for ever and ever.
Every day will I bless you* and praise your Name for ever and ever.
Great is the LORD and greatly to be praised;* there is no end to his greatness.
One generation shall praise your works to another* and shall declare your power.

I will ponder the glorious splendor of your majesty* and all your marvelous works.

They shall speak of the might of your wondrous acts,* and I will tell of your greatness.

They shall publish the remembrance of your great goodness;* they shall sing of your righteous deeds.

The LORD is gracious and full of compassion,* slow to anger and of great kindness.

The LORD is loving to everyone* and his compassion is over all his works.

All your works praise you, O LORD,* and your faithful servants bless you.

They make known the glory of your kingdom* and speak of your power;

That the peoples may know of your power* and the glorious splendor of your kingdom.

Your kingdom is an everlasting kingdom;* your dominion endures throughout all ages.

Psalm 145:1–13

The Refrain
"I will appoint a time," says God;* "I will judge with equity. . . ."

The Cry of the Church
Even so, come, Lord Jesus!

The Lord's Prayer

The Prayer Appointed for the Week
Stir up your power, O Lord, and with great might come among us; and, because we are sorely hindered by our sins, let your bountiful grace and mercy speedily help and deliver us; through Jesus Christ our Lord, to whom, with you and the Holy Spirit, be honor and glory now and for ever. *Amen.*†

The Concluding Prayer of the Church
O God, the source of eternal light: Shed forth your unending day upon all of us who watch for you, that our lips may praise you, our lives may bless you, and our worship may give you glory; through Jesus Christ our Lord. *Amen.*†

The Vespers Office   **To Be Observed on the Hour or Half Hour
Between 5 and 8 p.m.**

The Call to Prayer
Come now and look upon the works of the LORD,* what awesome things he has done on earth.

Psalm 46:9

The Request for Presence
Hear my cry, O God,* and listen to my prayer.
I call upon you from the ends of the earth . . .

Psalm 61:1–2

The Greeting

O ruler of the universe, Lord God, great deeds are they that you have done, surpassing human understanding.

Your ways are ways of righteousness and truth, O King of all the ages.

Traditional

The Hymn

When morning gilds the skies, my heart awaking cries,
May Jesus Christ be praised!
Alike at work and prayer, to Jesus I repair;
May Jesus Christ be praised.

Whenever the church bell peals over hill and dell,
May Jesus Christ be praised!
O hark to what it sings, as joyously it rings,
May Jesus Christ be praised.

The night becomes as day, when from the heart we say,
May Jesus Christ be praised!
The powers of darkness fear, when this sweet chant they hear,
May Jesus Christ be praised.

In heaven's eternal bliss the loveliest strain is this,
May Jesus Christ be praised!
Let earth, and sea, and sky, from depth to height reply,
May Jesus Christ be praised.

German

The Refrain for the Vespers Lessons

Happy are those who act with justice* and always do what is right!

Psalm 106:3

The Vespers Psalm   The LORD Comes in Holiness

The Lord gave the word;* great was the company of women who bore the tidings:
"Kings with their armies are fleeing away;* the women at home are dividing the spoils."
Though you lingered among the sheepfolds,* you shall be like a dove whose wings are covered with silver, whose feathers are like green gold.
When the Almighty scattered kings,* it was like snow falling in Zalmon.
O mighty mountain, O hill of Bashan!* O rugged mountain, O hill of Bashan!
Why do you look with envy, O rugged mountain, at the hill which God chose for his resting place?* truly, the LORD will dwell there for ever.
The chariots of God are twenty thousand, even thousands of thousands;* the Lord comes in holiness from Sinai.
You have gone up on high and led captivity captive; you have received gifts even from your enemies,* that the LORD God might dwell among them.
Blessed be the Lord day by day,* the God of our salvation, who bears our burdens.

He is our God, the God of our salvation;* God is the LORD, by whom we escape
death.

Psalm 68:11–20

The Refrain
Happy are those who act with justice* and always do what is right!

The Cry of the Church
Even so, come, Lord Jesus!

The Lord's Prayer

The Prayer Appointed for the Week
Stir up your power, O Lord, and with great might come among us; and, because
we are sorely hindered by our sins, let your bountiful grace and mercy speedily help and deliver us; through Jesus Christ our Lord, to whom, with you and
the Holy Spirit, be honor and glory now and for ever. *Amen.*†

The Concluding Prayer of the Church
Almighty God, who after the creation of the world rested from all your works and
sanctified a day of rest for all your creatures: Grant that I, putting away all
earthly anxieties, may be duly prepared for the service of public worship, and
grant as well that my Sabbath upon earth may be a preparation for the eternal
rest promised to your people in heaven; through Jesus Christ our Lord. *Amen.*†

∽❦∾

The Morning Office   **To Be Observed on the Hour or Half Hour
Between 6 and 9 a.m.**

The Call to Prayer
Sing to the LORD and bless his Name;* proclaim the good news of his salvation
from day to day.
Declare his glory among the nations* and his wonders among all peoples.
For great is the LORD and greatly to be praised;* he is more to be feared than all
gods.

Psalm 96:2–4

The Request for Presence
Satisfy us by your loving-kindness in the morning;* so shall we rejoice and be glad
all the days of our life.

Psalm 90:14

The Greeting

Awesome things will you show us in your righteousness, O God of our salvation,*
  O Hope of all the ends of the earth and of the seas that are far away.

Psalm 65:5

The Refrain for the Morning Lessons

You shall not be afraid of any terror by night,* nor of the arrow that flies by day.

Psalm 91:5

A Reading *During the fourth and final week of Advent, the Church is mindful in particular of the life and role of St. Joseph, husband of the Virgin and earthly father to our Lord.*

This is how Jesus Christ came to be born. His mother Mary was betrothed to
  Joseph; but before they came to live together she was found to be with child
  through the Holy Spirit. Her husband Joseph, being an upright man and wanting to spare her disgrace, decided to divorce her informally. He had made up
  his mind to do this when suddenly the angel of the Lord appeared to him in a
  dream and said, 'Joseph son of David, do not be afraid to take Mary home as
  your wife, because she has conceived what is in her by the Holy Spirit. She will
  give birth to a son and you must name him Jesus, because he is the one who is
  to save his people from their sins.' Now all this took place to fulfill what the
  Lord had spoken through the prophet: *Look! The virgin is with child and will give
  birth to a son whom they will call Immanuel,* a name which means 'God-is-with-
  us.' When Joseph woke up he did what the angel of the Lord had told him to
  do: he took his wife to his home; he had not had intercourse with her when she
  gave birth to a son; and he named him Jesus.

Matthew 1:18–25

The Refrain

You shall not be afraid of any terror by night,* nor of the arrow that flies by day.

The Morning Psalm *Let the Name of the Lord Be Blessed*

Hallelujah! Give praise, you servants of the Lord;* praise the Name of the Lord.
Let the Name of the Lord be blessed,* from this time forth for evermore.
From the rising of the sun to its going down* let the Name of the Lord be praised.
The Lord is high above all nations,* and his glory above the heavens.
Who is like the Lord our God, who sits enthroned on high* but stoops to behold
  the heavens and the earth?
He takes up the weak out of the dust* and lifts up the poor from the ashes.
He sets them with the princes,* with the princes of his people.
He makes the woman of a childless house* to be a joyful mother of children.

Psalm 113

The Refrain

You shall not be afraid of any terror by night,* nor of the arrow that flies by day.

The Cry of the Church
O Lord, hear my prayer and let my cry come unto you. Thanks be to God.

THE SHORT BREVIARY

The Lord's Prayer

The Prayer Appointed for the Week
Purify my conscience, Almighty God, by your daily visitation, that your Son Jesus
Christ, at his coming, may find in me a mansion prepared for himself; who
lives and reigns with you and the Holy Spirit, one God, now and for ever.
Amen.†

The Concluding Prayer of the Church
Lord God, almighty and everlasting Father, you have brought me in safety to this
new day: Preserve me with your mighty power, that I may not fall into sin, nor
be overcome by adversity; and in all I do direct me to the fulfilling of your purpose; through Jesus Christ my Lord. *Amen.*†

The Midday Office   **To Be Observed on the Hour or Half Hour**
Between 11 a.m. and 2 p.m.

The Call to Prayer
God has gone up with a shout,* the LORD with the sound of the ram's-horn.
Sing praises to God, sing praises;* sing praises to our King, sing praises.
For God is King of all the earth;* sing praises with all your skill.
God reigns over the nations;* God sits upon his holy throne.

Psalm 47:5–8

The Request for Presence
Let the peoples praise you, O God;* let all the peoples praise you.

Psalm 67:3

The Greeting
For you alone are the Holy One, you alone are the Lord, you alone are the Most
High, Jesus Christ, with the Holy Spirit, in the glory of God the Father.

The Refrain for the Midday Lessons
Tell it out among the nations: "The LORD is King!"

Psalm 96:10

A Reading
Look, the days are coming, YAHWEH declares, when I shall raise an upright Branch
of David; he will reign as king and be wise, doing what is just and upright in
the country. In his days Judah will triumph and Israel live in safety. And this is
the name he will be called, 'Yahweh-is-our-Saving-Justice.'

Jeremiah 23:5–6

The Refrain
Tell it out among the nations: "The LORD is King!"

The Midday Psalm   *Great Are the Deeds of the* LORD

Hallelujah! I will give thanks to the LORD with my whole heart,* in the assembly of the upright, in the congregation.

Great are the deeds of the LORD!* they are studied by all who delight in them.

His work is full of majesty and splendor,* and his righteousness endures for ever.

He makes his marvelous works to be remembered;* the LORD is gracious and full of compassion.

He gives food to those who fear him;* he is ever mindful of his covenant.

He has shown his people the power of his works* in giving them the lands of the nations.

The works of his hands are faithfulness and justice;* all his commandments are sure.

They stand fast for ever and ever,* because they are done in truth and equity.

He sent redemption to his people; he commanded his covenant for ever;* holy and awesome is his Name.

The fear of the LORD is the beginning of wisdom;* those who act accordingly have a good understanding; his praise endures for ever.

Psalm 111

The Refrain
Tell it out among the nations: "The LORD is King!"

The Cry of the Church
Even so, come, Lord Jesus!

The Lord's Prayer

The Prayer Appointed for the Week
Purify my conscience, Almighty God, by your daily visitation, that your Son Jesus Christ, at his coming, may find in me a mansion prepared for himself; who lives and reigns with you and the Holy Spirit, one God, now and for ever. *Amen.*†

The Concluding Prayer of the Church
O God, you make me glad with the weekly remembrance of the glorious resurrection of your Son my Lord: Give me this day such blessing through my worship of you, that the week to come may be spent in your favor; through Jesus Christ our Lord. *Amen.*†

The Vespers Office   **To Be Observed on the Hour or Half Hour**
                                        Between 5 and 8 p.m.

The Call to Prayer
Open my lips, O LORD,* and my mouth shall proclaim your praise.

Psalm 51:16

The Request for Presence
"Hear, O LORD, and have mercy upon me;* O LORD, be my helper."

Psalm 30:11

The Greeting

Blessed be the Lord GOD, the God of Israel,* who alone does wondrous deeds!
And blessed be his glorious Name for ever!* and may all the earth be filled with
    his glory. Amen. Amen.

Psalm 72:18–19

The Hymn

Savior of the nations, come;	Not by human flesh and blood;
Virgin's Son, here make your home!	By the Spirit of our God
Marvel now, O heaven and earth,	Was the word of God made flesh,
That the Lord chose such a birth.	Woman's offspring, pure and fresh.

Martin Luther

The Refrain for the Vespers Lessons

It is better to rely on the LORD* than to put any trust in flesh.
It is better to rely on the LORD* than to put any trust in rulers.

Psalm 118:8–9

The Vespers Psalm   *This God Is Our God For Ever*

Your praise, like your Name, O God, reaches to the world's end;* your right hand
    is full of justice.
Let Mount Zion be glad and the cities of Judah rejoice,* because of your
    judgments.
Make the circuit of Zion; walk round about her;* count the number of her towers.
Consider well her bulwarks; examine her strongholds;* that you may tell those
    who come after.
This God is our God for ever and ever;* he shall be our guide for evermore.

Psalm 48:9–13

The Refrain

It is better to rely on the LORD* than to put any trust in flesh.
It is better to rely on the LORD* than to put any trust in rulers.

The Small Verse

Their sound goes forth to all the earth and their speech to the end of the world.

adapted from THE SHORT BREVIARY

The Lord's Prayer

The Prayer Appointed for the Week

Purify my conscience, Almighty God, by your daily visitation, that your Son Jesus
    Christ, at his coming, may find in me a mansion prepared for himself; who
    lives and reigns with you and the Holy Spirit, one God, now and for ever.
    Amen.†

Concluding Prayers of the Church

Almighty God, by whose grace and power your disciple Thomas triumphed over
    doubt and was faithful: Grant me, who now remember him in thanksgiving,
    to also come to be so faithful in my witness to you in this world, that I may

receive with him the crown of life; through Jesus Christ our Lord, who lives and reigns with you and the Holy Spirit, one God for ever and ever. *Amen.*✝

Lord God, whose Son our Savior Jesus Christ, triumphed over the powers of death and prepared for us our place in the new Jerusalem: Grant that I, who have this day given thanks for his resurrection, may praise you in the City of which he is the light, and where he lives and reigns for ever and ever. *Amen.*✝

The Morning Office   **To Be Observed on the Hour or Half Hour**
Between 6 and 9 a.m.

The Call to Prayer
Love the Lord, all you who worship him;* the Lord protects the faithful, but repays to the full those who act haughtily.
Be strong and let your heart take courage,* all you who wait for the Lord.

Psalm 31:23–24

The Request for Presence
Be my strong rock, a castle to keep me safe, for you are my crag and my strong-hold;* for the sake of your Name, lead me and guide me.

Psalm 31:3

The Greeting
How great is your goodness, O Lord!* which you have laid up for those who fear you; which you have done in the sight of all.

Psalm 31:19

The Refrain for the Morning Lessons
Be strong and let your heart take courage,* all you who wait for the Lord.

Psalm 31:24

A Reading   *On December 21, the Church recalls and gives thanks for St. Thomas, the Apostle known as "Thomas the Doubter" for his questioning of Christ's resurrection. Thomas was also the first to proclaim Christ's divinity after the resurrection.*

Thomas, called the Twin, who was one of the Twelve, was not with them when Jesus came. So the other disciples said to him, 'We have seen the Lord,' but he answered, 'Unless I can see the holes that the nails made in his hands and can put my finger into the holes they made, and unless I can put my hand into his side, I refuse to believe.' Eight days later the disciples were in the house again and Thomas was with them. The doors were closed, but Jesus came in and stood among them. 'Peace be with you,' he said. Then he spoke to Thomas, 'Put your finger here; look here are my hands. Give me your hand; put it into my side. Do not be unbelieving any more but believe.' Thomas replied, 'My Lord and my God!' Jesus said to him: 'You believe because you can see me. Blessed are those who have not seen and yet believe.'

John 20:24–29

The Refrain
Be strong and let your heart take courage,* all you who wait for the LORD.

The Morning Psalm   Those Who Sowed with Tears Will Reap with Songs of Joy
When the LORD restored the fortunes of Zion,* then were we like those who
  dream.
Then was our mouth filled with laughter,* and our tongue with shouts of joy.
Then they said among the nations,* "The LORD has done great things for them."
The LORD has done great things for us,* and we are glad indeed.
Restore our fortunes, O LORD,* like the watercourses of the Negev.
Those who sowed with tears* will reap with songs of joy.
Those who go out weeping, carrying the seed,* will come again with joy,
  shouldering their sheaves.

Psalm 126

The Refrain
Be strong and let your heart take courage,* all you who wait for the LORD.

The Cry of the Church
In the evening, in the morning, and at noonday, I will complain and lament,* and
  he will hear my voice.

Psalm 55:18

The Lord's Prayer

The Prayer Appointed for the Week
Purify my conscience, Almighty God, by your daily visitation, that your Son Jesus
  Christ, at his coming, may find in me a mansion prepared for himself; who
  lives and reigns with you and the Holy Spirit, one God, now and for ever.
  Amen.†

Concluding Prayers of the Church
Everliving God, who strengthened your apostle Thomas with firm and certain
  faith in your Son's resurrection: Grant me so perfectly and without doubt to
  believe in Jesus Christ, our Lord and our God, that my faith may never be
  found wanting in your sight; through him who lives and reigns with you and
  the Holy Spirit, one God, now and for ever. *Amen.*†

Lord God, almighty and everlasting Father, you have brought me in safety to this
  new day: Preserve me with your mighty power, that I may not fall into sin, nor
  be overcome by adversity; and in all I do direct me to the fulfilling of your purpose; through Jesus Christ my Lord. *Amen.*†

The Midday Office   **To Be Observed on the Hour or Half Hour**
                                 Between 11 a.m. and 2 p.m.

The Call to Prayer
Sing to the LORD with the harp,* with the harp and the voice of song.

With trumpets and the sound of the horn* shout with joy before the King, the
LORD.

Psalm 98:6–7

The Request for Presence
Show us the light of your countenance, O God,* and come to us.

based on Psalm 67:1

The Greeting
O LORD, what are we that you should care for us?* mere mortals that you should
think of us?
We are like a puff of wind;* our days are like a passing shadow.

Psalm 144:3–4

The Refrain for the Midday Lessons
Shout with joy to the LORD, all you lands;* lift up your voice, rejoice, and sing.

Psalm 98:5

A Reading
Do not lose your fearlessness now, then, since the reward is so great. You will need
perseverance if you are to do God's will and gain what he has promised. Only *a
little while now, a very little while, for come he certainly will before too long. My
upright person will live through faith but if he draws back, my soul will take no pleasure
in him.* We are not the sort of people who *draw back,* and are lost by it; we are the
sort who keep faith until our souls are saved. Only faith can guarantee the blessings that we hope for, or prove the existence of realities that are unseen.

Hebrews 10:35–11:1

The Refrain
Shout with joy to the LORD, all you lands;* lift up your voice, rejoice, and sing.

The Midday Psalm   *The Faithfulness of the LORD Endures*
Praise the LORD, all you nations;* laud him, all you peoples.
For his loving-kindness toward us is great,* and the faithfulness of the LORD
endures for ever. Hallelujah!

Psalm 117

The Refrain
Shout with joy to the LORD, all you lands;* lift up your voice, rejoice, and sing.

The Cry of the Church
Even so, come, Lord Jesus!

The Lord's Prayer

The Prayer Appointed for the Week
Purify my conscience, Almighty God, by your daily visitation, that your Son Jesus
Christ, at his coming, may find in me a mansion prepared for himself; who
lives and reigns with you and the Holy Spirit, one God, now and for ever.
Amen.†

Concluding Prayers of the Church

Almighty God, by your Holy Spirit you have made us one with your saints in heaven and on earth: Grant that in my earthly pilgrimage I may always be supported by this fellowship of love and prayer, and know myself to be surrounded by their witness to your power and mercy. I ask this for the sake of Jesus Christ, in whom all my intercessions are acceptable through the Spirit, and who lives and reigns for ever and ever. *Amen.*†

Almighty and everlasting God, who willed that our Savior should take upon Him our flesh and suffer death upon the Cross, that all mankind should follow the example of His great humility, mercifully grant that we may both follow the example of His patience and also be made partakers of His resurrection. Through the same Jesus Christ. *Amen.*

adapted from THE SHORT BREVIARY

The Vespers Office   **To Be Observed on the Hour or Half Hour**
                               Between 5 and 8 p.m.

The Call to Prayer

Be joyful in God, all you lands;* sing the glory of his Name; sing the glory of his praise.
Say to God, "How awesome are your deeds! . . .
All the earth bows down before you,* sings to you, sings out your Name."

Psalm 66:1–3

The Request for Presence

Let your loving-kindness, O LORD, be upon us,* as we have put our trust in you.

Psalm 33:22

The Greeting

Blessed is the LORD!* for he has heard the voice of my prayer.

Psalm 28:7

The Hymn

How often, Lord, your face has shone
On doubting souls whose wills were true!
You Christ of Peter and of John
You are the Christ of Thomas too.

He loved you well, and firmly said,
"Come, let us go, and die with him";
Yet when your Easter news was spread,
Mid all its light his faith was dim.

His brethren's word he would not take,
But craved to touch those hands of thine;
When you did your appearance make,
He saw, and hailed his Lord Divine.

He saw you risen; at once he rose
To full belief's unclouded height;
And still through his confession flows
To Christian souls your life and light.

O Savior, make your presence known
To all who doubt your Word and thee;
And teach us in that Word alone
To find the truth that sets us free.

adapted from William Bright

The Refrain for the Vespers Lessons

Turn again to your rest, O my soul,* for the LORD has treated you well.

For you have rescued my life from death,* my eyes from tears, and my feet from stumbling.

Psalm 116:6–7

The Vespers Psalm　　　　　　　　*I Will Declare Your Name to My Brethren*

I am poured out like water,* all my bones are out of joint; my heart within my breast is melting wax.

My mouth is dried out like a pot-shard; my tongue sticks to the roof of my mouth;* and you have laid me in the dust of the grave.

Packs of dogs close me in, and gangs of evildoers circle around me;* they pierce my hands and my feet; I can count all my bones.

They stare and gloat over me;* they divide my garments among them; they cast lots for my clothing.

Be not far away, O LORD;* you are my strength; hasten to help me.

Save me from the sword,* my life from the power of the dog.

Save me from the lion's mouth,* my wretched body from the horns of wild bulls.

I will declare your Name to my brethren;* in the midst of the congregation I will praise you.

Psalm 22:14–21

The Refrain

Turn again to your rest, O my soul,* for the LORD has treated you well.

For you have rescued my life from death,* my eyes from tears, and my feet from stumbling.

The Cry of the Church

O Lord, hear my prayer and let my cry come unto you. Thanks be to God.

THE SHORT BREVIARY

The Lord's Prayer

The Prayer Appointed for the Week

Purify my conscience, Almighty God, by your daily visitation, that your Son Jesus Christ, at his coming, may find in me a mansion prepared for himself; who lives and reigns with you and the Holy Spirit, one God, now and for ever. *Amen.*†

Concluding Prayers of the Church

Almighty God, you have surrounded me with a great cloud of witnesses: Grant that I, encouraged by the good example of your servant Thomas, may persevere in running the race that is set before me, until at last I may with him attain to your eternal joy; through Jesus Christ, the pioneer and perfecter of our faith, who lives and reigns with you and the Holy Spirit, one God, for ever and ever. *Amen.*†

Grant me and all of your people the gift of your Spirit, that we may know Christ and make him known; and through him, at all times and in all places, may give thanks to you in all things. *Amen.*†

The Morning Office   **To Be Observed on the Hour or Half Hour**
Between 6 and 9 a.m.

The Call to Prayer
Come and listen, all you who fear God,* and I will tell you what he has done for me.
Psalm 66:14

The Request for Presence
May God be merciful to us and bless us,* show us the light of his countenance and
come to us.
Let your ways be known upon earth,* your saving health among all nations.
Psalm 67:1–2

The Greeting
Your statutes have been like songs to me* wherever I have lived as a stranger.
Psalm 119:54

The Refrain for the Morning Lessons
Create in me a clean heart, O God,* and renew a right spirit within me.
Psalm 51:11

A Reading
Jesus taught us, saying: "But the hour is coming—indeed is already here—when
true worshippers will worship the Father in spirit and truth: that is the kind of
worshipper the Father seeks. God is spirit, and those who worship must worship in spirit and truth."
John 4:23–24

The Refrain
Create in me a clean heart, O God,* and renew a right spirit within me.

The Morning Psalm   *You, O God, Have Heard My Vows*
Hear my cry, O God,* and listen to my prayer.
I call upon you from the ends of the earth* with heaviness in my heart; set me
upon the rock that is higher than I.
For you have been my refuge,* a strong tower against the enemy.
I will dwell in your house for ever;* I will take refuge under the cover of your
wings.
For you, O God, have heard my vows;* you have granted me the heritage of those
who fear your Name.
Psalm 61:1–5

The Refrain
Create in me a clean heart, O God,* and renew a right spirit within me.

The Cry of the Church
Even so, come, Lord Jesus!

The Lord's Prayer

The Prayer Appointed for the Week

Purify my conscience, Almighty God, by your daily visitation, that your Son Jesus Christ, at his coming, may find in me a mansion prepared for himself; who lives and reigns with you and the Holy Spirit, one God, now and for ever. *Amen.*†

The Concluding Prayer of the Church

Lord God, almighty and everlasting Father, you have brought me in safety to this new day: Preserve me with your mighty power, that I may not fall into sin, nor be overcome by adversity; and in all I do direct me to the fulfilling of your purpose; through Jesus Christ my Lord. *Amen.*†

The Midday Office   **To Be Observed on the Hour or Half Hour Between 11 a.m. and 2 p.m.**

The Call to Prayer

Praise Him from whom all blessings flow; praise Him all creatures here below; praise Him you heavenly hosts; praise Father, Son and Holy Ghost.

Traditional

The Request for Presence

Be my strong rock, a castle to keep me safe, for you are my crag and my stronghold;* for the sake of your Name, lead me and guide me.

Psalm 31:3

The Greeting

To you, O LORD, I lift up my soul;* my God, I put my trust in you . . .

Psalm 25:1

The Refrain for the Midday Lessons

Happy are they all who fear the LORD,* and who follow in his ways!

Psalm 28:1

A Reading

Joyfully you will draw water from the springs of salvation and, that day, you will say, 'Praise YAHWEH, invoke his name. Proclaim his deeds to the people, declare his name sublime. Sing of YAHWEH, for his works are majestic, make them known throughout the world. Cry and shout for joy, you who live in Zion, For the Holy One of Israel is among you in his greatness.'

Isaiah 12:3–6

The Refrain

Happy are they all who fear the LORD,* and who follow in his ways!

The Midday Psalm   *The LORD Will Bless Both Small and Great Who Trust Him*

Not to us, O LORD, not to us, but to your Name give glory;* because of your love and because of your faithfulness.

Why should the heathen say,* "Where then is their God?"

Our God is in heaven;* whatever he wills to do he does.

Their idols are silver and gold,* the work of human hands.

They have mouths, but they cannot speak;* eyes have they, but they cannot see;

They have ears, but they cannot hear;* noses, but they cannot smell;

They have hands, but they cannot feel; feet, but they cannot walk;* they make no
sound with their throat.

Those who make them are like them,* and so are all who put their trust in them.

O Israel, trust in the LORD;* he is their help and their shield.

O house of Aaron, trust in the LORD;* he is their help and their shield.

You who fear the LORD, trust in the LORD;* he is their help and their shield.

The LORD has been mindful of us, and he will bless us;* he will bless the house of
Israel; he will bless the house of Aaron;

He will bless those who fear the LORD,* both small and great together.

Psalm 115:1–13

The Refrain
Happy are they all who fear the LORD,* and who follow in his ways!

The Small Verse
The Lord is king. He has put on glorious apparel. Let all the nations praise him.
Let those of every tongue bow before him. Alleluia, alleluia, alleluia.

Traditional

The Lord's Prayer

The Prayer Appointed for the Week
Purify my conscience, Almighty God, by your daily visitation, that your Son Jesus
Christ, at his coming, may find in me a mansion prepared for himself; who
lives and reigns with you and the Holy Spirit, one God, now and for ever.
Amen.†

The Concluding Prayer of the Church
Come forth, O Christ, and help me. For your name's sake deliver me.

Traditional

The Vespers Office
**To Be Observed on the Hour or Half Hour
Between 5 and 8 p.m.**

The Call to Prayer
Praise God, from whom all blessings flow; praise him, all creatures here below;
praise him above, you heavenly hosts; praise Father, Son and Holy Ghost.

Doxology

The Request for Presence
Show your goodness, O LORD, to those who are good* and to those who are true of
heart.

Psalm 125:4

The Greeting

Out of the mouths of infants and children* your majesty is praised above the
heavens.

Psalm 8:2

The Hymn

Lord Jesus Christ, be present now,
And let your Holy Spirit bow
All hearts in love and truth today
To hear your word and keep your way.

May your glad tidings always bring
Good news to men, that they may sing
Of how you came to save all men.
Instruct us till you come again.

To God the Father and the Son
And Holy Spirit, three in one;
To you, O blessed Trinity,
Be praise throughout eternity.

*Anonymous, translated
by Catherine Winkworth*

The Refrain for the Vespers Lessons

We have heard with our ears, O God, our forefathers have told us,* the deeds you
did in their days, in the days of old.

Psalm 44:1

The Vespers Psalm

Let the Nations Be Glad and Sing for Joy

May God be merciful to us and bless us,* show us the light of his countenance and
come to us.

Let your ways be known upon earth,* your saving health among all nations.

Let the peoples praise you, O God;* let all the peoples praise you.

Let the nations be glad and sing for joy,* for you judge the peoples with equity and
guide all the nations upon earth.

Let the peoples praise you, O God;* let all the peoples praise you.

The earth has brought forth her increase;* may God, our own God, give us his
blessing.

May God give us his blessing,* and may all the ends of the earth stand in awe of
him.

Psalm 67

The Refrain

We have heard with our ears, O God, our forefathers have told us,* the deeds you
did in their days, in the days of old.

The Call to Prayer

Even so, come, Lord Jesus!

The Lord's Prayer

The Prayer Appointed for the Week

Purify my conscience, Almighty God, by your daily visitation, that your Son Jesus
Christ, at his coming, may find in me a mansion prepared for himself; who
lives and reigns with you and the Holy Spirit, one God, now and for ever.
Amen.†

The Concluding Prayer of the Church

Almighty and eternal God, ruler of all things in heaven and earth: Mercifully
accept my prayer, and strengthen me to do your will; through Jesus Christ our
Lord. *Amen.*†

The Morning Office   **To Be Observed on the Hour or Half Hour**
Between 6 and 9 a.m.

The Call to Prayer

Praise God from whom all blessings flow; praise him, all creatures here below;
praise him above, you heavenly hosts; praise Father, Son and Holy Ghost.

Doxology

The Request for Presence

Send out your light and your truth, that they may lead me,* and bring me to your
holy hill and to your dwelling;
That I may go to the altar of God, to the God of my joy and gladness;* and on the
harp I will give thanks to you, O God my god.

Psalm 43:3–4

The Greeting

Splendor and honor and kingly power are yours by right, O Lord our God,
For you created everything that is, and by your will they were created and have
their being.

A Song to the Lamb

The Refrain for the Morning Lessons

For one day in your courts is better than a thousand in my own room,* and to
stand at the threshold of the house of my God than to dwell in the tents of the
wicked.

Psalm 84:9

A Reading

. . . the angel said to her, 'Mary, do not be afraid; you have won God's favor. Look!
You are to conceive in your womb and bear a son, and you must name him
Jesus. He will be great and will be called Son of the Most High. The Lord God
will give him the throne of his ancestor David; he will rule over the House of
Jacob for ever and his reign will have no end.' Mary said to the angel, 'But how
can this come about, since I have no knowledge of man?' The angel answered,
'The Holy Spirit will come upon you, and the power of the Most High will
cover you with its shadow. And so the child will be holy and will be called Son
of God. And I tell you this too: your cousin Elizabeth also, in her old age, has
conceived a son, and she whom people called barren is now in her sixth month,
for nothing is impossible to God.' Mary said, 'You see before you the Lord's servant, let it happen to me as you have said.' And the angel left her.

Luke 1:30–38

The Refrain

For one day in your courts is better than a thousand in my own room,* and to stand at the threshold of the house of my God than to dwell in the tents of the wicked.

The Morning Psalm   *Who Can Stand in His Holy Place*

The earth is the LORD's and all that is in it,* the world and all who dwell therein.

For it is he who founded it upon the seas* and made it firm upon the rivers of the deep.

"Who can ascend the hill of the LORD?* and who can stand in his holy place?"

"Those who have clean hands and a pure heart,* who have not pledged themselves to falsehood, nor sworn by what is a fraud.

They shall receive a blessing from the LORD* and a just reward from the God of their salvation."

Such is the generation of those who seek him,* of those who seek your face, O God of Jacob.

Psalm 24:1–6

The Refrain

For one day in your courts is better than a thousand in my own room,* and to stand at the threshold of the house of my God than to dwell in the tents of the wicked.

The Small Verse

The people that walked in darkness have seen a great light; on those who live in a land of deep shadow a light has shone.

Isaiah 9:1

The Lord's Prayer

The Prayer Appointed for the Week

Purify my conscience, Almighty God, by your daily visitation, that your Son Jesus Christ, at his coming, may find in me a mansion prepared for himself; who lives and reigns with you and the Holy Spirit, one God, now and for ever. *Amen.*†

The Concluding Prayer of the Church

Lord God, almighty and everlasting Father, you have brought me in safety to this new day: Preserve me with your mighty power, that I may not fall into sin, nor be overcome by adversity; and in all I do direct me to the fulfilling of your purpose; through Jesus Christ my Lord. *Amen.*†

The Midday Office   **To Be Observed on the Hour or Half Hour**
                                      Between 11 a.m. and 2 p.m.

The Call to Prayer

Hallelujah! Praise the LORD, O my soul!* I will praise the LORD as long as I live, I will sing praises to my God while I have my being.

Psalm 146:1

The Request for Presence

Remember me, O LORD, with the favor you have for your people,* and visit me
　　with your saving help;

That I may see the prosperity of your elect and be glad with the gladness of your
　　people,* that I may glory with your inheritance.

Psalm 106:4–5

The Greeting

You are to be praised, O God, in Zion . . .

To you that hear prayer shall all flesh come,* because of their transgressions.

Psalm 65:1–2

The Refrain for the Midday Lessons

Your statutes have been like songs to me* wherever I have lived like a stranger.

Psalm 119:54

A Reading

Besides, you know the time has come; the moment is here for you to stop sleeping
　　and wake up, because by now our salvation is nearer than when we first began
　　to believe. The night is nearly over, daylight is on the way; so let us throw off
　　everything that belongs to darkness and equip ourselves for the light.

Romans 13:11–12

The Refrain

Your statutes have been like songs to me* wherever I have lived like a stranger.

The Midday Psalm　　　　　　　　　　*Such Knowledge Is Too Wonderful for Me*

LORD, you have searched me out and known me;* you know my sitting down and
　　my rising up; you discern my thoughts from afar.

You trace my journeys and my resting-places* and are acquainted with all my
　　ways.

Indeed, there is not a word on my lips,* but you, O LORD, know it altogether.

You press upon me behind and before* and lay your hand upon me.

Such knowledge is too wonderful for me;* it is so high that I cannot attain to it.

Where can I go then from your Spirit?* where can I flee from your presence?

If I climb up to heaven, you are there;* if I make the grave my bed, you are there
　　also.

If I take the wings of the morning* and dwell in the uttermost parts of the sea,

Even there your hand will lead me* and your right hand hold me fast.

Psalm 139:1–9

The Refrain

Your statutes have been like songs to me* wherever I have lived like a stranger.

The Small Verse

Keep me, Lord, as the apple of your eye and carry me under the shadow of your
　　wings.

Traditional

The Lord's Prayer

The Prayer Appointed for the Week
Purify my conscience, Almighty God, by your daily visitation, that your Son Jesus
  Christ, at his coming, may find in me a mansion prepared for himself; who lives
  and reigns with you and the Holy Spirit, one God, now and for ever. *Amen.*†

The Concluding Prayer of the Church
May God himself order my days and make them acceptable in his sight. Blessed
  be the Lord always, my strength and my redeemer.

Traditional

The Vespers Office   **To Be Observed on the Hour or Half Hour**
                                          Between 5 and 8 p.m.

The Call to Prayer
But I will call upon God,* and the LORD will deliver me.
In the evening, in the morning, and at noonday, I will complain and lament,* and
  he will hear my voice.
He will bring me safely back . . .
God, who is enthroned of old, will hear me.

Psalm 55:17ff

The Request for Presence
I cry out to you, O LORD;* I say, "You are my refuge, my portion in the land of the
  living."

Psalm 142:5

The Greeting
I will confess you among the peoples, O LORD;* I will sing praises to you among
  the nations.

Psalm 108:3

The Hymn
Love divine, all loves excelling, joy of heaven, to earth come down;
Fix us in your humble dwelling; all your faithful mercies crown!
Jesus, you are all compassion, pure, unbounded love you art;
Visit us with your salvation; enter every trembling heart.

Breathe, O breathe your loving Spirit into every troubled breast!
Let us all in you inherit; let us find that second rest.
Take away our bent to sinning; Alpha and Omega be;
End of faith, as its beginning, set our hearts at liberty.

Come, Almighty to deliver, let us all your life receive;
Suddenly return and never, nevermore your temples leave.
You we would be always blessing, serve you as your hosts above,
Pray and praise you without ceasing, glory in your perfect love.

Finish, then, your new creation; pure and spotless let us be.
Let us see your great salvation perfectly restored in thee;
Changed from glory into glory, till in heaven we take our place,
Till we cast our crowns before thee, lost in wonder, love, and praise.

Charles Wesley

The Refrain for the Vespers Lessons

The LORD will hear the desire of the humble;* you will strengthen their heart and
your ears shall hear.

Psalm 10:18

The Vespers Psalm   *Let All Who Seek You Rejoice*

You are the LORD; do not withhold your compassion from me;* let your love and
your faithfulness keep me safe for ever,

For innumerable troubles have crowded upon me; my sins have overtaken me,
and I cannot see;* they are more in number than the hairs of my head, and my
heart fails me.

Be pleased, O LORD, to deliver me;* O LORD, make haste to help me.

Let them be ashamed and altogether dismayed who seek after my life to destroy
it;* let them draw back and be disgraced who take pleasure in my misfortune.

Let those who say "Aha!" and gloat over me be confounded* because they are
ashamed.

Let all who seek you rejoice in you and be glad;* let those who love your salvation
continually say, "Great is the LORD!"

Though I am poor and afflicted,* the Lord will have regard for me.

You are my helper and my deliverer,* do not tarry, O my God.

Psalm 40:12–19

The Refrain

The LORD will hear the desire of the humble;* you will strengthen their heart and
your ears shall hear.

The Small Verse

The Lord is my shepherd and nothing is wanting to me. In green pastures He hath
settled me.

THE SHORT BREVIARY

The Lord's Prayer

The Prayer Appointed for the Week

Purify my conscience, Almighty God, by your daily visitation, that your Son Jesus
Christ, at his coming, may find in me a mansion prepared for himself; who
lives and reigns with you and the Holy Spirit, one God, now and for ever.
Amen.†

The Concluding Prayer of the Church

Lead me not into temptation. Deliver me from evil. Yours are the kingdom and the
glory.

The Morning Office   **To Be Observed on the Hour or Half Hour**
Between 6 and 9 a.m.

The Call to Prayer
Come, let us bow down, and bend the knee,* and kneel before the LORD our
    Maker.
For he is our God,* and we are the people of his pasture and the sheep of his
    hand . . .

Psalm 95:6–7

The Request for Presence
So teach us to number our days* that we may apply our hearts to wisdom.

Psalm 90:12

The Greeting
My God, my rock in whom I put my trust,* my shield, the horn of my salvation,
    and my refuge; you are worthy of praise.

Psalm 18:2

The Refrain for the Morning Lessons
My eyes are upon the faithful in the land, that they may dwell with me . . .

Psalm 101:6

A Reading
Jesus taught the people saying: "Were I to testify on my own behalf, my testimony
    would not be true; but there is another witness who speaks on my behalf, and I
    know that his testimony is true. You sent messengers to John, and he gave his
    testimony to the truth—not that I depend on human testimony; no, it is for
    your salvation that I mention it. John was a lamp lit and shining and for a time
    you were content to enjoy the light that he gave. But my testimony is greater
    than John's: the deeds my Father has given me to perform, these same deeds of
    mine testify that the Father has sent me."

John 5:31–36

The Refrain
My eyes are upon the faithful in the land, that they may dwell with me . . .

The Morning Psalm   *The Eye of the LORD Is Upon Those Who Fear Him*
The LORD looks down from heaven,* and beholds all the people in the world.
From where he sits enthroned he turns his gaze* on all who dwell on the earth.
He fashions all the hearts of them* and understands all their works.
There is no king that can be saved by a mighty army;* a strong man is not
    delivered by his great strength.
The horse is a vain hope for deliverance;* for all its strength it cannot save.
Behold, the eye of the LORD is upon those who fear him,* on those who wait upon
    his love,
To pluck their lives from death,* and to feed them in time of famine.
Our soul waits for the LORD;* he is our help and our shield.

Indeed, our heart rejoices in him,* for in his holy Name we put our trust.
Let your loving-kindness, O LORD, be upon us,* as we have put our trust in you.

Psalm 33:13–22

The Refrain
My eyes are upon the faithful in the land, that they may dwell with me . . .

The Cry of the Church
O God, come to my assistance! O Lord, make haste to help me!

The Lord's Prayer

The Prayer Appointed for the Week
Purify my conscience, Almighty God, by your daily visitation, that your Son Jesus
   Christ, at his coming, may find in me a mansion prepared for himself; who lives
   and reigns with you and the Holy Spirit, one God, now and for ever. *Amen.*†

The Concluding Prayer of the Church
Lord God, almighty and everlasting Father, you have brought me in safety to this
   new day: Preserve me with your mighty power, that I may not fall into sin, nor
   be overcome by adversity; and in all I do direct me to the fulfilling of your purpose; through Jesus Christ my Lord. *Amen.*†

The Midday Office   **To Be Observed on the Hour or Half Hour**
                                  Between 11 a.m. and 2 p.m.

The Call to Prayer
Search for the LORD and his strength;* continually seek his face.

Psalm 105:4

The Request for Presence
You are good and you bring forth good;* instruct me in your statutes.

Psalm 119:68

The Greeting
When your word goes forth it gives light;* it gives understanding to the simple.

Psalm 119:130

The Refrain for the Midday Lessons
You strengthen me more and more; you enfold and comfort me.

Psalm 71:21

A Reading
YAHWEH, God of the House of Jacob, Abraham's redeemer, says this, 'No longer
   shall Jacob be disappointed, no more shall his face grow pale, for when he sees
   his children, my creatures, home again with him, he will acknowledge my
   name as holy, he will acknowledge the Holy One of Jacob to be holy and will
   hold the God of Israel in awe. Erring spirits will learn to understand and mur-
   murers accept instruction.'

Isaiah 29:22–24

The Refrain
You strengthen me more and more;* you enfold and comfort me.

The Midday Psalm   ***Hear, O Shepherd of Israel, Leading Joseph Like a Flock***
Hear, O Shepherd of Israel, leading Joseph like a flock;* shine forth, you that are
   enthroned upon the cherubim.
In the presence of Ephraim, Benjamin, and Manasseh,* stir up your strength and
   come to help us.
Restore us, O God of hosts;* show the light of your countenance, and we shall be
   saved.
Let your hand be upon the man of your right hand,* the son of man you have
   made so strong for yourself.
And so will we never turn away from you;* give us life, that we may call upon
   your Name.
Restore us, O LORD God of hosts;* show the light of your countenance, and we
   shall be saved.

Psalm 80:1–3, 16–18

The Refrain
You strengthen me more and more;* you enfold and comfort me.

The Cry of the Church
Even so, come, Lord Jesus!

The Lord's Prayer

The Prayer Appointed for the Week
Purify my conscience, Almighty God, by your daily visitation, that your Son Jesus
   Christ, at his coming, may find in me a mansion prepared for himself; who lives
   and reigns with you and the Holy Spirit, one God, now and for ever. *Amen.*†

The Concluding Prayer of the Church
O God, author of peace and lover of concord, to know you is eternal life and to
   serve you is perfect freedom: Defend me, your humble servant, in all assaults
   of my enemies; that I, surely trusting in your defense, may not fear the power
   of any adversary; through the might of Jesus Christ my Lord. *Amen.*†

The Vespers Office   **To Be Observed on the Hour or Half Hour**
                               Between 5 and 8 p.m.

The Call to Prayer
Behold now, bless the LORD, all you servants of the LORD,* you that stand by night
   in the house of our LORD.

Psalm 134:1

The Request for Presence
For God alone my soul in silence waits;* from him comes my salvation.

Psalm 62:1

The Greeting

Yours is the day, yours also the night;* you established the moon and the sun.
You fixed all the boundaries of the earth;* you made both summer and winter.

Psalm 74:15–16

The Hymn

Praise to the Lord, Almighty, the King of creation:
O my soul, praise him, for he is your health and salvation.
All you who hear,
Now to his altar draw near,
Joining in glad adoration.

Praise to the Lord who does prosper your work and defend you;
Surely his goodness and mercy shall daily attend you.
Ponder anew
What the Almighty can do,
Who with his love does befriend you.

Praise to the Lord, O let all that is in me adore him!
All that has life and breath come now in praises before him!
Let the Amen
Sound from his people again:
Now as we worship before him.

J. Neander

The Refrain for the Vespers Lessons

The LORD's will stands fast for ever,* and the designs of his heart from age to age.

Psalm 33:11

The Vespers Psalm   *The LORD Shall Reign For Ever*

Hallelujah! Praise the LORD, O my soul!* I will praise the LORD as long as I live; I
will sing praises to my God while I have my being.
Put not your trust in rulers, nor in any child of earth,* for there is no help in them.
When they breathe their last, they return to earth,* and in that day their thoughts
perish.
Happy are they who have the God of Jacob for their help!* whose hope is in the
LORD their God;
Who made heaven and earth, the seas, and all that is in them;* who keeps his
promise for ever;
Who gives justice to those who are oppressed,* and food to those who hunger.
The LORD sets the prisoners free; the LORD opens the eyes of the blind;* the LORD
lifts up those who are bowed down;
The LORD loves the righteous; the LORD cares for the stranger;* he sustains the
orphan and widow, but frustrates the way of the wicked.
The LORD shall reign for ever,* your God, O Zion, throughout all generations.
Hallelujah!

Psalm 146

The Refrain
The Lord's will stands fast for ever,* and the designs of his heart from age to age.

The Cry of the Church
Even so, come, Lord Jesus!

The Lord's Prayer

The Prayer Appointed for the Week
Purify my conscience, Almighty God, by your daily visitation, that your Son Jesus
    Christ, at his coming, may find in me a mansion prepared for himself; who
    lives and reigns with you and the Holy Spirit, one God, now and for ever.
    Amen.†

The Concluding Prayer of the Church
May Almighty God grant me a peaceful night and a perfect end. *Amen.*

| The Morning Office | To Be Observed on the Hour or Half Hour Between 6 and 9 a.m. |

The Call to Prayer
Hallelujah! Praise the Name of the Lord;* give praise, you servants of the Lord,
You who stand in the house of the Lord,* in the courts of the house of our God.
Praise the Lord, for the Lord is good;* sing praises to his Name, for it is lovely.
Psalm 136:1–3

The Request for Presence
I have said to the Lord, "You are my God;* listen, O Lord, to my supplication."
Psalm 140:6

The Greeting
You are the Lord, most high over all the earth;* you are exalted far above all gods.
Psalm 97:9

The Refrain for the Morning Lessons
Everyone will stand in awe and declare God's deeds;* they will recognize his
    works.
Psalm 64:9

A Reading
Now a great sign appeared in heaven: a woman, robed with the sun, standing on
    the moon, and on her head a crown of twelve stars. She was pregnant, and in
    labor, crying aloud in the pangs of childbirth. Then a second sign appeared in
    the sky: there was a huge red dragon with seven heads and ten horns, and each
    of the seven heads crowned with a coronet. Its tail swept a third of the *stars
    from the sky and hurled them to the ground,* and the dragon stopped in front of the
    woman as she was at the point of giving birth, so that he could eat the child as
    soon as it was born. The woman *was delivered of a boy,* the son who was *to rule*

the nations with an iron scepter, and the child was taken straight up to God and to his throne, while the woman escaped into the desert, where God has prepared a place for her to be looked after for twelve hundred and sixty days.

Revelation 12:1–6

The Refrain

Everyone will stand in awe and declare God's deeds;* they will recognize his works.

The Morning Psalm

The LORD Has Pleasure in Those Who Await His Gracious Favor

Hallelujah! How good it is to sing praises to our God!* how pleasant it is to honor him with praise!

The LORD rebuilds Jerusalem;* he gathers the exiles of Israel.

He heals the brokenhearted* and binds up their wounds.

He counts the number of the stars* and calls them all by their names.

Great is our LORD and mighty in power;* there is no limit to his wisdom.

The LORD lifts up the lowly,* but casts the wicked to the ground.

Sing to the LORD with thanksgiving;* make music to our God upon the harp.

He covers the heavens with clouds* and prepares rain for the earth;

He makes grass to grow upon the mountains* and green plants to serve mankind.

He provides food for flocks and herds* and for the young ravens when they cry.

He is not impressed by the might of a horse;* he has no pleasure in the strength of a man;

But the LORD has pleasure in those who fear him,* in those who await his gracious favor.

Psalm 147:1–12

The Refrain

Everyone will stand in awe and declare God's deeds;* they will recognize his works.

The Cry of the Church

O God, come to my assistance! O Lord, make haste to help me!

The Lord's Prayer

The Prayer Appointed for the Week

Purify my conscience, Almighty God, by your daily visitation, that your Son Jesus Christ, at his coming, may find in me a mansion prepared for himself; who lives and reigns with you and the Holy Spirit, one God, now and for ever. Amen.†

The Concluding Prayer of the Church

Lord God, almighty and everlasting Father, you have brought me in safety to this new day: Preserve me with your mighty power, that I may not fall into sin, nor be overcome by adversity; and in all I do direct me to the fulfilling of your purpose; through Jesus Christ my Lord. Amen.†

The Midday Office   **To Be Observed on the Hour or Half Hour**
                                          Between 11 a.m. and 2 p.m.

The Call to Prayer
Bless God in the congregation;* bless the LORD, you that are of the fountain of
   Israel.

                                                                    Psalm 68:26

The Request for Presence
Accept, O LORD, the willing tribute of my lips,* and teach me your judgments.

                                                                   Psalm 119:108

The Greeting
Let the words of my mouth and the meditation of my heart be acceptable in your
   sight,* O LORD, my strength and my redeemer.

                                                                    Psalm 19:14

The Refrain for the Midday Lessons
Hallelujah! Happy are they who fear the Lord* and have great delight in his commandments.

                                                                    Psalm 112:1

A Reading
Jerusalem, turn your eyes to the east, see the joy that is coming to you from God.
   Look, the children you watched go away are on their way home; reassembled
   from east and west, they are on their way home at the Holy One's command,
   rejoicing in God's glory.

                                                                 Baruch 4:36–37

The Refrain
Hallelujah! Happy are they who fear the Lord* and have great delight in his commandments.

The Midday Psalm   *He Has Raised Up Strength for His People*
Praise the LORD from the earth,* you sea-monsters and all deeps;
Fire and hail, snow and fog,* tempestuous wind, doing his will;
Mountains and all hills,* fruit trees and all cedars;
Wild beasts and all cattle,* creeping things and winged birds;
Kings of the earth and all peoples,* princes and all rulers of the world;
Young men and maidens,* old and young together.
Let them praise the Name of the LORD,* for his Name only is exalted, his splendor
   is over earth and heaven.
He has raised up strength for his people and praise for all his loyal servants,* the
   children of Israel, a people who are near him. Hallelujah!

                                                                 Psalm 148:7–14

The Refrain
Hallelujah! Happy are they who fear the Lord* and have great delight in his commandments.

The Cry of the Church

O Lord, hear my prayer and let my cry come unto you. Thanks be to God.

THE SHORT BREVIARY

The Lord's Prayer

The Prayer Appointed for the Week

Purify my conscience, Almighty God, by your daily visitation, that your Son Jesus
Christ, at his coming, may find in me a mansion prepared for himself; who lives
and reigns with you and the Holy Spirit, one God, now and for ever. *Amen.*†

The Concluding Prayer of the Church

Lord Jesus Christ, by your death you took away the sting of death: Grant me to so
follow in faith where you have led the way, that I may at length fall asleep peacefully in you and wake in your likeness; for your tender mercies' sake. *Amen.*†

The Vespers Office   **To Be Observed on the Hour or Half Hour
Between 5 and 8 p.m.**

The Call to Prayer

The LORD is my strength and my shield;* my heart trusts in him, and I have been
helped;
Therefore my heart dances for joy,* and in my song will I praise him.

Psalm 28:8–9

The Request for Presence

I have gone astray like a sheep that is lost;* search for your servant, for I do not
forget your commandments.

Psalm 119:176

The Greeting

How great is your goodness, O LORD! which you have laid up for those who fear
you;* which you have done in the sight of all for those who put their trust in
you.

Psalm 31:19

The Hymn

All praise to you, O God, this night
For all the blessings of the light;
Keep us, we pray, O king of kings,
Beneath your own almighty wings.

Forgive us, Lord, through Christ your Son,
Whatever wrong this day we've done;
Your peace give to the world, O Lord,
That men might live in one accord.

Enlighten us, O blessed Light,
And give us rest throughout this night.
O strengthen us, that for your sake,
We all may serve you when we wake.

Thomas Ken

The Refrain for the Vespers Lessons
Mercy and truth have met together;* righteousness and peace have kissed each other.

Psalm 85:10

The Vespers Psalm   *He Redeems Our Life*
Bless the LORD, O my soul,* and all that is within me, bless his holy Name.
Bless the LORD, O my soul,* and forget not all his benefits.
He forgives all your sins* and heals all your infirmities;
He redeems your life from the grave* and crowns you with mercy and loving-
    kindness;
He satisfies you with good things,* and your youth is renewed like an eagle's.
The LORD executes righteousness* and judgment for all who are oppressed.
He made his ways known to Moses* and his works to the children of Israel.
The LORD is full of compassion and mercy,* slow to anger and of great kindness.
He will not always accuse us,* nor will he keep his anger for ever.
He has not dealt with us according to our sins,* nor rewarded us according to our
    wickedness.
For as the heavens are high above the earth,* so is his mercy great upon those who
    fear him.
As far as the east is from the west,* so far has he removed our sins from us.
As a father cares for his children,* so does the LORD care for those who fear him.
For he himself knows whereof we are made;* he remembers that we are but dust.

Psalm 103:1–14

The Refrain
Mercy and truth have met together;* righteousness and peace have kissed each other.

The Small Verse
My help is in the Name of the Lord who made heaven and earth and all that is in
    them. Thanks be to God.

Traditional

The Lord's Prayer

The Prayer Appointed for the Week
Purify my conscience, Almighty God, by your daily visitation, that your Son Jesus
    Christ, at his coming, may find in me a mansion prepared for himself; who lives
    and reigns with you and the Holy Spirit, one God, now and for ever. *Amen.*†

Concluding Prayers of the Church
Almighty God, who has promised to hear the petitions of those who ask in your
    Son's Name: I beseech you mercifully to incline your ear to me who have made
    my prayers and supplications to you; and grant that those things which I have
    faithfully asked according to your will, I may effectually obtain, to the relief of
    my necessity, and to the setting forth of your glory; through Jesus Christ my
    Lord. *Amen.*†

May the souls of the faithful departed, through the mercy of God, rest in eternal
    peace. *Amen.*

Advent Compline

Sunday
The Night Office   To Be Observed Before Retiri▮

The Call to Prayer

May the Lord Almighty grant me and those I love a peaceful night and a perfect
end. *Amen.*†

The Request for Presence

Our help is in the Name of the Lord; the maker of heaven and earth.

The Greeting

Almighty God, my heavenly Father: I have sinned against you, through my own
fault, in thought, and word, and deed, in what I have done and what I have le▮
undone. For the sake of your Son our Lord Jesus Christ, forgive me all my
offenses; and grant that I may serve you in newness of life, to the glory of you▮
Name. *Amen.*†

The Reading   *The Magnific▮*

My soul doth magnify the Lord,
And my spirit hath rejoiced in God my Savior;
For he hath regarded the low estate of his handmaiden:
For, behold, henceforth all generations shall call me blessed,
For he that is mighty hath done to me great things;
And holy is his name,
And his mercy is on them that fear him from generation to generation.
He hath showed strength with his arm;
He hath scattered the proud in the imagination of their hearts.
He hath put down the mighty from their seats, and exalted them of low degree.
He hath filled the hungry with good things; and the rich he hath sent away empt▮
He hath holpen his servant Israel, in remembrance of his mercy
As he spake to our fathers, to Abraham, and to his seed for ever.

Luke 1:46–55 (KJ▮

The Cry of the Church

Come, thou long expected Jesus!

The Psalm   *I Will Sing and Make Melo▮*

My heart is firmly fixed, O God, my heart is fixed;* I will sing and make melody.
Wake up, my spirit; awake, lute and harp;* I myself will waken the dawn.
I will confess you among the peoples, O LORD;* I will sing praises to you among
the nations.
For your loving-kindness is greater than the heavens,* and your faithfulness
reaches to the clouds.
Exalt yourself above the heavens, O God,* and your glory over all the earth.

Psalm 108:1–▮

The Cry of the Church

Even so, come, Lord Jesus!

The Small Verse

Into your hands, O Lord, I commend my spirit; for you have redeemed me, O
 Lord, O God of truth. Keep me, O Lord, as the apple of your eye; hide me
 under the shadow of your wings.†

The Lord's Prayer

The Petition

Watch, O Lord, with those who wake, or watch, or weep tonight, and give Your
 angels and saints charge over those who sleep. Tend Your sick ones, O Lord
 Christ. Rest Your weary ones. Bless Your dying ones. Soothe Your suffering
 ones. Shield Your joyous ones, and all for Your love's sake. *Amen.*§

The Final Thanksgiving

Lord, you now have set your servant free to go in peace as you have promised; for
 these eyes of mine have seen the Savior, whom you have prepared for all the
 world to see: a Light to enlighten the nations, and the glory of your people
 Israel. Glory to the Father, and to the Son, and to the Holy Spirit: as it was in the
 beginning, is now, and will be for ever. *Amen.*

Monday
The Night Office   **To Be Observed Before Retiring**

The Call to Prayer

May the Lord Almighty grant me and those I love a peaceful night and a perfect
 end. *Amen.*†

The Request for Presence

Our help is in the Name of the Lord; the maker of heaven and earth.

The Greeting

Almighty God, my heavenly Father: I have sinned against you, through my own
 fault, in thought, and word, and deed, in what I have done and what I have left
 undone. For the sake of your Son our Lord Jesus Christ, forgive me all my
 offenses; and grant that I may serve you in newness of life, to the glory of your
 Name. *Amen.*†

The Reading   *The General Thanksgiving*

Almighty God, Father of all mercies,
We your unworthy servants
Do give you most humble and hearty thanks
For all your goodness and loving-kindness

To us and to all men.
We bless you for our creation, preservation,
And all the blessings of this life;
But above all for your inestimable love
In the redemption of the world by our Lord Jesus Christ,
For the means of grace, and for the hope of glory.
And, we beseech you,
Give us that due sense of all your mercies,
That our hearts may be unfeignedly thankful;
And that we show forth your praise,
Not only with our lips, but in our lives,
By giving up ourselves to your service,
And by walking before you
In holiness and righteousness all our days;
Through Jesus Christ our Lord,
To whom, with you and the Holy Ghost,
Be all honor and glory, world without end. *Amen.*†

The Cry of the Church
Come, thou long expected Jesus!

The Psalm   *May God Come to Us*
May God be merciful to us and bless us,* show us the light of his countenance and
    come to us.
Let your ways be known upon earth,* your saving health among all nations.
Let the peoples praise you, O God;* let all the peoples praise you.
Let the nations be glad and sing for joy,* for you judge the peoples with equity and
    guide all the nations upon earth.
Let the peoples praise you, O God;* let all the peoples praise you.
The earth has brought forth her increase;* may God, our own God, give us his
    blessing.
May God give us his blessing,* and may all the ends of the earth stand in awe of him.
Psalm 67

The Cry of the Church
Even so, come, Lord Jesus!

The Small Verse
Into your hands, O Lord, I commend my spirit; for you have redeemed me, O
    Lord, O God of truth. Keep me, O Lord, as the apple of your eye; hide me
    under the shadow of your wings.†

The Lord's Prayer

The Petition
Watch, O Lord, with those who wake, or watch, or weep tonight, and give Your
    angels and saints charge over those who sleep. Tend Your sick ones, O Lord

Christ. Rest Your weary ones. Bless Your dying ones. Soothe Your suffering ones. Shield Your joyous ones, and all for Your love's sake. *Amen*.§

The Final Thanksgiving

Lord, you now have set your servant free to go in peace as you have promised; for these eyes of mine have seen the Savior, whom you have prepared for all the world to see: a Light to enlighten the nations, and the glory of your people Israel. Glory to the Father, and to the Son, and to the Holy Spirit: as it was in the beginning, is now, and will be for ever. *Amen.*

Tuesday
The Night Office   To Be Observed Before Retiring

The Call to Prayer

May the Lord Almighty grant me and those I love a peaceful night and a perfect end. *Amen.*†

The Request for Presence

Our help is in the Name of the Lord; the maker of heaven and earth.

The Greeting

Almighty God, my heavenly Father: I have sinned against you, through my own fault, in thought, and word, and deed, in what I have done and what I have left undone. For the sake of your Son our Lord Jesus Christ, forgive me all my offenses; and grant that I may serve you in newness of life, to the glory of your Name. *Amen.*†

The Reading

The people that walked in darkness have seen a great light;
On the inhabitants of a country in shadow dark as death light has blazed forth.
You have enlarged the nation, you have increased its joy;
They rejoice before you as people rejoice at harvest time,
As they exult when they are dividing the spoils.
For the yoke that weighed on it, the bar across its shoulders,
The rod of its oppressor,
These you have broken as on the day of Midian.
For all the footgear clanking over the ground
And all the clothing rolled in blood,
Will be burnt, will be food for the flames.
For a son has been born for us, a son has been given to us,
And dominion has been laid on his shoulders;

And this is the name he has been given,
'Wonder-Counselor, Mighty-God,
Eternal-Father, Prince-of-Peace,'
To extend his dominion in boundless peace,
Over the throne of David and over his kingdom
To make it secure and sustain it
In fair judgment and integrity.
From this time onwards and for ever,
The jealous love of YAHWEH Sabaoth will do this.

Isaiah 9:1–6

The Cry of the Church
Come, thou long expected Jesus!

The Psalm   *Behold, I Come*
Great things are they that you have done, O LORD my God! how great your
   wonders and your plans for us!* there is none who can be compared with
   you.
Oh, that I could make them known and tell them!* but they are more than I can
   count.
In sacrifice and offering you take no pleasure* (you have given me ears to hear you);
Burnt-offering and sin-offering you have not required,* and so I said, "Behold, I
   come.
In the roll of the book it is written concerning me:* 'I love to do your will, O my
   God; your law is deep in my heart.' "

Psalm 40:5–9

The Cry of the Church
Even so, come, Lord Jesus!

The Small Verse
Into your hands, O Lord, I commend my spirit; for you have redeemed me,
   O Lord, O God of truth. Keep me, O Lord, as the apple of your eye; hide me
   under the shadow of your wings.†

The Lord's Prayer

The Petition
Watch, O Lord, with those who wake, or watch, or weep tonight, and give Your
   angels and saints charge over those who sleep. Tend Your sick ones, O Lord
   Christ. Rest Your weary ones. Bless Your dying ones. Soothe Your suffering
   ones. Shield Your joyous ones, and all for Your love's sake. *Amen.*§

The Final Thanksgiving
Lord, you now have set your servant free to go in peace as you have promised; for
   these eyes of mine have seen the Savior, whom you have prepared for all the
   world to see: a Light to enlighten the nations, and the glory of your people
   Israel. Glory to the Father, and to the Son, and to the Holy Spirit: as it was in the
   beginning, is now, and will be for ever. *Amen.*

❧

Wednesday
The Night Office   **To Be Observed Before Retiring**

The Call to Prayer
May the Lord Almighty grant me and those I love a peaceful night and a perfect
end. *Amen*.†

The Request for Presence
Our help is in the Name of the Lord; the maker of heaven and earth.

The Greeting
Almighty God, my heavenly Father: I have sinned against you, through my own
fault, in thought, and word, and deed, in what I have done and what I have left
undone. For the sake of your Son our Lord Jesus Christ, forgive me all my
offenses; and grant that I may serve you in newness of life, to the glory of your
Name. *Amen*.†

The Hymn   *The Divine Image*

To Mercy, Pity, Peace, and Love   Then every man, of every clime,
All pray in their distress;   That prays in his distress,
And to these virtues of delight   Prays to the human form divine,
Return their thankfulness.   Love, Mercy, Pity, Peace.

For Mercy, Pity, Peace, and Love   And all must love the human form,
Is God, our Father dear,   In heathen, Turk, or Jew:
And Mercy, Pity, Peace, and Love   Where Mercy, Love, and Pity dwell
Is man, His child and care.   There God is dwelling too.

For Mercy has a human heart,   *William Blake*
Pity a human face.
And Love, the human form divine,
And Peace, the human dress.

The Cry of the Church
Come, thou long expected Jesus!

The Psalm   *God, Your God, Has Anointed You*
Your throne, O God, endures for ever and ever,* a scepter of righteousness is the
scepter of your kingdom; you love righteousness and hate iniquity.
Therefore God, your God, has anointed you* with the oil of gladness above your
fellows.
All your garments are fragrant with myrrh, aloes, and cassia,* and the music of
strings from ivory palaces makes you glad.

Kings' daughters stand among the ladies of the court;* on your right hand is the
queen, adorned with the gold of Ophir.

Psalm 45:7–10

The Cry of the Church
Even so, come, Lord Jesus!

The Small Verse
Into your hands, O Lord, I commend my spirit; for you have redeemed me,
O Lord, O God of truth. Keep me, O Lord, as the apple of your eye; hide me
under the shadow of your wings.†

The Lord's Prayer

The Petition
Watch, O Lord, with those who wake, or watch, or weep tonight, and give Your
angels and saints charge over those who sleep. Tend Your sick ones, O Lord
Christ. Rest Your weary ones. Bless Your dying ones. Soothe Your suffering
ones. Shield Your joyous ones, and all for Your love's sake. *Amen.*§

The Final Thanksgiving
Lord, you now have set your servant free to go in peace as you have promised; for
these eyes of mine have seen the Savior, whom you have prepared for all the
world to see: a Light to enlighten the nations, and the glory of your people
Israel. Glory to the Father, and to the Son, and to the Holy Spirit: as it was in the
beginning, is now, and will be for ever. *Amen.*

Thursday
The Night Office   **To Be Observed Before Retiring**

The Call to Prayer
May the Lord Almighty grant me and those I love a peaceful night and a perfect
end. *Amen.*†

The Request for Presence
Our help is in the Name of the Lord; the maker of heaven and earth.

The Greeting
Almighty God, my heavenly Father: I have sinned against you, through my own
fault, in thought, and word, and deed, in what I have done and what I have left
undone. For the sake of your Son our Lord Jesus Christ, forgive me all my
offenses; and grant that I may serve you in newness of life, to the glory of your
Name. *Amen.*†

The Reading

Here is my servant whom I uphold,
My chosen one in whom my soul delights.
I have sent my spirit upon him,
He will bring fair judgment to the nations.
He does not cry out or raise his voice,
His voice is not heard in the street;
He does not break the crushed reed
Or snuff the faltering wick.
Faithfully he presents his fair judgment;
He will not grow faint, he will not be crushed
Until he has established fair judgment on earth,
And the coasts and islands are waiting for his instruction.

Isaiah 42:1–4

The Cry of the Church

Come, thou long expected Jesus!

The Psalm
The LORD Will Show Us His Covenant

Gracious and upright is the LORD;* therefore he teaches sinners in his way.
He guides the humble in doing right* and teaches his way to the lowly.
All the paths of the LORD are love and faithfulness* to those who keep his
    covenant and his testimonies.
For your Name's sake, O LORD,* forgive my sin, for it is great.
Who are they who fear the LORD?* he will teach them the way that they should choose.
The LORD is a friend to those who fear him* and will show them his covenant.

Psalm 25:7–11, 13

The Cry of the Church

Even so, come, Lord Jesus!

The Small Verse

Into your hands, O Lord, I commend my spirit; for you have redeemed me,
    O Lord, O God of truth. Keep me, O Lord, as the apple of your eye; hide me
    under the shadow of your wings.†

The Lord's Prayer

The Petition

Watch, O Lord, with those who wake, or watch, or weep tonight, and give Your
    angels and saints charge over those who sleep. Tend Your sick ones, O Lord
    Christ. Rest Your weary ones. Bless Your dying ones. Soothe Your suffering
    ones. Shield Your joyous ones, and all for Your love's sake. *Amen.*§

The Final Thanksgiving

Lord, you now have set your servant free to go in peace as you have promised; for
    these eyes of mine have seen the Savior, whom you have prepared for all the
    world to see: a Light to enlighten the nations, and the glory of your people
    Israel. Glory to the Father, and to the Son, and to the Holy Spirit: as it was in the
    beginning, is now, and will be for ever. *Amen.*

Friday
The Night Office   **To Be Observed Before Retiring**

The Call to Prayer
May the Lord Almighty grant me and those I love a peaceful night and a perfect
    end. *Amen.*†

The Request for Presence
Our help is in the Name of the Lord; the maker of heaven and earth.

The Greeting
Almighty God, my heavenly Father: I have sinned against you, through my own
    fault, in thought, and word, and deed, in what I have done and what I have left
    undone. For the sake of your Son our Lord Jesus Christ, forgive me all my
    offenses; and grant that I may serve you in newness of life, to the glory of your
    Name. *Amen.*†

The Reading   *Catherine of Siena on the Virgin*
If I consider your own great counsel, eternal Trinity, I see that in your light you
    saw the dignity and nobility of the human race. So, just as love compelled you
    to draw us out of yourself, so that same love compelled you to buy us back
    when we were lost. In fact, you showed that you loved us before we existed,
    when you chose to draw us out of yourself only for love. But you have shown
    us greater love still by giving us yourself, shutting yourself up today in the
    pouch of humanity. And what more could you have given us than to give your
    very self? So you can truly ask us, "What should I or could I have done for you
    that I have not done?" I see, then, that whatever your wisdom saw, in that great
    council of yours, as best for our salvation, is what your mercy willed, and what
    your power has today accomplished. So in that council your power, your wis-
    dom, and your mercy agreed to our salvation, O eternal Trinity. In that council
    your great mercy chose to be merciful to your creature, and you, O eternal
    Trinity, chose to fulfill your truth in us by giving us eternal life. For this you
    had created us, that we might share and be glad in you. But your justice dis-
    agreed with us, protesting in the great council that justice, which lasts for ever,
    is just as much your hallmark as is mercy. Therefore, since your justice leaves
    no evil unpunished nor any good unrewarded, we could not be saved because
    we could not make satisfaction to you for our sin.
So what do you do? What way did your eternal unfathomable Wisdom find to fulfill
    your truth and be merciful, and to satisfy your justice as well? What remedy did
    you give us? O see what a fitting remedy! You arranged to give us the Word, your
    only-begotten Son. He would take on the clay of our flesh which had offended
    you so that when he suffered in that humanity your justice would be satisfied—
    not by humanity's power, but by the power of divinity united with that human-
    ity. And so your truth was fulfilled, and both justice and mercy were satisfied.

O Mary, I see this Word given to you, living in you yet not separated from the Father—just as the word one has in one's mind does not leave one's heart or become separated from it even though the word is externalized and communicated to others. In these things our human dignity is revealed—that God should have done such and so great things for us.

And even more: in you, O Mary, our human strength and freedom are today revealed, for after the deliberation of such and so great a council, the angel was sent to you to announce to you the mystery of divine counsel and to seek to know your will, and God's son did not come down to your womb until you had given your will's consent. He waited at the door for you to open to him; for he wanted to come into you, but he would never have entered unless you had opened to him, saying, "Here I am, God's servant; let it be done to me as you have said."

The strength and freedom of the will is clearly revealed, then, for no good nor any evil can be done without that will. Nor is there any devil or other creature that can drive it to the guilt of deadly sin without its consent. Nor, on the other hand, can it be driven to do anything good unless it so chooses. The eternal Godhead, O Mary, was knocking at your door, but unless you had opened that door of your will, God would not have taken flesh in you. Blush, my soul, when you see that today God has become your relative in Mary. Today you have been shown that even though you were made without your help, you will not be saved without your help, for today God is knocking at the door of Mary's will and waiting for her to open to Him.

O Mary, my tenderest love! In you is written the Word from whom we have the teaching of life. You are the tablet that sets this teaching before us. I see that this Word, once written in you, was never without the cross of holy desire. Even as He was conceived within you, desire to die for the salvation of humankind was engrafted and bound into Him. This is why He had been made flesh. So it was a great cross for Him to carry for such a long time that desire, when He would have liked to see it realized at once. In fact, the Godhead was united even with Christ's body in the tomb and with His soul in limbo, and afterwards with both his soul and body. The relationship was so entered into and sealed that it will never be dissolved, any more than it has been broken up to now.

Catherine of Siena

The Cry of the Church
Come, thou long expected Jesus!

The Psalm   *For God Alone My Soul in Silence Waits*
For God alone my soul in silence waits;* truly, my hope is in him.
He alone is my rock and my salvation,* my stronghold, so that I shall not be shaken.
In God is my safety and my honor;* God is my strong rock and my refuge.
Put your trust in him always, O people,* pour out your hearts before him, for God is our refuge.
God has spoken once, twice have I heard it,* that power belongs to God.

Psalm 62:6–9, 13

The Cry of the Church
Even so, come, Lord Jesus!

The Small Verse
Into your hands, O Lord, I commend my spirit; for you have redeemed me,
O Lord, O God of truth. Keep me, O Lord, as the apple of your eye; hide me
under the shadow of your wings.†

The Lord's Prayer

The Petition
Watch, O Lord, with those who wake, or watch, or weep tonight, and give Your
angels and saints charge over those who sleep. Tend Your sick ones, O Lord
Christ. Rest Your weary ones. Bless Your dying ones. Soothe Your suffering
ones. Shield Your joyous ones, and all for Your love's sake. *Amen.*§

The Final Thanksgiving
Lord, you now have set your servant free to go in peace as you have promised; for
these eyes of mine have seen the Savior, whom you have prepared for all the
world to see: a Light to enlighten the nations, and the glory of your people
Israel. Glory to the Father, and to the Son, and to the Holy Spirit: as it was in the
beginning, is now, and will be for ever. *Amen.*

Saturday
The Night Office   **To Be Observed Before Retiring**

The Call to Prayer
May the Lord Almighty grant me and those I love a peaceful night and a perfect
end. *Amen.*†

The Request for Presence
Our help is in the Name of the Lord; the maker of heaven and earth.

The Greeting
Almighty God, my heavenly Father: I have sinned against you, through my own
fault, in thought, and word, and deed, in what I have done and what I have left
undone. For the sake of your Son our Lord Jesus Christ, forgive me all my
offenses; and grant that I may serve you in newness of life, to the glory of your
Name. *Amen.*†

The Reading
". . . for my thoughts are not your thoughts and your ways are not my ways,"
declares Yahweh. "For the heavens are as high above the earth as my ways are

above your ways, my thoughts above your thoughts. For, as the rain and the snow come down from the sky and do not return before having watered the earth, fertilizing it and making it germinate to provide seed for the sower and food to eat, so it is with the word that goes from my mouth: it will not return to me unfulfilled or before having carried out my good pleasure and having achieved what it was sent to do."

Isaiah 55:8–11

The Cry of the Church
Come, thou long expected Jesus!

The Psalm
Out of Zion, Perfect in Its Beauty

The LORD, the God of gods, has spoken;* he has called the earth from the rising of the sun to its setting.

Out of Zion, perfect in its beauty,* God reveals himself in glory.

Our God will come and will not keep silence;* before him there is a consuming flame, and round about him a raging storm.

He calls the heavens and the earth from above* to witness the judgment of his people.

"Gather before me my loyal followers,* those who have made a covenant with me and sealed it with sacrifice."

Let the heavens declare the rightness of his cause;* for God himself is judge.

Psalm 50:1–6

The Cry of the Church
Even so, come, Lord Jesus!

The Small Verse
Into your hands, O Lord, I commend my spirit; for you have redeemed me, O Lord, O God of truth. Keep me, O Lord, as the apple of your eye; hide me under the shadow of your wings.†

The Lord's Prayer

The Petition
Watch, O Lord, with those who wake, or watch, or weep tonight, and give Your angels and saints charge over those who sleep. Tend Your sick ones, O Lord Christ. Rest Your weary ones. Bless Your dying ones. Soothe Your suffering ones. Shield Your joyous ones, and all for Your love's sake. *Amen.*§

The Final Thanksgiving
Lord, you now have set your servant free to go in peace as you have promised; for these eyes of mine have seen the Savior, whom you have prepared for all the world to see: a Light to enlighten the nations, and the glory of your people Israel. Glory to the Father, and to the Son, and to the Holy Spirit: as it was in the beginning, is now, and will be for ever. *Amen.*

The Gloria

Glory be to God the Father, God the Son, and God the Holy Spirit. As it was in the beginning, so it is now and so it shall ever be, world without end. Alleluia. *Amen.*

The Lord's Prayer

Our Father, who art in heaven, hallowed be your Name.
May your kingdom come, and your will be done, on earth as in heaven.
Give us today our daily bread.
Forgive us our sins as we forgive those who sin against us.
Lead us not into temptation, but deliver us from evil;
for yours are the kingdom and the power and the glory
forever and ever. *Amen.*

Compline Prayers for the First Week of Christmas Are Located on Page 183.

The Following Holy Days Occur within the first week of Christmas:
The Eve of the Nativity of Our Lord: *December 24*
The Feast of The Nativity of Our Lord: Christmas Day: *December 25*
The Feast of St. Stephen: *December 26*
The Feast of St. John: *December 27*
The Commemoration of the Holy Innocents: *December 28*
The Fifth Day of the Octave of Christmas: *December 29*
The Feast of the Holy Family: *December 30*
The Eve of the Feast of the Holy Name: *December 31*

The First Week
of Christmas

The Morning Office

To Be Observed on the Hour or Half Hour
Between 6 and 9 a.m.

The Call to Prayer
Wake up, my spirit; awake, lute and harp;* I myself will waken the dawn.

Psalm 57:8

The Request for Presence
O Lamb of God, that takes away the sins of the world, have mercy upon me.
O Lamb of God, that takes away the sins of the world, have mercy upon me.
O Lamb of God, that takes away the sins of the world, grant me your peace.

Agnus Dei

The Greeting
For you alone are the Holy One, you alone are the Lord, you alone are the Most
    High, Jesus Christ, with the Holy Spirit, in the Glory of God the Father.

The Refrain for the Morning Lessons
Be strong and let your heart take courage,* all you who wait for the Lord.

Psalm 31:24

A Reading   The Prophecy of the Priest Zechariah, Father of John the Baptizer
Zechariah was filled with the Holy Spirit and spoke this prophecy: "*Blessed be the
    Lord, the God of Israel*, for he has visited his people, he has *set them free*, and he
    has established for us a saving power in the House of his servant David, just as
    he proclaimed, by the mouth of his holy prophets from ancient times, that he
    would save us from our *enemies and from the hands of all those who hate us*, and
    show *faithful love to our ancestors, and so keep in mind his holy covenant.* This was
    the oath he swore to our father Abraham, that he would grant us, free from
    fear, to be delivered from the hands of our enemies, to serve him in holiness
    and uprightness in his presence, all our days."

Luke 1:67–75

The Refrain
Be strong and let your heart take courage,* all you who wait for the Lord.

The Morning Psalm   In the Roll of the Book It Is Written Concerning Me
In sacrifice and offering you take no pleasure* (you have given me ears to hear you);
Burnt-offering and sin-offering you have not required,* and so I said, "Behold, I
    come.
In the roll of the book it is written concerning me:* 'I love to do your will, O my
    God; your law is deep in my heart.' "

Psalm 40:7–9

The Refrain
Be strong and let your heart take courage,* all you who wait for the Lord.

The Cry of the Church
Even so, come, Lord Jesus!

The Lord's Prayer

The Prayer Appointed for the Week
Purify my conscience, Almighty God, by your daily visitation, that your Son Jesus
Christ, at his coming, may find in me a mansion prepared for himself; who
lives and reigns with you and the Holy Spirit, one God, now and for ever.
Amen.†

The Concluding Prayer of the Church
Lord God, almighty and everlasting Father, you have brought me in safety to this
new day: Preserve me with your mighty power, that I may not fall into sin, nor
be overcome by adversity; and in all I do direct me to the fulfilling of your purpose; through Jesus Christ my Lord. *Amen.*†

The Midday Office   **To Be Observed on the Hour or Half Hour**
                                          Between 11 a.m. and 2 p.m.

The Call to Prayer
Ascribe to the LORD, you families of the peoples;* ascribe to the LORD honor and
power.
Ascribe to the LORD the honor due his Name;* bring offerings and come into his
courts.
Worship the LORD in the beauty of holiness . . .

Psalm 96:7–9

The Request for Presence
For God alone my soul in silence waits;* truly, my hope is in him.

Psalm 62:6

The Greeting
Happy are the people whose strength is in you!* whose hearts are set on the pilgrims' way.

Psalm 84:4

The Refrain for the Midday Lessons
My heart, therefore, is glad, and my spirit rejoices;* my body also shall rest in
hope.

Psalm 16:9

A Reading
YAHWEH declares, "Because of this, my people will know my name, because of this
they will know when the day comes, that it is I saying, 'Here I am!' How beautiful on the mountains, are the feet of the messenger announcing peace, of the
messenger of good news, who proclaims salvation and says to Zion, 'Your God
is king!' The voices of your watchmen! Now they raise their voices, shouting
for joy together, for with their own eyes they have seen YAHWEH returning to
Zion. Break into shouts together, shouts for joy, you ruins of Jerusalem; for
YAHWEH has consoled his people, he has redeemed Jerusalem. YAHWEH has

bared his holy arm for all the nations to see, and all the ends of the earth have seen the salvation of our God."

Isaiah 52:6–10

The Refrain
My heart, therefore, is glad, and my spirit rejoices;* my body also shall rest in hope.

The Midday Psalm   The Lord of Hosts Is with Us
There is a river whose streams make glad the city of God,* the holy habitation of the Most High.

God is in the midst of her; she shall not be overthrown;* God shall help her at the break of day.

The nations make much ado, and the kingdoms are shaken;* God has spoken, and the earth shall melt away.

The Lord of hosts is with us;* the God of Jacob is our stronghold.

Psalm 46:5–8

The Refrain
My heart, therefore, is glad, and my spirit rejoices;* my body also shall rest in hope.

The Small Verse
'I am the Alpha and the Omega,' says the Lord God, who is, who was, and who is to come, the Almighty.

Revelation 1:8

The Lord's Prayer

The Prayer Appointed for the Week
Purify my conscience, Almighty God, by your daily visitation, that your Son Jesus Christ, at his coming, may find in me a mansion prepared for himself; who lives and reigns with you and the Holy Spirit, one God, now and for ever. *Amen.*†

The Concluding Prayer of the Church
O God, the source of eternal light: Shed forth your unending day upon all of us who watch for you, that our lips may praise you, our lives may bless you, and our worship may give you glory; through Jesus Christ our Lord. *Amen.*†

The Vespers Office   **To Be Observed on the Hour or Half Hour Between 5 and 8 p.m.**

The Call to Prayer
Give thanks to the Lord, for he is good,* and his mercy endures for ever.

Psalm 107:1

The Request for Presence
So teach us to number our days* that we may apply our hearts to wisdom.

Psalm 90:12

The Greeting

Remember not the sins of my youth and my transgressions;* remember me
according to your love and for the sake of your goodness, O LORD.

Psalm 25:6

The Hymn   Silent Night

Silent night, Holy night,   Silent night, Holy night,
All is calm, all is bright.   Son of God, love's pure light
Round yon virgin mother and child.   Radiant beams from thy holy face,
Holy infant, so tender and mild,   With the dawn of redeeming grace,
Sleep in heavenly peace.   Jesus, Lord, at thy birth.
Sleep in heavenly peace.   Jesus, Lord, at thy birth.

Silent night, Holy night,   *Joseph Mohr*
Shepherds quake at the sight,
Glories stream from heaven afar,
Heavenly hosts sing alleluia;
Christ the Savior is born!
Christ the Savior is born!

The Refrain for the Vespers Lessons

Behold, God is my helper;* it is the LORD who sustains my life.

Psalm 54:4

The Vespers Psalm   Come Now and Look Upon the Works of the LORD

Come now and look upon the works of the LORD,* what awesome things he has
done on earth.

"Be still, then, and know that I am God;* I will be exalted among the nations; I will
be exalted in the earth."

The LORD of hosts is with us;* the God of Jacob is our stronghold.

Psalm 46:9, 11–12

The Refrain

Behold, God is my helper;* it is the LORD who sustains my life.

The Small Verse

The Lord is my shepherd and nothing is wanting to me. In green pastures He hath
settled me.

THE SHORT BREVIARY

The Lord's Prayer

The Prayer Appointed for the Week

Purify my conscience, Almighty God, by your daily visitation, that your Son Jesus
Christ, at his coming, may find in me a mansion prepared for himself; who
lives and reigns with you and the Holy Spirit, one God, now and for ever.
Amen.†

The Concluding Prayer of the Church

O God, you make us glad by the yearly festival of the birth of your only Son Jesus Christ: Grant that I, who joyfully receive him as my Redeemer, may with sure confidence behold him when he comes to be our Judge; who lives and reigns with you and the Holy Spirit, one God, now and for ever. *Amen.*†

◈

The Morning Office   **To Be Observed on the Hour or Half Hour Between 6 and 9 a.m.**

The Call to Prayer

Be glad, you righteous, and rejoice in the LORD;* shout for joy, all who are true of heart.

Psalm 32:12

The Request for Presence

Let the peoples praise you, O God;* let all the peoples praise you.

Let the nations be glad and sing for joy,* for you judge the peoples with equity and guide all the nations upon earth.

Let the peoples praise you, O God;* let all the peoples praise you.

Psalm 67:3–5

The Greeting

. . . O LORD my God, I will give you thanks for ever.

Psalm 30:13

The Refrain for the Morning Lessons

In the roll of the book it is written concerning me . . .

Psalm 40:9

A Reading

Now it happened that at this time Caesar Augustus issued a decree that a census should be made of the whole inhabited world. This census—the first—took place while Quirinius was governor of Syria, and everyone went to be registered, each to his own town. So Joseph set out from the town of Nazareth in Galilee for Judaea, to David's town called Bethlehem, since he was of David's House and line, in order to be registered together with Mary, his betrothed, who was with child. Now it happened that, while they were there, the time came for her to have her child, and she gave birth to a son, her first-born. She wrapped him in swaddling clothes and laid him in a manger because there was no room for them in the living-space. In the countryside close by there were shepherds out in the fields keeping guard over their sheep during the watches of the night. An angel of the Lord stood over them and the glory of the Lord shone around them. They were terrified, but the angel said, 'Do not be afraid. Look, I bring you news of great joy, a joy to be shared by the whole people. Today in the town of David, a Savior has been born to you; he is Christ the Lord. And here is a sign for you: you will find a baby wrapped in swaddling clothes and lying in a manger.' And all at once with the angel there was a great throng of the hosts of heaven, praising God with the words: Glory to God in the highest heaven, and on earth peace for those he favors. Now it happened that when the angels had gone from them into heaven, the shepherds said to one another, 'Let us go to Bethlehem and see this event which the Lord has made known to us.' So they hurried away and found Mary and Joseph, and the baby lying in the manger. When they saw the child they repeated what they had been told about him, and everyone who heard it was astonished at what the shepherds said to them. As for Mary, she treasured all these things and pondered them in her heart. And the shepherds went back glorifying and praising God for all they had heard and seen, just as they had been told.

Luke 2:1–20

The Refrain
In the roll of the book it is written concerning me . . .

The Morning Psalm   *Shout with Joy to the LORD*
Sing to the LORD a new song,* for he has done marvelous things.

With his right hand and his holy arm* has he won for himself the victory.

The LORD has made known his victory;* his righteousness has he openly shown in the sight of the nations.

He remembers his mercy and faithfulness to the house of Israel,* and all the ends of the earth have seen the victory of our God.

Shout with joy to the LORD, all you lands;* lift up your voice, rejoice, and sing.

Sing to the LORD with the harp,* with the harp and the voice of song.

With trumpets and the sound of the horn* shout with joy before the King, the LORD.

Let the sea make a noise and all that is in it,* the lands and those who dwell therein.

Let the rivers clap their hands,* and let the hills ring out with joy before the LORD, when he comes to judge the earth.

In righteousness shall he judge the world* and the peoples with equity.

Psalm 98

The Refrain
In the roll of the book it is written concerning me . . .

The Gloria

The Lord's Prayer

The Prayer Appointed for the Week
Almighty God, you have given your only-begotten Son to take our nature upon him, and to be born this day of a pure virgin: Grant that I, who have been born

again and made your child by adoption and grace, may daily be renewed by
your Holy Spirit; through my Lord Jesus Christ, to whom with you and the
same Spirit be honor and glory, now and for ever. *Amen.*†

The Concluding Prayer of the Church

O God, you have caused the holy night to shine with the brightness of the true
Light: Grant that I, who have known the mystery of that Light on earth, may
also enjoy him perfectly in heaven; where with you and the Holy Spirit he lives
and reigns, one God, in glory everlasting. *Amen.*†

The Midday Office **To Be Observed on the Hour or Half Hour
Between 11 a.m. and 2 p.m.**

The Call to Prayer

Come, let us bow down, and bend the knee,* and kneel before the LORD our
Maker.
For he is our God, and we are the people of his pasture and the sheep of his hand.*
Oh, that today you would hearken to his voice!

Psalm 95:6–7

The Request for Presence

My merciful God comes to meet me . . .

Psalm 59:11

The Greeting

I will give you thanks for what you have done* and declare the goodness of your
Name in the presence of the godly.

Psalm 52:9

The Refrain for the Midday Lessons

Let me announce the decree of the LORD:* he said to me, "You are my Son; this day
have I begotten you."

Psalm 2:7

A Reading

My dear friends, let us love each other, since love is from God and everyone who
loves is a child of God and knows God. Whoever fails to love does not know
God, because God is love. This is the revelation of God's love for us, that God
sent his only Son into the world that we might have life through him. Love
consists in this: it is not we who loved God, but God loved us and sent his Son
to expiate our sins.

1 John 4:7–10

The Refrain

Let me announce the decree of the LORD:* he said to me, "You are my Son; this day
have I begotten you."

The Midday Psalm *Righteousness and Peace Have Kissed Each Other*

I will listen to what the LORD God is saying,* for he is speaking peace to his faithful
people and to those who turn their hearts to him.

Truly, his salvation is very near to those who fear him,* that his glory may dwell in
our land.

Mercy and truth have met together;* righteousness and peace have kissed each
other.

Truth shall spring up from the earth,* and righteousness shall look down from
heaven.

The LORD will indeed grant prosperity,* and our land will yield its increase.

Righteousness shall go before him,* and peace shall be a pathway for his feet.

Psalm 85:8–13

The Refrain

Let me announce the decree of the LORD:* he said to me, "You are my Son; this day
have I begotten you."

The Gloria

The Lord's Prayer

The Prayer Appointed for the Week

Almighty God, you have given your only-begotten Son to take our nature upon
him, and to be born this day of a pure virgin: Grant that I, who have been born
again and made your child by adoption and grace, may daily be renewed by
your Holy Spirit; through my Lord Jesus Christ, to whom with you and the
same Spirit be honor and glory, now and for ever. *Amen.*†

The Concluding Prayer of the Church

O God, you have caused the holy night to shine with the brightness of the true
Light: Grant that I, who have known the mystery of that Light on earth, may
also enjoy him perfectly in heaven; where with you and the Holy Spirit he lives
and reigns, one God, in glory everlasting. *Amen.*†

The Vespers Office **To Be Observed on the Hour or Half Hour**
Between 5 and 8 p.m.

The Call to Prayer

Sing to the LORD a new song;* sing to the LORD, all the whole earth.

Sing to the LORD and bless his Name;* proclaim the good news of his salvation
from day to day.

Declare his glory among the nations* and his wonders among all peoples.

Psalm 96:1–3

The Request for Presence

Exalt yourself above the heavens, O God,* and your glory over all the earth.

Psalm 57:6

The Greeting

I will offer you a freewill sacrifice* and praise your Name, O Lord, for it is good.
For you have rescued me from every trouble . . .

Psalm 54:6–7

The Hymn   *Joy to the World*

Joy to the world! The Lord is come:
Let earth receive her King;
Let every heart prepare him room,
And heaven and nature sing,
And heaven and nature sing,
And heaven and nature sing.

Joy to the world! The Savior reigns;
Let us our songs employ,
While fields and floods, rocks, hills, and plains,
Repeat the sounding joy,
Repeat the sounding joy,
Repeat the sounding joy.

No more let sins or sorrows grow,
Nor thorns infest the ground;
He comes to make his blessings flow
Far as the curse is found,
Far as the curse is found,
Far as the curse is found.

He rules the world with truth and grace,
And makes the nations prove
The glories of his righteousness,
And wonders of his love,
And wonders of his love,
And wonders of his love.

Isaac Watts

The Refrain for the Vespers Lessons

I lie down and go to sleep;* I wake again, because the Lord sustains me.

Psalm 3:5

The Vespers Psalm   *My Heart Is Glad, My Spirit Rejoices,*
My Body Shall Rest in Peace

O Lord, you are my portion and my cup;* it is you who uphold my lot.
My boundaries enclose a pleasant land;* indeed, I have a goodly heritage.
I will bless the Lord who gives me counsel;* my heart teaches me, night after
  night.
I have set the Lord always before me;* because he is at my right hand I shall not
  fall.
My heart, therefore, is glad, and my spirit rejoices;* my body also shall rest in hope.

For you will not abandon me to the grave,* nor let your holy one see the Pit.
You will show me the path of life;* in your presence there is fullness of joy, and in
your right hand are pleasures for evermore.

Psalm 16:5–11

The Refrain
I lie down and go to sleep;* I wake again, because the LORD sustains me.

The Gloria

The Lord's Prayer

The Prayer Appointed for the Week
Almighty God, you have given your only-begotten Son to take our nature upon
him, and to be born this day of a pure virgin: Grant that I, who have been born
again and made your child by adoption and grace, may daily be renewed by
your Holy Spirit; through my Lord Jesus Christ, to whom with you and the
same Spirit be honor and glory, now and for ever. *Amen.*†

The Concluding Prayer of the Church
O God, you have caused the holy night to shine with the brightness of the true
Light: Grant that I, who have known the mystery of that Light on earth, may
also enjoy him perfectly in heaven; where with you and the Holy Spirit he lives
and reigns, one God, in glory everlasting. *Amen.*†

The Morning Office **To Be Observed on the Hour or Half Hour**
Between 6 and 9 a.m.

The Call to Prayer
Hallelujah! Praise the LORD, O my soul!* I will praise the LORD as long as I live; I
will sing praises to my God while I have my being.

Psalm 146:1

The Request for Presence
Set a watch before my mouth, O LORD, and guard the door of my lips;* let not my
heart incline to any evil thing.
Let me not be occupied in wickedness with evildoers,* nor eat of their choice
foods.
Let the righteous smite me in friendly rebuke;* let not the oil of the unrighteous
anoint my head.

Psalm 141:3–5

The Greeting
Not to us, O LORD, not to us, but to your Name give glory;* because of your love
and because of your faithfulness.

Psalm 115:1

The Refrain for the Morning Lessons
. . . the testimony of the LORD is sure and gives wisdom to the innocent.

Psalm 19:7b

A Reading   *St. Stephen, who was one of the first class of seven deacons appointed*
by the Apostles in Jerusalem, was also the first Christian martyr.
Because of his testimony as the first to die for the faith of Christ, the
Church observes his feast day immediately after that which cele-
brates the birth of Stephen's Lord.

Jesus said to the people: "This is why—look—I am sending you prophets and wise
men and scribes; some you will slaughter and crucify, some you will scourge in
the synagogues and hunt from town to town; and so you will draw down on
yourselves the blood of every upright person that has been shed on the earth,
from the blood of Abel to the holy blood of Zechariah son of Barachiah whom
you murdered between the sanctuary and the altar. In truth I tell you, it will all
recoil on this generation."

Matthew 23:34–36

The Refrain
. . . the testimony of the LORD is sure and gives wisdom to the innocent.

The Morning Psalm   *Into Your Hands I Commend My Spirit*
In you, O LORD, have I taken refuge; let me never be put to shame;* deliver me in
your righteousness.
Incline your ear to me;* make haste to deliver me.
Be my strong rock, a castle to keep me safe, for you are my crag and my
stronghold;* for the sake of your Name, lead me and guide me.
Take me out of the net that they have secretly set for me,* for you are my tower of
strength.
Into your hands I commend my spirit,* for you have redeemed me, O LORD, O
God of truth.

Psalm 31:1–5

The Refrain
. . . the testimony of the LORD is sure and gives wisdom to the innocent.

The Cry of the Church
O God, come to my assistance! O Lord, make haste to help me!

The Lord's Prayer

The Prayer Appointed for the Week

Almighty God, you have given your only-begotten Son to take our nature upon
him, and to be born of a pure virgin: Grant that I, who have been born again
and made your child by adoption and grace, may daily be renewed by your
Holy Spirit; through my Lord Jesus Christ, to whom with you and the same
Spirit be honor and glory, now and for ever. *Amen.*†

Concluding Prayers of the Church

I give you thanks, O Lord of Glory, for the example of the first martyr Stephen,
who looked up to heaven and prayed for his persecutors to your Son Jesus
Christ, who stands at your right hand; where he lives and reigns with you and
the Holy Spirit, one God, in glory everlasting. *Amen.*†

Lord God, almighty and everlasting Father, you have brought me in safety to this
new day: Preserve me with your mighty power, that I may not fall into sin, nor
be overcome by adversity; and in all I do direct me to the fulfilling of your purpose; through Jesus Christ my Lord. *Amen.*†

The Midday Office

**To Be Observed on the Hour or Half Hour
Between 11 a.m. and 2 p.m.**

The Call to Prayer

Come and listen, all you who fear God,* and I will tell you what he has done for me.

Psalm 66:14

The Request for Presence

I call upon you, O God, for you will answer me;* incline your ear to me and hear
my words.

Psalm 17:6

The Greeting

The Lord is in his holy temple; let all the earth keep silence before him. Amen.

Traditional

The Refrain for the Midday Lessons

The LORD is my strength and my song,* and he has become my salvation.

Psalm 118:14

A Reading

Stephen was filled with grace and power and began to work miracles and great
signs among the people. Then certain people came forward to debate with
Stephen, some from Cyrene and Alexandria who were members of the synagogue called the Synagogue of Freedmen, and others from Cilicia and Asia.
They found they could not stand up against him because of his wisdom, and
the Spirit that prompted what he said. So they procured some men to say, 'We
heard him using blasphemous language against Moses and against God.'
Having turned people against him as well as the elders and scribes, they took
Stephen by surprise, and arrested him and brought him before the Sanhedrin.

There they put up false witnesses to say, 'This man is always making speeches against this holy place and the Law. We have heard him say that Jesus, the Nazarene, is going to destroy this Place and alter the traditions that Moses handed down to us.' The members of the Sanhedrin all looked intently at Stephen, and his face appeared to them like the face of an angel . . . They were infuriated . . . and ground their teeth at him. But Stephen, filled with the Holy Spirit, gazed into heaven and saw the glory of God, and Jesus standing at God's right hand. 'Look! I can see heaven thrown open,' he said, 'and the Son of man standing at the right hand of God.' All the members of the council shouted out and stopped their ears with their hands; then they made a concerted rush at him, thrust him out of the city and stoned him. The witnesses put down their clothes at the feet of a young man called Saul. As they were stoning him, Stephen said in invocation, 'Lord Jesus, receive my spirit.' Then he knelt down and said aloud, 'Lord, do not hold this sin against them.' And with these words he fell asleep.

Acts 6:8–15, 7:54–60

The Refrain
The LORD is my strength and my song,* and he has become my salvation.

The Midday Psalm   *My Times Are in Your Hands*
I have become a reproach to all my enemies and even to my neighbors,* a dismay
    to those of my acquaintance; when they see me in the street they avoid me.
I am forgotten like a dead man, out of mind;* I am as useless as a broken pot.
For I have heard the whispering of the crowd; fear is all around;* they put their
    heads together against me; they plot to take my life.
But as for me, I have trusted in you, O LORD.* I have said, "You are my God.
My times are in your hand;* rescue me from the hand of my enemies, and from
    those who persecute me.
Make your face to shine upon your servant.*"

Psalm 31:11–16

The Refrain
The LORD is my strength and my song,* and he has become my salvation.

The Gloria

The Lord's Prayer

The Prayer Appointed for the Week
Almighty God, you have given your only-begotten Son to take our nature upon
    him, and to be born of a pure virgin: Grant that I, who have been born again
    and made your child by adoption and grace, may daily be renewed by your
    Holy Spirit; through my Lord Jesus Christ, to whom with you and the same
    Spirit be honor and glory, now and for ever. *Amen.*†

The Concluding Prayers of Church

Almighty God, who gave to your servant Stephen boldness to confess the Name of our Savior Jesus Christ before the rulers of this world, and courage to die for this faith: Grant that I may always be ready to give a reason for the hope that is in me, and to suffer gladly for the sake of our Lord Jesus Christ; who lives and reigns with you and the Holy Spirit, one God, for ever and ever. *Amen.†*

The Vespers Office   **To Be Observed on the Hour or Half Hour**
                                          Between 5 and 8 p.m.

The Call to Prayer

Hallelujah! Praise the LORD from the heavens;* praise him in the heights.

Psalm 148:1

The Request for Presence

You are my helper and my deliverer,* O LORD, do not tarry.

Psalm 70:6

The Greeting

O LORD, I am your servant;* I am your servant and the child of your handmaid; you have freed me from my bonds.

Psalm 116:14

The Hymn   *Good King Wenceslaus*

Good King Wenceslaus looked out on the feast of Stephen.
When the snow lay round about, deep and crisp and even.
Brightly shone the moon that night, though the frost was cruel,
When a poor man came in sight gathering winter fuel.

"Hither, page, and stand by me if you know it telling.
Yonder peasant, who is he, where and what his dwelling?"
"Sire, he lives a good league hence, underneath the mountain
Right against the forest fence, by Saint Agnes' fountain."

"Bring me flesh and bring me wine, bring me pine-logs hither.
You and I will see him dine when we bear them thither."
Page and monarch forth they went, forth they went together.
Through the rude winds' wild lament, and the bitter weather.

"Sire, the night is darker now, and the wind blows stronger.
Fails my heart I know not how, I can go no longer."
"Mark my footsteps, my good page, tread now in them boldly.
You shall find the winter's rage freeze your blood less coldly."

In his master's steps he trod where the snow lay dented.
Heat was in the very sod which the saint had printed.
Therefore, Christian men, be sure, wealth or rank possessing.
You who now will bless the poor, shall yourselves find blessing.

Unknown

The Refrain for the Vespers Lessons

Be strong and let your heart take courage,* all you who wait for the Lord.

Psalm 31:24

The Vespers Psalm   *Come, Children, and Listen to Me*

Fear the Lord, you that are his saints,* for those who fear him lack nothing.

The young lions lack and suffer hunger,* but those who seek the Lord lack
    nothing that is good.

Come, children, and listen to me;* I will teach you the fear of the Lord.

Many are the troubles of the righteous,* but the Lord will deliver him out of them
    all.

The Lord ransoms the life of his servants,* and none will be punished who trust in
    him.

Psalm 34:9–11, 19, 22

The Refrain

Be strong and let your heart take courage,* all you who wait for the Lord.

The Gloria

The Lord's Prayer

The Prayer Appointed for the Week

Almighty God, you have given your only-begotten Son to take our nature upon
    him, and to be born of a pure virgin: Grant that I, who have been born again
    and made your child by adoption and grace, may daily be renewed by your
    Holy Spirit; through my Lord Jesus Christ, to whom with you and the same
    Spirit be honor and glory, now and for ever. *Amen.*†

The Concluding Prayer of the Church

Almighty God, by your Holy Spirit you have made me one with your saints in
    heaven and on earth: Grant that in my earthly pilgrimage I may always be sup-
    ported by this fellowship of love and prayer, and know myself to be sur-
    rounded by their witness to your power and mercy. I ask this for the sake of
    Jesus Christ, in whom all my intercessions are acceptable through the Spirit,
    and who lives and reigns for ever and ever. *Amen.*†

The Morning Office   **To Be Observed on the Hour or Half Hour
Between 6 and 9 a.m.**

The Call to Prayer

Bless the Lord, you angels of his, you mighty ones who do his bidding,* and hear-
    ken to the voice of his word.

Bless the LORD, all you his hosts,* you ministers of his who do his will.
Bless the LORD, all you works of his,* in all places of his dominion . . .

Psalm 103:20–22

The Request for Presence
Be seated on your lofty throne, O Most High;* O LORD, judge the nations.

Psalm 7:8

The Greeting
Not to us, O LORD, not to us, but to your Name give glory;* because of your love
and because of your faithfulness.

Psalm 115:1

The Refrain for the Morning Lessons
The LORD is my strength and my song,* and he has become my salvation.

Psalm 118:14

A Reading   *On the second day of Christmas, the Church celebrates the life of St. John, whom Scripture refers to as "the beloved disciple." The only one of the original twelve to not suffer martyrdom, St. John spent all of his long life writing and preaching.*

Peter turned and saw the disciple whom Jesus loved following them—the one
who had leaned back close to his chest at the supper and had said to him,
'Lord, who is it that will betray you?' Seeing him, Peter said to Jesus, 'What
about him, Lord?' Jesus answered, 'If I want him to stay behind until I come,
what does it matter to you? You are to follow me.' The rumor then went out
among the brothers that this disciple would not die. Yet Jesus had not said to
Peter, 'He will not die,' but, 'If I want him to stay behind till I come.' This disciple is the one who vouches for these things and has written them down, and
we know that his testimony is true. There was much else that Jesus did; if it
were written down in detail. I do not suppose the world itself would hold all
the books that would be written.

The Conclusion of the Gospel of St. John (21:20–25)

The Refrain
The LORD is my strength and my song,* and he has become my salvation.

The Morning Psalm   *It Is a Good Thing to Tell of Your Loving-kindness in the Morning*

It is a good thing to give thanks to the LORD,* and to sing praises to your Name, O
Most High;
To tell of your loving-kindness early in the morning* and of your faithfulness in
the night season;
On the psaltery, and on the lyre,* and to the melody of the harp.
For you have made me glad by your acts, O LORD;* and I shout for joy because of
the works of your hands.

Psalm 92:1–4

The Refrain
The LORD is my strength and my song,* and he has become my salvation.

The Cry of the Church
Let us praise the Lord, whom the Angels are praising, whom the Cherubim and Seraphim proclaim: Holy, holy, holy!

THE SHORT BREVIARY

The Lord's Prayer

The Prayer Appointed for the Week
Almighty God, you have given your only-begotten Son to take our nature upon him, and to be born of a pure virgin: Grant that I, who have been born again and made your child by adoption and grace, may daily be renewed by your Holy Spirit; through my Lord Jesus Christ, to whom with you and the same Spirit be honor and glory, now and for ever. *Amen.*†

Concluding Prayers of the Church
Shed upon your Church, O Lord, the brightness of your light, that we, being illumined by the teaching of your apostle and evangelist John, may walk in the light of your truth, that at length we may attain to the fullness of eternal life; through Jesus Christ our Lord, who lives and reigns with you and the Holy Spirit, one God, for ever and ever. *Amen.*

Lord God, almighty and everlasting Father, you have brought me in safety to this new day: Preserve me with your mighty power, that I may not fall into sin, nor be overcome by adversity; and in all I do direct me to the fulfilling of your purpose; through Jesus Christ my Lord. *Amen.*†

The Midday Office
To Be Observed on the Hour or Half Hour Between 11 a.m. and 2 p.m.

The Call to Prayer
Bless the LORD, you angels of his, you mighty ones who do his bidding,* and hearken to the voice of his word.
Bless the LORD, all you his hosts,* you ministers of his who do his will.
Bless the LORD, all you works of his, in all places of his dominion;* bless the LORD, O my soul.

Psalm 103:20–22

The Request for Presence
I am a stranger here on earth;* do not hide your commandments from me.

Psalm 119:19

The Greeting
I am bound by the vow I made to you, O God;* I will present to you thank-offerings;

For you have rescued my soul from death and my feet from stumbling,* that I may
walk before God in the light of the living.

Psalm 56:11–12

The Refrain for the Midday Lessons

Glory be to him whose power, working in us, can do infinitely more than we can
ask or imagine; glory be to him from generation to generation in the Church
and in Christ Jesus for ever and ever. Amen.

Ephesians 3:20–21

A Reading

Something which has existed since the beginning, which we have heard, which
we have seen with our own eyes, which we have watched and touched with
our own hands, the Word of life—this is our theme. That life was made visible;
we saw it and are giving our testimony, declaring to you the eternal life, which
was present to the Father and has been revealed to us. We are declaring to you
what we have seen and heard, so that you too may share our life. Our life is
shared with the Father and with his Son Jesus Christ. We are writing this to you
so that our joy may be complete.

1 John 1:1–4

The Refrain

Glory be to him whose power, working in us, can do infinitely more than we can
ask or imagine; glory be to him from generation to generation in the Church
and in Christ Jesus for ever and ever. Amen.

The Midday Psalm   The Righteous Shall Spread Abroad Like a Cedar of Lebanon

The righteous shall flourish like a palm tree,* and shall spread abroad like a cedar
of Lebanon.

Those who are planted in the house of the LORD* shall flourish in the courts of our
God;

They shall still bear fruit in old age;* they shall be green and succulent;

That they may show how upright the LORD is,* my Rock, in whom there is no fault.

Psalm 92:11–14

The Refrain

Glory be to him whose power, working in us, can do infinitely more than we can
ask or imagine; glory be to him from generation to generation in the Church
and in Christ Jesus for ever and ever. Amen.

The Gloria

The Lord's Prayer

The Prayer Appointed for the Week

Almighty God, you have given your only-begotten Son to take our nature upon
him, and to be born of a pure virgin: Grant that I, who have been born again
and made your child by adoption and grace, may daily be renewed by your

Holy Spirit; through my Lord Jesus Christ, to whom with you and the same Spirit be honor and glory, now and for ever. *Amen*.†

Concluding Prayers of the Church

I thank you, heavenly Father, for the witness of your apostle and evangelist John to the Gospel of your Son my Savior; and I pray that after his example, I may with ready will and heart obey the calling of my Lord, who lives and reigns with you and the Holy Spirit, one God, now and for ever. *Amen*.†

Almighty God, you have poured upon us the new light of your incarnate Word: Grant that this light, enkindled in my heart, may shine forth in my life; through Jesus Christ our Lord, who lives and reigns with you, in the unity of the Holy Spirit, one God, now and for ever. *Amen*.†

The Vespers Office   **To Be Observed on the Hour or Half Hour Between 5 and 8 p.m.**

The Call to Prayer

Let the Name of the Lord be blessed,* from this time forth for evermore.
From the rising of the sun to its going down* let the Name of the Lord be praised.

Psalm 113:2–3

The Request for Presence

Hear my prayer, O God;* do not hide yourself from my petition.
Listen to me and answer me . . .

Psalm 55:1–2

The Greeting

The Lord is in his holy temple; let all the earth keep silence before him.

Traditional

The Hymn

Come sing, your choirs exultant, those messengers of God,
Through whom the living Gospels came sounding all abroad!
Whose voice proclaimed salvation that poured upon the night,
And drove away the shadows, and filled the world with light.

In one harmonious witness the chosen four combine,
While each his own commission fulfills in every line;
As, in the prophet's vision from out the amber flame
In mystic form and image four living creatures came.

Four-square on this foundation the Church of Christ remains,
A house to stand unshaken by floods or winds or rains.
How blessed this habitation of gospel liberty,
Where with a holy people God dwells in Unity.

Latin, 12th Century

The Refrain for the Vespers Lessons

Why are you so full of heaviness, O my soul?* and why are you so disquieted
within me?

Put your trust in God;* for I will yet give thanks to him, who is the help of my
countenance, and my God.

Psalm 42:6–7

The Vespers Psalm   *He Is Bound to Me in Love*

Because you have made the Lord your refuge,* and the Most High your
habitation,

There shall no evil happen to you,* neither shall any plague come near your
dwelling.

For he shall give his angels charge over you,* to keep you in all your ways.

They shall bear you in their hands,* lest you dash your foot against a stone.

You shall tread upon the lion and adder;* you shall trample the young lion and the
serpent under your feet.

Because he is bound to me in love, therefore will I deliver him;* I will protect him,
because he knows my Name.

He shall call upon me, and I will answer him;* I am with him in trouble; I will
rescue him and bring him to honor.

With long life will I satisfy him,* and show him my salvation.

Psalm 91:9–16

The Refrain

Why are you so full of heaviness, O my soul?* and why are you so disquieted
within me?

Put your trust in God;* for I will yet give thanks to him, who is the help of my
countenance, and my God.

The Cry of the Church

O God, come to my assistance! O Lord, make haste to help me!

The Lord's Prayer

The Prayer Appointed for the Week

Almighty God, you have given your only-begotten Son to take our nature upon
him, and to be born of a pure virgin: Grant that I, who have been born again
and made your child by adoption and grace, may daily be renewed by your
Holy Spirit; through my Lord Jesus Christ, to whom with you and the same
Spirit be honor and glory, now and for ever. *Amen.*†

Concluding Prayers of the Church

Almighty God, whose will it is to be glorified in your saints, and who raised up
your servant John to be a light in the world: Shine, we pray, in our hearts, that
we also in our generation may show forth your praise, who called us out of
darkness into your marvelous light; through Jesus Christ our Lord, who lives
and reigns with you and the Holy Spirit, one God, now and for ever. *Amen.*†

Save me, Lord, while I am awake and keep me while I sleep, that I may wake with Christ and rest in peace. *Amen.*

ᕷᴥ

The Morning Office   **To Be Observed on the Hour or Half Hour Between 6 and 9 a.m.**

The Call to Prayer
Come, let us sing to the LORD;* let us shout for joy to the Rock of our salvation.

Psalm 95:1

The Request for Presence
Bow your heavens, O LORD, and come down;* touch the mountains, and they shall smoke.

Psalm 144:5

The Greeting
My lips will sing with joy when I play to you,* and so will my soul, which you have redeemed.

Psalm 71:23

The Refrain for the Morning Lessons
Remember, LORD, how short life is,* how frail you have made all flesh.

Psalm 89:47

A Reading   *On December 28, the Church remembers with sorrow the slaughter of the male infants of Bethlehem. They were indeed the first victims of the persecution of Christians.*

After they had left, suddenly the angel of the Lord appeared to Joseph in a dream and said, 'Get up, take the child and his mother with you, and escape into Egypt, and stay there until I tell you, because Herod intends to search for the child and do away with him.' So Joseph got up and, taking the child and his mother with him, left that night for Egypt, where he stayed until Herod was dead. This was to fulfill what the Lord had spoken through the prophet: *I called my son out of Egypt.* Herod was furious on realizing that he had been fooled by the wise men, and in Bethlehem and its surrounding district he had all the male children killed who were two years old or less, reckoning by the date he had been careful to ask the wise men. Then were fulfilled the words spoken through the prophet Jeremiah: *A voice is heard in Ramah, lamenting and weeping bitterly: it is Rachel weeping for her children, refusing to be comforted because they are no more.*

Matthew 2:13–18

The Refrain
Remember, LORD, how short life is,* how frail you have made all flesh.

The Morning Psalm   *Show Your Splendor to Our Children*
Return, O LORD; how long will you tarry?* be gracious to your servants.
Satisfy us by your loving-kindness in the morning;* so shall we rejoice and be glad
    all the days of our life.
Make us glad by the measure of the days that you afflicted us* and the years in
    which we suffered adversity.
Show your servants your works* and your splendor to their children.
May the graciousness of the LORD our God be upon us;* prosper the work of our
    hands; prosper our handiwork.

Psalm 90:13–17

The Refrain
Remember, LORD, how short life is,* how frail you have made all flesh.

The Gloria

The Lord's Prayer

The Prayer Appointed for the Week
Almighty God, you have given your only-begotten Son to take our nature upon
    him, and to be born of a pure virgin: Grant that I, who have been born again
    and made your child by adoption and grace, may daily be renewed by your
    Holy Spirit; through my Lord Jesus Christ, to whom with you and the same
    Spirit be honor and glory, now and for ever. *Amen.*†

Concluding Prayers of the Church
We remember today, O God, the slaughter of the holy innocents of Bethlehem by
    King Herod. Receive, we pray, into the arms of your mercy all innocent vic-
    tims; and by your great might frustrate the designs of evil tyrants and establish
    your rule of justice, love, and peace; through Jesus Christ our Lord, who lives
    and reigns with you, in the unity of the Holy Spirit, one God, for ever and ever.
    Amen.

Lord God, almighty and everlasting Father, you have brought me in safety to this
    new day: Preserve me with your mighty power, that I may not fall into sin, nor
    be overcome by adversity; and in all I do direct me to the fulfilling of your pur-
    pose; through Jesus Christ my Lord. *Amen.*†

The Midday Office   **To Be Observed on the Hour or Half Hour**
                                   Between 11 a.m. and 2 p.m.

The Call to Prayer
Praise God from whom all blessings flow; praise him, all creatures here below;
    praise him above, you heavenly hosts; praise Father, Son and Holy Ghost.

Doxology

The Request for Presence
May the glory of the LORD endure for ever;* may the LORD rejoice in all his works.

Psalm 104:32

The Greeting
Hosanna, LORD, hosanna!* LORD, send us now success.
Blessed is he who comes in the name of the Lord . . .
God is the LORD; he has shined upon us;* form a procession with branches up to
the horns of the altar.

Psalm 118:25–27

The Refrain for the Midday Lessons
Those who go out weeping, carrying the seed,* will come again in joy, shouldering
their sheaves.

Psalm 126:7

A Reading
YAHWEH says this, "A voice is heard in Ramah, lamenting and weeping bitterly: it
is Rachel weeping for her children, refusing to be comforted for her children,
because they are no more." YAHWEH says this, "Stop your lamenting, dry your
eyes, for your labor will have a reward," YAHWEH declares, "and they will
return from your enemy's country. There is a hope for your future after all,"
YAHWEH declares, "your children will return to their homeland."

Jeremiah 31:15–17

The Refrain
Those who go out weeping, carrying the seed,* will come again in joy, shouldering
their sheaves.

The Midday Psalm　　　　　　　　　　　　　　　　*Our Eyes Look to the LORD Our God*
To you I lift up my eyes,* to you enthroned in the heavens.
As the eyes of servants look to the hand of their masters,* and the eyes of a maid to
the hand of her mistress,
So our eyes look to the LORD our God,* until he shows us his mercy.
Have mercy upon us, O LORD, have mercy,* for we have had more than enough of
contempt,
Too much of the scorn of the indolent rich,* and of the derision of the proud.

Psalm 123

The Refrain
Those who go out weeping, carrying the seed,* will come again in joy, shouldering
their sheaves.

The Cry of the Church
Lord, have mercy on us; Christ, have mercy on us; Lord, have mercy on us.

The Lord's Prayer

The Prayer Appointed for the Week

Almighty God, you have given your only-begotten Son to take our nature upon
him, and to be born of a pure virgin: Grant that I, who have been born again
and made your child by adoption and grace, may daily be renewed by your
Holy Spirit; through my Lord Jesus Christ, to whom with you and the same
Spirit be honor and glory, now and for ever. *Amen.*†

Concluding Prayers of the Church

O God, whose beloved Son took children into his arms and blessed them: Give me
the grace to entrust the holy innocents of Bethlehem to your never-failing care
and love, and bring me to your heavenly kingdom; through Jesus Christ our
Lord, who lives and reigns with you and the Holy Spirit, one God, now and for
ever. *Amen.*†

Almighty and eternal God, ruler of all things in heaven and earth: Mercifully
accept the prayers of your people everywhere, and strengthen each of us to do
your will; through Jesus Christ my Lord. *Amen.*†

The Vespers Office **To Be Observed on the Hour or Half Hour**
Between 5 and 8 p.m.

The Call to Prayer

Praise the LORD, all you nations;* laud him, all you peoples.
For his loving-kindness toward us is great,* and the faithfulness of the LORD
endures for ever. . . .

Psalm 117:1–2

The Request for Presence

O LORD, do not forsake me;* be not far from me, O my God.
Make haste to help me,* O LORD of my salvation.

Psalm 38:21–22

The Greeting

You are my refuge and shield;* my hope is in your word.

Psalm 119:114

The Hymn

Lully, lullay, you little tiny child,
bye-bye, lully lullay
O sisters, too,
how may we do
for to preserve this day
this poor youngling
for whom we sing
bye-bye, lully, lullay?

Lully, lullay, you little tiny child,
bye-bye, lully lullay
Herod the King,
in his raging charged
he had this day
his men of might,
in his own sight,
all young children to slay.

Lully, lullay, you little tiny child,
bye-bye, lully lullay
That woe is me,
poor child for thee!
And every morn and day,
for thy parting
nor say nor sing
bye-bye, lully lullay.

15th Century

The Refrain for the Vespers Lessons
. . . it is good for me to be near God;* I have made the Lord GOD my refuge.

Psalm 73:28

The Vespers Psalm
But the souls of the upright are in the hands of God,
And no torment can touch them.
To the unenlightened, they appeared to die,
Their departure was regarded as a disaster,
Their leaving us like annihilation;
But they are at peace.
If, as it seemed to us, they suffered punishment,
Their hope was rich with immortality;
Slight was their correction, great will their blessings be.
He has tested them like gold in a furnace,
And accepted them as a perfect burnt offering.
At their time of visitation, they will shine out;
As sparks run through stubble, so will they.
They will judge nations, rule over peoples,
And the Lord will be their king for ever.
Those who trust in him will understand the truth,
Those who are faithful will live with him in love;
For grace and mercy await his holy ones,
And he intervenes on behalf of his chosen.

Wisdom 3:1ff

The Refrain
. . . it is good for me to be near God;* I have made the Lord GOD my refuge.

The Gloria

The Lord's Prayer

The Prayer Appointed for the Week
Almighty God, you have given your only-begotten Son to take our nature upon
him, and to be born of a pure virgin: Grant that I, who have been born again
and made your child by adoption and grace, may daily be renewed by your

Holy Spirit; through my Lord Jesus Christ, to whom with you and the same Spirit be honor and glory, now and for ever. *Amen.*†

Concluding Prayers of the Church
Give rest, O Christ, to your servants, where sorrow and pain are no more, neither sighing, but life everlasting. *Amen.*†

Save me, O Lord, while I am awake, and keep me while I sleep that I may wake in Christ and rest in peace.

adapted from THE SHORT BREVIARY

The Morning Office   **To Be Observed on the Hour or Half Hour Between 6 and 9 a.m.**

The Call to Prayer
My mouth shall speak the praise of the LORD;* let all flesh bless his holy Name for ever and ever.

Psalm 145:22

The Request for Presence
O Lamb of God, that takes away the sins of the world, have mercy on me.
O Lamb of God, that takes away the sins of the world, have mercy on me.
O Lamb of God, that takes away the sins of the world, grant me your peace.

Agnus Dei

The Greeting
Your love, O LORD, reaches to the heavens,* and your faithfulness to the clouds.

Psalm 36:5

The Refrain for the Morning Lessons
I will exalt you, O God my King,* and bless your Name for ever and ever.

Psalm 145:1

A Reading
On the last day, the great day of the festival, Jesus stood and cried out: 'Let anyone who is thirsty come to me! Let anyone who believes in me come and drink! As scripture says, "From his heart shall flow streams of living water." ' He was speaking of the Spirit which those who believe in him were to receive; for there was no Spirit as yet because Jesus had not yet been glorified. Some of the crowd who had been listening said, 'He is indeed the prophet,' and some said, 'He is the Christ,' but others said, 'Would the Christ come from Galilee? Does not scripture say that the Christ must be descended from David and come from

Believers come to me + drink

Bethlehem, the village where David was?' So the people could not agree about him. Some wanted to arrest him, but no one actually laid a hand on him.

John 7:37–44

The Refrain
I will exalt you, O God my King,* and bless your Name for ever and ever.

The Morning Psalm   *I Love You, O LORD*
I love you, O LORD my strength,* O LORD my stronghold, my crag, and my haven.
My God, my rock in whom I put my trust,* my shield, the horn of my salvation, and my refuge; you are worthy of praise.
As for God, his ways are perfect; the words of the LORD are tried in the fire;* he is a shield to all who trust in him.
For who is God, but the LORD?* who is the Rock, except our God?

Psalm 18:1–2, 31–32

The Refrain
I will exalt you, O God my King,* and bless your Name for ever and ever.

The Cry of the Church
O God, come to my assistance! O Lord, make haste to help me!

The Lord's Prayer

The Prayer Appointed for the Week
Almighty God, you have given your only-begotten Son to take our nature upon him, and to be born of a pure virgin: Grant that I, who have been born again and made your child by adoption and grace, may daily be renewed by your Holy Spirit; through my Lord Jesus Christ, to whom with you and the same Spirit be honor and glory, now and for ever. *Amen.†*

The Concluding Prayer of the Church
Lord God, almighty and everlasting Father, you have brought me in safety to this new day: Preserve me with your mighty power, that I may not fall into sin, nor be overcome by adversity; and in all I do direct me to the fulfilling of your purpose; through Jesus Christ my Lord. *Amen.†*

The Midday Office   **To Be Observed on the Hour or Half Hour**
                                         Between 11 a.m. and 2 p.m.

The Call to Prayer
Bless the LORD, O my soul,* and all that is within me, bless his holy Name.

Psalm 103:1

The Request for Presence
Hearken to my voice, O LORD, when I call;* have mercy on me and answer me.
You speak in my heart and say, "Seek my face."* Your face, LORD, will I seek.
Hide not your face from me,* nor turn away your servant in displeasure.

Psalm 27:10–12

The Greeting

I restrain my feet from every evil way,* that I may ke

P.

The Refrain for the Midday Lessons

For one day in your courts is better than a thousand in my ow
stand at the threshold of the house of my God than to dwell
wicked.

:9

A Reading

There are many deceivers at large in the world, refusing to acknowledge Jesus
Christ as coming in human nature. They are the Deceiver; they are the
Antichrist. Watch yourselves, or all our work will be lost and you will forfeit
your full reward. If anybody does not remain in the teaching of Christ but goes
beyond it, he does not have God with him: only those who remain in what he
taught can have the Father and the Son with them. If anyone comes to you
bringing a different doctrine, you must not receive him into your house or even
give him a greeting. Whoever greets him has a share in his wicked activities.

2 John: 7–10

The Refrain

For one day in your courts is better than a thousand in my own room,* and to
stand at the threshold of the house of my God than to dwell in the tents of the
wicked.

The Midday Psalm   *It Is God Who Makes My Way Secure*

It is God who girds me about with strength* and makes my way secure.
He makes me sure-footed like a deer* and lets me stand firm on the heights.
He trains my hands for battle* and my arms for bending even a bow of bronze.
You have given me your shield of victory;* your right hand also sustains me; your
loving care makes me great.
You lengthen my stride beneath me,* and my ankles do not give way.
The LORD lives! Blessed is my Rock!* Exalted is the God of my salvation!

Psalm 18:33–37, 46

The Refrain

For one day in your courts is better than a thousand in my own room,* and to
stand at the threshold of the house of my God than to dwell in the tents of the
wicked.

The Cry of the Church

O Lamb of God, that takes away the sins of the world, have mercy upon me.
O Lamb of God, that takes away the sins of the world, have mercy upon me.
O Lamb of God, that takes away the sins of the world, grant me your peace.

rayer Appointed for the Week

Almighty God, you have given your only-begotten Son to take our nature upon
him, and to be born of a pure virgin: Grant that I, who have been born again
and made your child by adoption and grace, may daily be renewed by your
Holy Spirit; through my Lord Jesus Christ, to whom with you and the same
Spirit be honor and glory, now and for ever. *Amen.*†

The Concluding Prayer of the Church

God of justice, God of mercy, bless all those who are surprised with pain this day
from suffering caused by their own weakness or that of others. Let what we
suffer teach us to be merciful; let our sins teach us to forgive. This we ask
through the intercession of Jesus and all who died forgiving those who
oppressed them. *Amen.*

THE NEW COMPANION TO THE BREVIARY

The Vespers Office **To Be Observed on the Hour or Half Hour**
Between 5 and 8 p.m.

The Call to Prayer

Praise the LORD, all you nations;* laud him, all you peoples.
For his loving-kindness toward us is great,* and the faithfulness of the LORD
endures for ever. Hallelujah!

Psalm 117

The Request for Presence

Gladden the soul of your servant,* for to you, O LORD, I lift up my soul.

Psalm 86:4

The Greeting

One generation shall praise your works to another* and shall declare your power.

Psalm 145:4

The Hymn

What child is this, who laid to rest,
On Mary's lap is sleeping?
Whom angels greet with anthems sweet,
While shepherds watch are keeping?
This, this is Christ the King,
Whom shepherds guard and angels sing:
Haste, haste to bring him laud,
The babe, the son of Mary.

Why lies he in such mean estate
Where ox and ass are feeding?
Good Christian, fear: for sinners here
The silent Word is pleading.
This, this is Christ the King,
Whom shepherds guard and angels sing:
Haste, haste to bring him laud,
The babe, the son of Mary.

So bring him incense, gold and myrrh,
Come, peasant, king, to own him;
The King of kings salvation brings,
Let loving hearts enthrone him.
This, this is Christ the King,
Whom shepherds guard and angels sing:
Haste, haste to bring him laud,
The babe, the son of Mary.

William Dix

The Refrain for the Vespers Lessons
Happy are they all who fear the LORD,* and who follow in his ways!

Psalm 128:1

The Vespers Psalm   *You Have Put Gladness in My Heart*
Answer me when I call, O God, defender of my cause;* you set me free when I am
  hard-pressed; have mercy on me and hear my prayer.
"You mortals, how long will you dishonor my glory;* how long will you worship
  dumb idols and run after false gods?"
Know that the LORD does wonders for the faithful;* when I call upon the LORD, he
  will hear me.
Tremble, then, and do not sin;* speak to your heart in silence upon your bed.
Offer the appointed sacrifices* and put your trust in the LORD.
Many are saying, "Oh, that we might see better times!"* Lift up the light of your
  countenance upon us, O LORD.
You have put gladness in my heart,* more than when grain and wine and oil
  increase.
I lie down in peace; at once I fall asleep;* for only you, LORD, make me dwell in
  safety.

Psalm 4

The Refrain
Happy are they all who fear the LORD,* and who follow in his ways!

The Gloria

The Lord's Prayer

The Prayer Appointed for the Week

Almighty God, you have given your only-begotten Son to take our nature upon him, and to be born of a pure virgin: Grant that I, who have been born again and made your child by adoption and grace, may daily be renewed by your Holy Spirit; through my Lord Jesus Christ, to whom with you and the same Spirit be honor and glory, now and for ever. *Amen.†*

The Concluding Prayer of the Church

May Almighty God grant me a peaceful night and a perfect end. *Amen.*

The Morning Office   **To Be Observed on the Hour or Half Hour Between 6 and 9 a.m.**

The Call to Prayer

Open my lips, O Lord,* and my mouth shall proclaim your praise.

Psalm 51:16

The Request for Presence

Bow down your ear, O Lord, and answer me . . .
Keep watch over my life, for I am faithful.

Psalm 86:1–2

The Greeting

Lord, you have been our refuge* from one generation to another.
Before the mountains were brought forth, or the land and the earth were born,*
    from age to age you are God.

Psalm 90:1–2

The Refrain for the Morning Lessons

Truly, his salvation is very near to those who fear him,* that his glory may dwell in our land.

Psalm 85:9

A Reading

When the day came for them to be purified in keeping with the Law of Moses, they took him [Jesus] up to Jerusalem to present him to the Lord . . . Now in Jerusalem there was a man named Simeon. He was an upright and devout man . . . and the Holy Spirit rested on him. It had been revealed to him by the Holy Spirit that he would not see death until he had set eyes on the Christ of the Lord. Prompted by the Spirit he came to the Temple; and when the parents brought in the Child Jesus . . . he took him into his arms and blessed God; and he said: "Now, Master, you are letting your servant go in peace as you promised; for my eyes have seen the salvation which you have made ready in the sight of the nations; a light of revelation for the gentiles and glory for your people Israel." As the child's father and mother were wondering at these things that were being said about him, Simeon blessed them and said to Mary his mother, "Look, he is destined for the fall and for the rise of many in Israel, destined to be a sign that is opposed—and a sword will pierce your soul too— so that the secret thoughts of many may be laid bare." There was a prophetess, too, Anna . . . she had been married seven years before becoming a widow. She was now eighty-four years old and never left the Temple, serving God night and day with fasting and prayer. She came up just at that moment and began to praise God; and she spoke of the child to all who looked forward to the deliverance of Jerusalem.

Luke 2:22–38

The Refrain

Truly, his salvation is very near to those who fear him,* that his glory may dwell in our land.

The Morning Psalm   *Holiness Adorns Your House For Ever*

The LORD is King; he has put on splendid apparel;* the LORD has put on his apparel and girded himself with strength.

He has made the whole world so sure* that it cannot be moved;

Ever since the world began, your throne has been established;* you are from everlasting.

The waters have lifted up, O LORD, the waters have lifted up their voice;* the waters have lifted up their pounding waves.

Mightier than the sound of many waters, mightier than the breakers of the sea,* mightier is the LORD who dwells on high.

Your testimonies are very sure,* and holiness adorns your house, O LORD, for ever and for evermore.

Psalm 93

The Refrain

Truly, his salvation is very near to those who fear him,* that his glory may dwell in our land.

The Gloria

The Lord's Prayer

The Prayer Appointed for the Week

Almighty God, you have given your only-begotten Son to take our nature upon him, and to be born of a pure virgin: Grant that I, who have been born again and made your child by adoption and grace, may daily be renewed by your Holy Spirit; through my Lord Jesus Christ, to whom with you and the same Spirit be honor and glory, now and for ever. *Amen.*†

The Concluding Prayer of the Church

Lord God, almighty and everlasting Father, you have brought me in safety to this new day: Preserve me with your mighty power, that I may not fall into sin, nor be overcome by adversity; and in all I do direct me to the fulfilling of your purpose; through Jesus Christ my Lord. *Amen.*†

The Midday Office   To Be Observed on the Hour or Half Hour
                                        Between 11 a.m. and 2 p.m.

The Call to Prayer

Sing to God, O kingdoms of the earth;* sing praises to the Lord.

He rides in the heavens, the ancient heavens;* he sends forth his voice, his mighty voice.

Psalm 68:33–34

The Request for Presence

For God alone my soul in silence waits;* from him comes my salvation.

Psalm 62:1

The Greeting

Awesome things will you show us in your righteousness,* O God of our salvation, O Hope of all the ends of the earth . . .

Psalm 65:5

The Refrain for the Midday Lessons

Happy are they who trust in the Lord!* they do not resort to evil spirits or turn to false gods.

Psalm 40:4

A Reading

Every day, as long as this *today* lasts, keep encouraging one another so that none of you is *hardened* by the lure of sin, because we have been granted a share with Christ only if we keep the grasp of our first confidence firm to the end. In this saying: *If only you would listen to him today; do not harden your hearts, as at the Rebellion,* who was it who *listened* and then *rebelled?* Surely all those whom Moses led out of Egypt. And with whom was he *angry for forty years?* Surely with those who sinned and whose *dead bodies fell in the desert.* To whom did he *swear they would never enter his place of rest?* Surely those who would not believe. So we see that it was their refusal to believe which prevented them from entering.

Hebrews 3:13–19

The Refrain

Happy are they who trust in the Lord!* they do not resort to evil spirits or turn to false gods.

The Midday Psalm   *The Lord Delivers the Righteous*

The eyes of the Lord are upon the righteous,* and his ears are open to their cry.

The face of the Lord is against those who do evil,* to root out the remembrance of them from the earth.

The righteous cry, and the LORD hears them* and delivers them from all their
  troubles.
The LORD is near to the brokenhearted* and will save those whose spirits are
  crushed.
Many are the troubles of the righteous,* but the LORD will deliver him out of them
  all.

Psalm 34:15–19

The Refrain
Happy are they who trust in the LORD!* they do not resort to evil spirits or turn to
  false gods.

The Cry of the Church
Be, Lord, my helper and forsake me not. Do not despise me, O God, my savior.

THE SHORT BREVIARY

The Lord's Prayer

The Prayer Appointed for the Week
Almighty God, you have given your only-begotten Son to take our nature upon
  him, and to be born of a pure virgin: Grant that I, who have been born again
  and made your child by adoption and grace, may daily be renewed by your
  Holy Spirit; through my Lord Jesus Christ, to whom with you and the same
  Spirit be honor and glory, now and for ever. *Amen.*†

The Concluding Prayer of the Church
May God have mercy on me, forgive me my sins and bring me to life everlasting.
  In Jesus' name. *Amen.*

The Vespers Office   **To Be Observed on the Hour or Half Hour**
Between 5 and 8 p.m.

The Call to Prayer
Let us come before his presence with thanksgiving* and raise a loud shout to him
  with psalms.

Psalm 95:2

The Request for Presence
Remember not our past sins; let your compassion be swift to meet us;* for we have
  been brought very low.
Help us, O God our Savior, for the glory of your Name;* deliver us and forgive us
  our sins, for your Name's sake.

Psalm 79:8–9

The Greeting
Exalt yourself above the heavens, O God,* and your glory over all the earth.

Psalm 57:11

The Hymn

Go, tell it on the mountain,
Over the hills and everywhere;
Go, tell it on the mountain,
That Jesus Christ is born.
While shepherds kept their watching
Over silent flocks by night,
Behold throughout the heavens
There shone a holy light.

Go, tell it on the mountain,
Over the hills and everywhere;
Go, tell it on the mountain,
That Jesus Christ is born.
The shepherds feared and trembled,
When lo! Above the earth,
Rang out the angel chorus
That hailed the Savior's birth.

Go, tell it on the mountain,
Over the hills and everywhere;
Go, tell it on the mountain,
That Jesus Christ is born.
Down in a lowly manger
The humble Christ was born,
And God sent us salvation
That blessed Christmas morn.

African-American Spiritual

The Refrain for the Vespers Lessons

When the LORD restores the fortunes of his people, Jacob will rejoice and Israel be
    glad.

Psalm 14:7b

The Vespers Psalm   *Who May Abide Upon Your Holy Hill?*

LORD, who may dwell in your tabernacle?* who may abide upon your holy hill?
Whoever leads a blameless life and does what is right,* who speaks the truth from
    his heart.
There is no guile upon his tongue; he does no evil to his friend;* he does not heap
    contempt upon his neighbor.
In his sight the wicked is rejected,* but he honors those who fear the LORD.
He has sworn to do no wrong* and does not take back his word.
He does not give his money in hope of gain,* nor does he take a bribe against the
    innocent.
Whoever does these things* shall never be overthrown.

Psalm 15

The Refrain

When the LORD restores the fortunes of his people, Jacob will rejoice and Israel be
    glad.

The Gloria

The Lord's Prayer

The Prayer Appointed for the Week

Almighty God, you have given your only-begotten Son to take our nature upon
    him, and to be born of a pure virgin: Grant that I, who have been born again

and made your child by adoption and grace, may daily be renewed by your
Holy Spirit; through my Lord Jesus Christ, to whom with you and the same
Spirit be honor and glory, now and for ever. *Amen.*†

The Concluding Prayer of the Church
Blessed be the Lord God of Israel for he has visited and delivered us. Alleluia,
alleluia, alleluia.

Traditional

The Morning Office — To Be Observed on the Hour or Half Hour Between 6 and 9 a.m.

The Call to Prayer
I will call upon God,* and the LORD will deliver me.
In the evening, in the morning, and at noonday, I will complain and lament,* and
he will hear my voice.
He will bring me safely back . . . * God, who is enthroned of old, will hear me.

Psalm 55:17ff

The Request for Presence
Be pleased, O God, to deliver me;* O LORD, make haste to help me.

Psalm 70:1

The Greeting
Happy are they whom you choose and draw to your courts to dwell there!* they
will be satisfied by the beauty of your house, by the holiness of your temple.

Psalm 65:4

The Refrain for the Morning Lessons
Bless the LORD, you angels of his, you mighty ones who do his bidding,* and hearken to the voice of his word.

Psalm 103:20

A Reading
And now I saw heaven open, and a white horse appear; its rider was called
Trustworthy and True; *in uprightness he judges* and makes war. His eyes were
flames of fire, and he was crowned with many coronets; the name written on
him was known only to himself, *his cloak was soaked in blood.* He is known by the
name, the Word of God. Behind him, dressed in linen of dazzling white, rode
the armies of heaven on white horses. From his mouth came a sharp sword
with which to strike at unbelievers; he is the one *who will rule them with an iron
scepter,* and tread out the wine of the Almighty's fierce retribution. On his cloak
and on his thigh a name was written: *King of kings* and *Lord of lords.*

Revelation 19:11–16

The Refrain

Bless the LORD, you angels of his, you mighty ones who do his bidding,* and hearken to the voice of his word.

The Morning Psalm   *Praise the LORD, All Creation, and Bless His Holy Name*

Hallelujah! Praise the LORD from the heavens;* praise him in the heights.

Praise him, all you angels of his;* praise him, all his host.

Praise him, sun and moon;* praise him, all you shining stars.

Praise him, heaven of heavens,* and you waters above the heavens.

Let them praise the Name of the LORD;* for he commanded, and they were created.

He made them stand fast for ever and ever;* he gave them a law which shall not pass away.

Praise the LORD from the earth,* you sea-monsters and all deeps;

Fire and hail, snow and fog,* tempestuous wind, doing his will;

Mountains and all hills,* fruit trees and all cedars;

Wild beasts and all cattle,* creeping things and winged birds;

Kings of the earth and all peoples,* princes and all rulers of the world;

Young men and maidens,* old and young together.

Let them praise the Name of the LORD,* for his Name only is exalted, his splendor is over earth and heaven.

He has raised up strength for his people and praise for all his loyal servants,* the children of Israel, a people who are near him. Hallelujah!

Psalm 148

The Refrain

Bless the LORD, you angels of his, you mighty ones who do his bidding,* and hearken to the voice of his word.

The Cry of the Church

Even so, come, Lord Jesus!

The Lord's Prayer

The Prayer Appointed for the Week

Almighty God, you have given your only-begotten Son to take our nature upon him, and to be born of a pure virgin: Grant that I, who have been born again and made your child by adoption and grace, may daily be renewed by your Holy Spirit; through my Lord Jesus Christ, to whom with you and the same Spirit be honor and glory, now and for ever. *Amen.*†

The Concluding Prayer of the Church

Lord God, almighty and everlasting Father, you have brought me in safety to this new day: Preserve me with your mighty power, that I may not fall into sin, nor be overcome by adversity; and in all I do direct me to the fulfilling of your purpose; through Jesus Christ my Lord. *Amen.*†

The Midday Office   **To Be Observed on the Hour or Half Hour**
Between 11 a.m. and 2 p.m.

The Call to Prayer
Sing to the LORD with thanksgiving;* make music to our God upon the harp.

Psalm 147:7

The Request for Presence
Hear, O Shepherd of Israel, leading Joseph like a flock;* shine forth, you that are enthroned upon the cherubim.

Psalm 80:1

The Greeting
Exalt yourself above the heavens, O God,* and your glory over all the earth.

Psalm 57:6

The Refrain for the Midday Lessons
The LORD has sworn and he will not recant:* "You are a priest for ever after the order of Melchizedek."

Psalm 110:4

A Reading
For look, I am going to create new heavens and a new earth, and the past will not be remembered and will come no more to mind. Rather be joyful, be glad for ever at what I am creating, for look, I am creating Jerusalem to be 'Joy' and my people to be 'Gladness.' I shall be joyful in Jerusalem and I shall rejoice in my people. No more will the sound of weeping be heard there, nor the sound of a shriek; never again will there be an infant there who lives only a few days, nor an old man who does not run his full course; for the youngest will die at a hundred, and at a hundred the sinner will be accursed. They will build houses and live in them, they will plant vineyards and eat their fruit. They will not build for others to live in, or plant for others to eat; for the days of my people will be like the days of a tree, and my chosen ones will themselves use what they have made. They will not toil in vain, nor bear children destined to disaster, for they are the race of YAHWEH's blessed ones and so are their offspring. Thus, before they call I shall answer, before they stop speaking I shall have heard. The wolf and the lamb will feed together, *the lion will eat hay like the ox,* and dust be the serpent's food. *No hurt, no harm will be done on all my holy mountain,* YAHWEH says.

Isaiah 65:17–25

The Refrain
The LORD has sworn and he will not recant:* "You are a priest for ever after the order of Melchizedek."

The Midday Psalm   *We Will Not Fear*
God is our refuge and strength,* a very present help in trouble.
Therefore we will not fear, though the earth be moved,* and though the mountains be toppled into the depths of the sea;
Though its waters rage and foam,* and though the mountains tremble at its tumult.

The Lord of hosts is with us;* the God of Jacob is our stronghold.

There is a river whose streams make glad the city of God,* the holy habitation of the Most High.

God is in the midst of her; she shall not be overthrown;* God shall help her at the break of day.

The nations make much ado, and the kingdoms are shaken;* God has spoken, and the earth shall melt away.

The Lord of hosts is with us;* the God of Jacob is our stronghold.

Psalm 46:1–8

The Refrain
The LORD has sworn and he will not recant:* "You are a priest for ever after the order of Melchizedek."

The Gloria

The Lord's Prayer

The Prayer Appointed for the Week
Almighty God, you have given your only-begotten Son to take our nature upon him, and to be born of a pure virgin: Grant that I, who have been born again and made your child by adoption and grace, may daily be renewed by your Holy Spirit; through my Lord Jesus Christ, to whom with you and the same Spirit be honor and glory, now and for ever. *Amen.*†

The Concluding Prayer of the Church
Lord Jesus Christ, by your death you took away the sting of death: Grant me to so follow in faith where you have led the way, that I may at length fall asleep peacefully in you and wake in your likeness; for your tender mercies' sake. *Amen.*†

The Vespers Office   **To Be Observed on the Hour or Half Hour**
Between 5 and 8 p.m.

The Call to Prayer
I will call upon the LORD,* and so shall I be saved from my enemies.

Psalm 18:3

The Request for Presence
I have said to the LORD, "You are my God;* Listen, O LORD, to my supplication."

Psalm 140:6

The Greeting
But you, O Lord my GOD, oh, deal with me according to your Name;* for your tender mercy's sake, deliver me.

For I am poor and needy,* and my heart is wounded within me.

Psalm 109:20–21

The Hymn

The people who in darkness walked have seen a glorious light;
On them broke forth the heavenly dawn who dwelt in death and night.
To hail your rising, Sun of life, the gathering nations come,
Joyous as when the reapers bear their harvest treasures home.
To us the promised Child is born, to us the Son is given;
Him shall the tribes of earth obey, and all the hosts of heaven.
His name shall be the Prince of Peace for evermore adored,
The Wonderful, the Counsellor. The mighty God and Lord.
His power increasing still shall spread, his reign no end shall know;
Justice shall guard his throne above, and peace abound below.

John Morison

The Refrain for the Vespers Lessons
. . . For the Lord has heard the sound of my weeping
The Lord has heard my supplication;* the Lord accepts my prayer.

Psalm 6:8–9

The Vespers Psalm   *Our God Will Not Keep Silence*
The Lord, the God of gods, has spoken;* he has called the earth from the rising of
  the sun to its setting.
Out of Zion, perfect in its beauty,* God reveals himself in glory.
Our God will come and will not keep silence;* before him there is a consuming
  flame, and round about him a raging storm.
He calls the heavens and the earth from above* to witness the judgment of his
  people.
"Gather before me my loyal followers,* those who have made a covenant with me
  and sealed it with sacrifice."
Let the heavens declare the rightness of his cause;* for God himself is judge.

Psalm 50:1–6

The Refrain
. . . For the Lord has heard the sound of my weeping
The Lord has heard my supplication;* the Lord accepts my prayer.

The Cry of the Church
Be, Lord, my helper and forsake me not. Do not despise me, O God, my savior.

The Short Breviary

The Lord's Prayer

The Prayer Appointed for the Week
Almighty God, you have given your only-begotten Son to take our nature upon
  him, and to be born of a pure virgin: Grant that I, who have been born again
  and made your child by adoption and grace, may daily be renewed by your
  Holy Spirit; through my Lord Jesus Christ, to whom with you and the same
  Spirit be honor and glory, now and for ever. *Amen.*†

Concluding Prayers of the Church

Eternal Father, you gave to your incarnate Son the holy name of Jesus to be the sign of our salvation: Plant in every heart, I pray, the love of him who is the Savior of the world, our Lord Jesus Christ; who lives and reigns with you and the Holy Spirit, one God, in glory everlasting. *Amen.*†

Almighty God, who has promised to hear the petitions of those who ask in your Son's Name: I beseech you mercifully to incline your ear to me who have made my prayers and supplications to you; and grant that those things which I have faithfully asked according to your will, I may effectually obtain, to the relief of my necessity, and to the setting forth of your glory; through Jesus Christ my Lord. *Amen.*†

May the souls of the faithful departed, through the mercy of God, rest in eternal peace. *Amen.*

Christmas Compline

Sunday
The Night Office   **To Be Observed Before Retiring**

The Call to Prayer
May the Lord Almighty grant me and those I love a peaceful night and a perfect
    end. *Amen.*†

The Request for Presence
Our help is in the Name of the Lord; the maker of heaven and earth.

The Greeting
Almighty God, my heavenly Father: I have sinned against you, through my own
    fault, in thought, and word, and deed, in what I have done and what I have left
    undone. For the sake of your Son our Lord Jesus Christ, forgive me all my
    offenses; and grant that I may serve you in newness of life, to the glory of your
    Name. *Amen.*†

The Reading
It is truly just, necessary and beneficent
to give you thanks, holy Lord, all-powerful Father,
Eternal God, through Jesus Christ our Lord.

In celebrating today the octave of your birth,
we celebrate, O Lord, your marvelous deeds,
because she who has given birth is mother and virgin,
and He who was born is infant and God.

For good reason, the heavens have spoken,
the angels have sung, the shepherds were joyful,
the Magi were transformed, the kings seized with fright,
and infants were crowned with the glory of blood.

Nourish, O mother, Him who is your nourishment.
Nourish the bread descended from Heaven
and placed in the manger like the fodder of animals.
The ox saw his Master; the donkey, the crib of his Lord.

He is worthy of circumcision in order to fulfill
all prophecies about Him, our Savior and Lord,
whom Simeon received into the Temple.

Thus let us sing with the angels and the archangels,
with the Thrones and Dominions, with all the choirs
of Heaven, this hymn of glory:

Holy, Holy, Holy, Lord God of Hosts,
Heaven and earth are filled with your glory.
Hosanna in the highest! Blessed is He who comes
in the name of the Lord. Hosanna in the highest!

                                        Galasian Sacramentary

The Gloria

The Psalm   *Who Is the King of Glory?*

Lift up your heads, O gates; lift them high, O everlasting doors;* and the King of
    glory shall come in.

"Who is this King of glory?"* "The LORD, strong and mighty, the LORD, mighty in
    battle."

Lift up your heads, O gates; lift them high, O everlasting doors;* and the King of
    glory shall come in.

"Who is he, this King of glory?"* "The LORD of hosts, he is the King of glory."

Psalm 24:7–10

The Gloria

The Small Verse

Into your hands, O Lord, I commend my spirit; for you have redeemed me, O
    Lord, O God of truth. Keep me, O Lord, as the apple of your eye; hide me
    under the shadow of your wings.†

The Lord's Prayer

The Petition

Watch, O Lord, with those who wake, or watch, or weep tonight, and give Your
    angels and saints charge over those who sleep. Tend Your sick ones, O Lord
    Christ. Rest Your weary ones. Bless Your dying ones. Soothe Your suffering
    ones. Shield Your joyous ones, and all for Your love's sake. *Amen*.§

The Final Thanksgiving

Lord, you now have set your servant free to go in peace as you have promised; for
    these eyes of mine have seen the Savior, whom you have prepared for all the
    world to see: a Light to enlighten the nations, and the glory of your people
    Israel. Glory to the Father, and to the Son, and to the Holy Spirit: as it was in the
    beginning, is now, and will be for ever. *Amen.*

Monday
The Night Office   **To Be Observed Before Retiring**

The Call to Prayer

May the Lord Almighty grant me and those I love a peaceful night and a perfect
    end. *Amen.*†

The Request for Presence

Our help is in the Name of the Lord; the maker of heaven and earth.

The Greeting

Almighty God, my heavenly Father: I have sinned against you, through my own
fault, in thought, and word, and deed, in what I have done and what I have left
undone. For the sake of your Son our Lord Jesus Christ, forgive me all my
offenses; and grant that I may serve you in newness of life, to the glory of your
Name. *Amen.*†

The Reading

How beautiful on the mountains,
Are the feet of the messenger announcing peace,
Of the messenger of good news,
Who proclaims salvation
And says to Zion,
'Your God is king!'
The voices of your watchmen!
Now they raise their voices,
Shouting for joy together,
For with their own eyes they have seen
YAHWEH returning to Zion.
Break into shouts together,
Shouts of joy, you ruins of Jerusalem;
For YAHWEH has consoled his people,
He has redeemed Jerusalem.
YAHWEH has bared his holy arm
For all the nations to see,
And all the ends of the earth
Have seen the salvation of our God.

Isaiah 52:7–10

The Gloria

The Psalm   *May All the Earth Be Filled with His Glory*

All kings shall bow down before him,* and all the nations do him service.
For he shall deliver the poor who cries out in distress,* and the oppressed who has
no helper.
He shall have pity on the lowly and poor;* he shall preserve the lives of the needy.
He shall redeem their lives from oppression and violence,* and dear shall their
blood be in his sight.
Long may he live! and may there be given to him gold from Arabia;* may prayer
be made for him always, and may they bless him all the day long.
May there be abundance of grain on the earth, growing thick even on the hilltops;*
may its fruit flourish like Lebanon, and its grain like grass upon the earth.
May his Name remain for ever and be established as long as the sun endures;*
may all the nations bless themselves in him and call him blessed.
Blessed be the Lord GOD, the God of Israel,* who alone does wondrous deeds!

And blessed be his glorious Name for ever!* and may all the earth be filled with his glory. Amen. Amen.

Psalm 72:11–19

The Gloria

The Small Verse

Into your hands, O Lord, I commend my spirit; for you have redeemed me, O Lord, O God of truth. Keep me, O Lord, as the apple of your eye; hide me under the shadow of your wings.†

The Lord's Prayer

The Petition

Watch, O Lord, with those who wake, or watch, or weep tonight, and give Your angels and saints charge over those who sleep. Tend Your sick ones, O Lord Christ. Rest Your weary ones. Bless Your dying ones. Soothe Your suffering ones. Shield Your joyous ones, and all for Your love's sake. *Amen.*§

The Final Thanksgiving

Lord, you now have set your servant free to go in peace as you have promised; for these eyes of mine have seen the Savior, whom you have prepared for all the world to see: a Light to enlighten the nations, and the glory of your people Israel. Glory to the Father, and to the Son, and to the Holy Spirit: as it was in the beginning, is now, and will be for ever. *Amen.*

Tuesday
The Night Office

To Be Observed Before Retiring

The Call to Prayer

May the Lord Almighty grant me and those I love a peaceful night and a perfect end. *Amen.*†

The Request for Presence

Our help is in the Name of the Lord; the maker of heaven and earth.

The Greeting

Almighty God, my heavenly Father: I have sinned against you, through my own fault, in thought, and word, and deed, in what I have done and what I have left undone. For the sake of your Son our Lord Jesus Christ, forgive me all my offenses; and grant that I may serve you in newness of life, to the glory of your Name. *Amen.*†

The Reading   *Gloria in Excelsis*

Glory to God in the highest,
and peace to his people on earth.
Lord God, heavenly King,
almighty God and Father,
we worship you, we give you thanks,
we praise you for your glory.
Lord Jesus Christ, only Son of the Father,
Lord God, Lamb of God.
you take away the sins of the world:
have mercy on us;
you are seated at the right hand of the Father:
receive our prayer.
For you alone are the Holy One,
you alone are the Lord,
you alone are the Most High,
Jesus Christ,
with the Holy Spirit,
in the glory of God the Father.

The Gloria

The Psalm   *Let Everything Having Breath Praise the* LORD

Hallelujah! Praise God in his holy temple;* praise him in the firmament of his
     power.
Praise him for his mighty acts;* praise him for his excellent greatness.
Praise him with the blast of the ram's-horn;* praise him with lyre and harp.
Praise him with timbrel and dance;* praise him with strings and pipe.
Praise him with resounding cymbals;* praise him with loud-clanging cymbals.
Let everything that has breath* praise the LORD. Hallelujah!

Psalm 150

The Gloria

The Small Verse

Into your hands, O Lord, I commend my spirit; for you have redeemed me,
     O Lord, O God of truth. Keep me, O Lord, as the apple of your eye; hide me
     under the shadow of your wings.†

The Lord's Prayer

The Petition

Watch, O Lord, with those who wake, or watch, or weep tonight, and give Your
     angels and saints charge over those who sleep. Tend Your sick ones, O Lord
     Christ. Rest Your weary ones. Bless Your dying ones. Soothe Your suffering
     ones. Shield Your joyous ones, and all for Your love's sake. *Amen.*§

The Final Thanksgiving

Lord, you now have set your servant free to go in peace as you have promised; for these eyes of mine have seen the Savior, whom you have prepared for all the world to see: a Light to enlighten the nations, and the glory of your people Israel. Glory to the Father, and to the Son, and to the Holy Spirit: as it was in the beginning, is now, and will be for ever. *Amen.*

Wednesday
The Night Office   **To Be Observed Before Retiring**

The Call to Prayer

May the Lord Almighty grant me and those I love a peaceful night and a perfect end. *Amen.*†

The Request for Presence

Our help is in the Name of the Lord; the maker of heaven and earth.

The Greeting

Almighty God, my heavenly Father: I have sinned against you, through my own fault, in thought, and word, and deed, in what I have done and what I have left undone. For the sake of your Son our Lord Jesus Christ, forgive me all my offenses; and grant that I may serve you in newness of life, to the glory of your Name. *Amen.*†

The Reading

Thus says God, YAHWEH,
Who created the heavens and spread them out,
Who hammered into shape the earth and what comes from it,
Who gave breath to the people on it,
And spirit to those who walk on it:
I, YAHWEH, have called you in saving justice,
I have grasped you by the hand and shaped you;
I have made you a covenant of the people
And light to the nations,
To open the eyes of the blind,
To free the captives from prison,
And those who live in darkness from the dungeon.
I am YAHWEH, that is my name!
I shall not yield my glory to another,
Nor my honor to idols.

See how the former predictions have come true.

Fresh things I now reveal;

Before they appear I tell you of them.

Isaiah 42:5–9

The Gloria

The Psalm
Come Now and See the Works of the LORD

Come now and see the works of God,* how wonderful he is in his doing toward all people.

He turned the sea into dry land, so that they went through the water on foot,* and there we rejoiced in him.

In his might he rules for ever; his eyes keep watch over the nations;* let no rebel rise up against him.

Bless our God, you peoples;* make the voice of his praise to be heard;

Who holds our souls in life,* and will not allow our feet to slip.

For you, O God, have proved us;* you have tried us just as silver is tried.

You brought us into the snare;* you laid heavy burdens upon our backs.

You let enemies ride over our heads; we went through fire and water;* but you brought us out into a place of refreshment.

Psalm 66:4–11

The Gloria

The Small Verse
Into your hands, O Lord, I commend my spirit; for you have redeemed me, O Lord, O God of truth. Keep me, O Lord, as the apple of your eye; hide me under the shadow of your wings.†

The Lord's Prayer

The Petition
Watch, O Lord, with those who wake, or watch, or weep tonight, and give Your angels and saints charge over those who sleep. Tend Your sick ones, O Lord Christ. Rest Your weary ones. Bless Your dying ones. Soothe Your suffering ones. Shield Your joyous ones, and all for Your love's sake. *Amen.*§

The Final Thanksgiving
Lord, you now have set your servant free to go in peace as you have promised; for these eyes of mine have seen the Savior, whom you have prepared for all the world to see: a Light to enlighten the nations, and the glory of your people Israel. Glory to the Father, and to the Son, and to the Holy Spirit: as it was in the beginning, is now, and will be for ever. *Amen.*

Thursday
The Night Office   **To Be Observed Before Retiring**

The Call to Prayer
May the Lord Almighty grant me and those I love a peaceful night and a perfect
  end. *Amen.*†

The Request for Presence
Our help is in the Name of the Lord; the maker of heaven and earth.

The Greeting
Almighty God, my heavenly Father: I have sinned against you, through my own
  fault, in thought, and word, and deed, in what I have done and what I have left
  undone. For the sake of your Son our Lord Jesus Christ, forgive me all my
  offenses; and grant that I may serve you in newness of life, to the glory of your
  Name. *Amen.*†

The Reading
He is the image of the unseen God,
The first-born of all creation,
For in him were created all things
In heaven and on earth:
Everything visible and everything invisible,
Thrones, ruling forces, sovereignties, powers—
All things were created through him and for him.
He exists before all things
And in him all things hold together,
And he is the Head of the Body,
That is, the Church.

                    Colossians 1:15–18

The Gloria

The Psalm   *I Have Found David My Servant*
You spoke once in a vision and said to your faithful people:* "I have set the crown
  upon a warrior and have exalted one chosen out of the people.
I have found David my servant;* with my holy oil have I anointed him.
My hand will hold him fast* and my arm will make him strong.
No enemy shall deceive him,* nor any wicked man bring him down.
I will crush his foes before him* and strike down those who hate him.
My faithfulness and love shall be with him,* and he shall be victorious through
  my Name.
I shall make his dominion extend* from the Great Sea to the River.
He will say to me, 'You are my Father,* my God, and the rock of my salvation.'
I will make him my firstborn* and higher than the kings of the earth.
I will keep my love for him for ever,* and my covenant will stand firm for him."

                    Psalm 89:19–28

The Gloria

The Small Verse
Into your hands, O Lord, I commend my spirit; for you have redeemed me,
    O Lord, O God of truth. Keep me, O Lord, as the apple of your eye; hide me
    under the shadow of your wings.†

The Lord's Prayer

The Petition
Watch, O Lord, with those who wake, or watch, or weep tonight, and give Your
    angels and saints charge over those who sleep. Tend Your sick ones, O Lord
    Christ. Rest Your weary ones. Bless Your dying ones. Soothe Your suffering
    ones. Shield Your joyous ones, and all for Your love's sake. *Amen.*§

The Final Thanksgiving
Lord, you now have set your servant free to go in peace as you have promised; for
    these eyes of mine have seen the Savior, whom you have prepared for all the
    world to see: a Light to enlighten the nations, and the glory of your people
    Israel. Glory to the Father, and to the Son, and to the Holy Spirit: as it was in the
    beginning, is now, and will be for ever. *Amen.*

Friday
The Night Office   **To Be Observed Before Retiring**

The Call to Prayer
May the Lord Almighty grant me and those I love a peaceful night and a perfect
    end. *Amen.*†

The Request for Presence
Our help is in the Name of the Lord; the maker of heaven and earth.

The Greeting
Almighty God, my heavenly Father: I have sinned against you, through my own
    fault, in thought, and word, and deed, in what I have done and what I have left
    undone. For the sake of your Son our Lord Jesus Christ, forgive me all my
    offenses; and grant that I may serve you in newness of life, to the glory of your
    Name. *Amen.*†

The Reading
My mouth will utter the praise of the Lord, of the Lord through whom all things
    have been made and who has been made amidst all things; who is the Revealer
    of His Father, Creator of His mother; who is the Son of God from His Father

without a mother, the Son of man through His mother without a father. He is as great as the Day of Angels, and as small as a day in the life of men; he is the Word of God before all ages, and the Word made flesh at the destined time. Maker of the sun, He is made beneath the sun. Disposing all the ages from the bosom of the Father, He consecrates this very day in the womb of His mother. In His Father He abides; from His mother He goes forth. Creator of heaven and earth, under the heavens He was born upon earth. Wise beyond all speech, as a speechless child, He is wise. Filling the whole world, He lies in a manger. Ruling the stars, He nurses at His mother's breast. He is great in the form of God and small in the form of a servant, so much so that His greatness is not diminished by His smallness, nor His smallness concealed by His greatness. For when He assumed a human body, He did not forsake divine works. He did not cease to be concerned mightily from one end of the universe to the other, and to order all things delightfully, when, having clothed Himself in the fragility of flesh, He was received into, not confined in, the Virgin's womb. So that, while the food of wisdom was not taken away from the angels, we were to taste how sweet is the Lord.

St. Augustine

The Gloria

The Psalm   *Let Your Saving Health Come to All Nations*
May God be merciful to us and bless us,* show us the light of his countenance and
 come to us.
Let your ways be known upon earth,* your saving health among all nations.
Let the peoples praise you, O God;* let all the peoples praise you.
Let the nations be glad and sing for joy,* for you judge the peoples with equity and
 guide all the nations upon earth.
Let the peoples praise you, O God;* let all the peoples praise you.
The earth has brought forth her increase;* may God, our own God, give us his
 blessing.
May God give us his blessing,* and may all the ends of the earth stand in awe of him.

Psalm 67

The Gloria

The Small Verse
Into your hands, O Lord, I commend my spirit; for you have redeemed me,
 O Lord, O God of truth. Keep me, O Lord, as the apple of your eye; hide me
 under the shadow of your wings.†

The Lord's Prayer

The Petition
Watch, O Lord, with those who wake, or watch, or weep tonight, and give Your
 angels and saints charge over those who sleep. Tend Your sick ones, O Lord
 Christ. Rest Your weary ones. Bless Your dying ones. Soothe Your suffering
 ones. Shield Your joyous ones, and all for Your love's sake. *Amen.*§

The Final Thanksgiving

Lord, you now have set your servant free to go in peace as you have promised; for these eyes of mine have seen the Savior, whom you have prepared for all the world to see: a Light to enlighten the nations, and the glory of your people Israel. Glory to the Father, and to the Son, and to the Holy Spirit: as it was in the beginning, is now, and will be for ever. *Amen.*

Saturday
The Night Office   **To Be Observed Before Retiring**

The Call to Prayer

May the Lord Almighty grant me and those I love a peaceful night and a perfect end. *Amen.*†

The Request for Presence

Our help is in the Name of the Lord; the maker of heaven and earth.

The Greeting

Almighty God, my heavenly Father: I have sinned against you, through my own fault, in thought, and word, and deed, in what I have done and what I have left undone. For the sake of your Son our Lord Jesus Christ, forgive me all my offenses; and grant that I may serve you in newness of life, to the glory of your Name. *Amen.*†

The Reading

There is no rose of such virtue
As is the rose that bore Jesu:
Alleluia.
For in this rose contained was
Heaven and earth in little space:
Ros miranda.
By that rose we may well see
There be one God in Persons Three:
Pares forma.
The angels sang, the shepherds too:
Gloria in excelsis Deo:
Gaudeamus.
Leave we all this world's mirth
And follow we this joyous birth
Transeamus.

> *Anonymous, c. 1400*

The Gloria

The Psalm   ***Tell It Out Among the Nations***

Ascribe to the LORD, you families of the peoples;* ascribe to the LORD honor and
  power.

Ascribe to the LORD the honor due his Name;* bring offerings and come into his
  courts.

Worship the LORD in the beauty of holiness;* let the whole earth tremble before
  him.

Tell it out among the nations: "The LORD is King!* he has made the world so firm
  that it cannot be moved; he will judge the peoples with equity."

Psalm 96:7–10

The Gloria

The Small Verse

Into your hands, O Lord, I commend my spirit; for you have redeemed me,
  O Lord, O God of truth. Keep me, O Lord, as the apple of your eye; hide me
  under the shadow of your wings.†

The Lord's Prayer

The Petition

Watch, O Lord, with those who wake, or watch, or weep tonight, and give Your
  angels and saints charge over those who sleep. Tend Your sick ones, O Lord
  Christ. Rest Your weary ones. Bless Your dying ones. Soothe Your suffering
  ones. Shield Your joyous ones, and all for Your love's sake. *Amen.*§

The Final Thanksgiving

Lord, you now have set your servant free to go in peace as you have promised; for
  these eyes of mine have seen the Savior, whom you have prepared for all the
  world to see: a Light to enlighten the nations, and the glory of your people
  Israel. Glory to the Father, and to the Son, and to the Holy Spirit: as it was in the
  beginning, is now, and will be for ever. *Amen.*

The Gloria
Glory be to God the Father, God the Son, and God the Holy Spirit. As it was in the beginning, so it is now and so it shall ever be, world without end. Alleluia. *Amen.*

The Lord's Prayer
Our Father, who art in heaven, hallowed be your Name.
May your kingdom come, and your will be done, on earth as in heaven.
Give us today our daily bread.
Forgive us our sins as we forgive those who sin against us.
Lead us not into temptation, but deliver us from evil;
for yours are the kingdom and the power and the glory
forever and ever. *Amen.*

Compline Prayers for January Are Located on Page 230.

The Following Holy Days Occur in January:
The Holy Name of Our Lord Jesus Christ and/or
The Feast of the Circumcision of Our Lord and/or
The Feast of Mary, Mother of God: *January 1*
The Epiphany of Our Lord Jesus Christ: *January 6*
The Confession of St. Peter, the Apostle: *January 18*
The Confession of St. Paul, the Apostle: *January 25*

January

The Morning Office

To Be Observed on the Hour or Half Hour
Between 6 and 9 a.m.

The Call to Prayer
Sing to the LORD a new song,* for he has done marvelous things.
Psalm 98:1

The Request for Presence
Create in me a clean heart, O God,* and renew a right spirit within me.
Psalm 51:11

The Greeting
I am small and of little account,* yet I do not forget your commandments.
Psalm 119:141

The Refrain for the Morning Lessons
Let my mouth be full of your praise* and your glory all the day long.
Psalm 71:8

A Reading
In all this Jesus spoke to the crowds in parables; indeed he would never speak to
them except in parables. This was to fulfill what was spoken by the prophet: *I
will speak in parables, unfold what has been hidden since the foundation of the
world. . . .* Jesus asked the people, saying, 'Have you understood all these?'
They said, 'Yes' And he said to them, 'Well then, every scribe who becomes a
disciple of the kingdom of Heaven is like a householder who brings out from
his storeroom new things as well as old.'
Matthew 13:34–35, 51–52

The Refrain
Let my mouth be full of your praise* and your glory all the day long.

The Morning Psalm   *Sing to the LORD a New Song*
Sing to the LORD a new song,* for he has done marvelous things.
With his right hand and his holy arm* has he won for himself the victory.
The LORD has made known his victory;* his righteousness has he openly shown in
the sight of the nations.
He remembers his mercy and faithfulness to the house of Israel,* and all the ends
of the earth have seen the victory of our God.
Shout with joy to the LORD, all you lands;* lift up your voice, rejoice, and sing.
Sing to the LORD with the harp,* with the harp and the voice of song.
With trumpets and the sound of the horn* shout with joy before the King, the LORD.
Let the sea make a noise and all that is in it,* the lands and those who dwell therein.
Let the rivers clap their hands,* and let the hills ring out with joy before the LORD,
when he comes to judge the earth.
In righteousness shall he judge the world* and the peoples with equity.
Psalm 98

The Refrain
Let my mouth be full of your praise* and your glory all the day long.

The Cry of the Church

O Lord, hear my prayer and let my cry come unto you. Thanks be to God.

The Short Breviary

The Lord's Prayer

The Prayer Appointed for the Week

O God, who wonderfully created, and yet more wonderfully restored, the dignity of human nature: Grant that we may share the divine life of him who humbled himself to share our humanity, your Son Jesus Christ; who lives and reigns with you, in the unity of the Holy Spirit, one God, for ever and ever. *Amen.*

The Concluding Prayer of the Church

Lord God, almighty and everlasting Father, you have brought me in safety to this new day: Preserve me with your mighty power, that I may not fall into sin, nor be overcome by adversity; and in all I do direct me to the fulfilling of your purpose; through Jesus Christ my Lord. *Amen.*†

The Midday Office   **To Be Observed on the Hour or Half Hour**

Between 11 a.m. and 2 p.m.

The Call to Prayer

Blessed be the LORD for evermore!* Amen, I say, Amen.

Psalm 89:52

The Request for Presence

May the graciousness of the LORD our God be upon us;* prosper the work of our hands; prosper our handiwork.

Psalm 90:17

The Greeting

Blessed are you, O LORD;* instruct me in your statutes.

Psalm 119:12

The Refrain for the Midday Lessons

"I will instruct you and teach you in the way that you should go;* I will guide you with my eye."

Psalm 32:9

A Reading

'This is the covenant I shall make with the House of Israel when those days have come, YAHWEH declares. Within them I shall plant my Law, writing it on their hearts. Then I shall be their God and they will be my people. There will be no further need for everyone to teach neighbor or brother, saying, "Learn to know YAHWEH!" No, they will all know me, from the least to the greatest, YAHWEH declares, since I shall forgive their guilt and never more call their sin to mind.'

Jeremiah 31:33–34

The Refrain

"I will instruct you and teach you in the way that you should go;* I will guide you with my eye."

The Midday Psalm   *I Will Dwell in the House of the LORD*

The LORD is my shepherd;* I shall not be in want.

He makes me lie down in green pastures* and leads me beside still waters.

He revives my soul* and guides me along right pathways for his Name's sake.

Though I walk through the valley of the shadow of death, I shall fear no evil;* for you are with me; your rod and your staff, they comfort me.

You spread a table before me in the presence of those who trouble me;* you have anointed my head with oil, and my cup is running over.

Surely your goodness and mercy shall follow me all the days of my life,* and I will dwell in the house of the LORD for ever.

Psalm 23

The Refrain

"I will instruct you and teach you in the way that you should go;* I will guide you with my eye."

The Small Verse

My help is in the name of the Lord who made heaven and earth and all that is in them. Thanks be to God.

Traditional

The Lord's Prayer

The Prayer Appointed for the Week

O God, who wonderfully created, and yet more wonderfully restored, the dignity of human nature: Grant that we may share the divine life of him who humbled himself to share our humanity, your Son Jesus Christ; who lives and reigns with you, in the unity of the Holy Spirit, one God, for ever and ever. *Amen.*

The Concluding Prayer of the Church

O God, you make me glad with the weekly remembrance of the glorious resurrection of your Son my Lord: Give me this day such blessing through my worship of you, that the week to come may be spent in your favor; through Jesus Christ our Lord. *Amen.*†

The Vespers Office   **To Be Observed on the Hour or Half Hour**
Between 5 and 8 p.m.

The Call to Prayer

Sing praise to the LORD who dwells in Zion;* proclaim to the peoples the things he has done.

Psalm 9:11

The Request for Presence
To you I lift up my eyes,* to you enthroned in the heavens.

Psalm 123:1

The Greeting
I put my trust in your mercy;* my heart is joyful because of your saving help.

Psalm 13:5

The Hymn
> For all the blessings of the year,
> For all the friends we hold so dear,
> For peace on earth, both far and near,
> We thank You, Lord
>
> For life and health, those common things,
> That every day and hour brings,
> For home, where our affection clings,
> We thank You, Lord
>
> For love of Yours which never tires,
> That all our better thought inspires
> And warms our lives with heavenly fires,
> We thank You, Lord

Albert Hutchinson

The Refrain for the Vespers Lessons
The angel of the LORD encompasses those who fear him,* and he will deliver them.

Psalm 34:7

The Vespers Psalm   *Let All Flesh Bless His Holy Name*
The LORD is near to those who call upon him,* to all who call upon him faithfully.
He fulfills the desire of those who fear him;* he hears their cry and helps them.
The LORD preserves all those who love him,* but he destroys all the wicked.
My mouth shall speak the praise of the LORD;* let all flesh bless his holy Name for
    ever and ever.

Psalm 145:19–22

The Refrain
The angel of the LORD encompasses those who fear him,* and he will deliver them.

The Cry of the Church
Lord, have mercy on us. Christ, have mercy on us. Lord, have mercy on us.

The Lord's Prayer

The Prayer Appointed for the Week
O God, who wonderfully created, and yet more wonderfully restored, the dignity
    of human nature: Grant that we may share the divine life of him who humbled

himself to share our humanity, your Son Jesus Christ; who lives and reigns
with you, in the unity of the Holy Spirit, one God, for ever and ever. *Amen.*

The Concluding Prayer of the Church

Lord God, whose Son our Savior Jesus Christ, triumphed over the powers of death
and prepared for us our place in the new Jerusalem: Grant that I, who have this
day given thanks for his resurrection, may praise you in the City of which he is
the light, and where he lives and reigns for ever and ever. *Amen.*†

The Morning Office	**To Be Observed on the Hour or Half Hour**
	Between 6 and 9 a.m.

The Call to Prayer

Proclaim with me the greatness of the LORD;* let us exalt his Name together.

Psalm 34:3

The Request for Presence

Open my eyes, that I may see* the wonders of your law.

Psalm 119:18

The Greeting

I will confess you among the peoples, O LORD;* I will sing praise to you among the
nations.

For your loving-kindness is greater than the heavens,* and your faithfulness
reaches to the clouds.

Psalm 57:9–10

The Refrain for the Morning Lessons

Save us, O LORD our God, and gather us from among the nations,* that we may
give thanks to your holy Name and glory in your praise.

Psalm 106:47

A Reading   *In accordance with Jewish law, Jesus was brought by his parents
to be circumcised eight days after his birth (January 1 on our
calendar) and was named by them at that time. Most of the contemporary American church observe these simultaneous events
on January 1 either as the Feast of the Holy Name or the Feast of
the Circumcision or as the Feast of Mary, Mother of God.*

When the eighth day came and the child was to be circumcised, they gave him the
name Jesus, the name the angel had given him before his conception.

Luke 2:21

The Refrain

Save us, O LORD our God, and gather us from among the nations,* that we may
give thanks to your holy Name and glory in your praise.

The Morning Psalm   *Glory in His Holy Name*

Give thanks to the LORD and call upon his Name;* make known his deeds among
    the peoples.

Sing to him, sing praises to him,* and speak of all his marvelous works.

Glory in his holy Name;* let the hearts of those who seek the LORD rejoice.

Search for the LORD and his strength;* continually seek his face.

Remember the marvels he has done,* his wonders and the judgments of his
    mouth,

He has always been mindful of his covenant,* the promise he made for a thousand
    generations:

The covenant he made with Abraham,* the oath that he swore to Isaac,

Which he established as a statute for Jacob,* an everlasting covenant for Israel.

Psalm 105:1–5, 8–10

The Refrain

Save us, O LORD our God, and gather us from among the nations,* that we may
    give thanks to your holy Name and glory in your praise.

The Gloria

The Lord's Prayer

The Prayer Appointed for the Week

O God, who wonderfully created, and yet more wonderfully restored, the dignity
    of human nature: Grant that we may share the divine life of him who humbled
    himself to share our humanity, your Son Jesus Christ; who lives and reigns
    with you, in the unity of the Holy Spirit, one God, for ever and ever. *Amen.*

Concluding Prayers of the Church

Eternal Father, you gave to your incarnate Son the holy name of Jesus to be the
    sign of our salvation: Plant in every heart, I pray, the love of him who is the
    Savior of the world, our Lord Jesus Christ; who lives and reigns with you and
    the Holy Spirit, one God, in glory everlasting. *Amen.*†

Lord God, almighty and everlasting Father, you have brought me in safety to this
    new day: Preserve me with your mighty power, that I may not fall into sin, nor
    be overcome by adversity; and in all I do direct me to the fulfilling of your pur-
    pose; through Jesus Christ my Lord. *Amen.*†

The Midday Office   **To Be Observed on the Hour or Half Hour**
                                        Between 11 a.m. and 2 p.m.

The Call to Prayer

'Come, we will go up to YAHWEH's mountain, to the Temple of the God of Jacob so
    that he may teach us his ways and we may walk in his paths.'

Micah 4:2

The Request for Presence

Hear, O Shepherd of Israel, leading Joseph like a flock;* shine forth, you that are
  enthroned upon the cherubim.

Psalm 80:1

The Greeting

The LORD lives! Blessed is my Rock!* Exalted is the God of my salvation!

Psalm 18:46

The Refrain for the Midday Lessons

We give you thanks, O God, we give you thanks,* calling upon your Name and
  declaring all your wonderful deeds.

Psalm 75:1

A Reading

Make your own the mind of Christ Jesus: Who, being in the form of God, did not
  count equality with God something to be grasped. But he emptied himself, taking the form of a slave, becoming as human beings are; and being in every way
  like a human being, he was humbler yet, even to accepting death, death on a
  cross. And for this God raised him high, and gave him the name which is above
  all other names; so that *all beings* in the heavens, on earth and in the under-
  world, *should bend the knee* at the name of Jesus.

Philippians 2:5–10

The Refrain

We give you thanks, O God, we give you thanks,* calling upon your Name and
  declaring all your wonderful deeds.

The Midday Psalm *The Righteous Are Like Trees Planted by Streams of Water*

Happy are they who have not walked in the counsel of the wicked,* nor lingered
  in the way of sinners, nor sat in the seats of the scornful!

Their delight is in the law of the LORD,* and they meditate on his law day and
  night.

They are like trees planted by streams of water, bearing fruit in due season, with
  leaves that do not wither;* everything they do shall prosper.

It is not so with the wicked;* they are like chaff which the wind blows away.

Therefore the wicked shall not stand upright when judgment comes,* nor the
  sinner in the council of the righteous.

For the LORD knows the way of the righteous,* but the way of the wicked is
  doomed.

Psalm 1

The Refrain

We give you thanks, O God, we give you thanks,* calling upon your Name and
  declaring all your wonderful deeds.

The Gloria

The Lord's Prayer

The Prayer Appointed for the Week

O God, who wonderfully created, and yet more wonderfully restored, the dignity of human nature: Grant that we may share the divine life of him who humbled himself to share our humanity, your Son Jesus Christ; who lives and reigns with you, in the unity of the Holy Spirit, one God, for ever and ever. *Amen.*

Concluding Prayers of the Church

O God, who appointed Your only-begotten Son to be the Savior of mankind and bid that He should be called Jesus, mercifully grant that we who venerate His holy Name on earth, may also enjoy the vision of Him in heaven. Through the same Jesus Christ. *Amen.*

adapted from THE SHORT BREVIARY

O God, the source of eternal light: Shed forth your unending day upon all of us who watch for you, that our lips may praise you, our lives may bless you, and our worship may give you glory; through Jesus Christ our Lord. *Amen.†*

The Vespers Office

To Be Observed on the Hour or Half Hour Between 5 and 8 p.m.

The Call to Prayer

Come now and look upon the works of the LORD,* what awesome things he has done on earth.

Psalm 46:9

The Request for Presence

Hear my cry, O God,* and listen to my prayer.
I call upon you from the ends of the earth . . .

Psalm 61:1–2

The Greeting

Remember your word to your servant,* because you have given me hope.
This is my comfort in my trouble,* that your promise gives me life.

Psalm 119:49–50

The Hymn

Ring out the old, ring in the new,
Ring, happy bells, across the snow:
The year is going, let him go;
Ring out false, ring in the true.

Ring out a slowly dying cause,
And ancient forms of party strife;
Ring in the nobler modes of life,
With sweeter manners, purer laws.

Ring out the shapes of foul disease,
Ring out the narrowing lust of gold;
Ring out the thousand wars of old,
Ring in the thousand years of peace.

Ring in the valiant man and free,
The larger heart, the kindlier hand;
Ring out the darkness of the land,
Ring in the Christ that is to be.

Alfred, Lord Tennyson

The Refrain for the Vespers Lessons

Help us, O God our Savior, for the glory of your Name;* deliver us and forgive us
our sins, for your Name's sake.

Psalm 79:9

The Vespers Psalm   *Take Delight in the LORD*

Do not fret yourself because of evildoers;* do not be jealous of those who do
wrong.

For they shall soon wither like the grass,* and like the green grass fade away.

Put your trust in the LORD and do good;* dwell in the land and feed on its riches.

Take delight in the LORD,* and he shall give you your heart's desire.

Commit your way to the LORD and put your trust in him,* and he will bring it to
pass.

He will make your righteousness as clear as the light* and your just dealing as the
noonday.

Be still before the LORD* and wait patiently for him.

Psalm 37:1-7

The Refrain

Help us, O God our Savior, for the glory of your Name;* deliver us and forgive us
our sins, for your Name's sake.

The Gloria

The Lord's Prayer

The Prayer Appointed for the Week

O God, who wonderfully created, and yet more wonderfully restored, the dignity
of human nature: Grant that we may share the divine life of him who humbled
himself to share our humanity, your Son Jesus Christ; who lives and reigns
with you, in the unity of the Holy Spirit, one God, for ever and ever. *Amen.*

The Concluding Prayer of the Church

Grant, O Father, I pray, that whatever I do in my words, my thoughts, or my work,
I may do all in the Name of the Lord Jesus, giving thanks to you and the Holy
Spirit through Him. *Amen.*

The Morning Office   **To Be Observed on the Hour or Half Hour**
Between 6 and 9 a.m.

The Call to Prayer

Love the LORD, all you who worship him;* the LORD protects the faithful, but
repays to the full those who act haughtily.

Psalm 31:23

The Request for Presence

Early in the morning I cry out to you,* for in your word is my trust.

Psalm 119:147

The Greeting

"You are my God, and I will thank you;* you are my God, and I will exalt you."

Psalm 118:28

The Refrain for the Morning Lessons

Our help is in the Name of the LORD,* the maker of heaven and earth.

Psalm 124:8

A Reading

Of John the Baptizer it is written: "When the Jews sent to him priests and Levites from Jerusalem to ask him, 'Who are you?' He declared, he did not deny but declared, 'I am not the Christ . . . I am, as Isaiah prophesied: *A voice of one that cries out in the desert: Prepare a way for the Lord. Make his paths straight.'* Now those who had been sent were Pharisees, and they put this question to him, 'Why are you baptizing if you are not the Christ, and not Elijah, and not the Prophet?' John answered them, 'I baptize with water, but standing among you—unknown to you—is the one who is coming after me; and I am not fit to undo the strap of his sandal.' This happened at Bethany, on the far side of the Jordan, where John was baptizing."

John 1:19–20, 23–28

The Refrain

Our help is in the Name of the LORD,* the maker of heaven and earth.

The Morning Psalm　　　　　　　*Tremble, O Earth, at the Presence of the LORD*

Hallelujah! When Israel came out of Egypt,* the house of Jacob from a people of strange speech,

Judah became God's sanctuary* and Israel his dominion.

The sea beheld it and fled;* Jordan turned and went back.

The mountains skipped like rams,* and the little hills like young sheep.

What ailed you, O sea, that you fled?* O Jordan, that you turned back?

You mountains, that you skipped like rams?* you little hills like young sheep?

Tremble, O earth, at the presence of the Lord,* at the presence of the God of Jacob,

Who turned the hard rock into a pool of water* and flint-stone into a flowing spring.

Psalm 114

The Refrain

Our help is in the Name of the LORD,* the maker of heaven and earth.

The Cry of the Church

Lord, have mercy on us. Christ, have mercy on us. Lord, have mercy on us.

The Lord's Prayer

The Prayer Appointed for the Week

O God, who wonderfully created, and yet more wonderfully restored, the dignity of human nature: Grant that we may share the divine life of him who humbled himself to share our humanity, your Son Jesus Christ; who lives and reigns with you, in the unity of the Holy Spirit, one God, for ever and ever. *Amen.*

The Concluding Prayer of the Church
Lord God, almighty and everlasting Father, you have brought me in safety to this new day: Preserve me with your mighty power, that I may not fall into sin, nor be overcome by adversity; and in all I do direct me to the fulfilling of your purpose; through Jesus Christ my Lord. *Amen.*†

The Midday Office **To Be Observed on the Hour or Half Hour**
Between 11 a.m. and 2 p.m.

The Call to Prayer
Hallelujah! Give praise, you servants of the LORD;* praise the Name of the LORD.
Psalm 113:1

The Request for Presence
Hear my voice, O LORD, according to your loving-kindness;* according to your judgments, give me life.
Psalm 119:149

The Greeting
O LORD of hosts,* happy are they who put their trust in you!
Psalm 84:12

The Refrain for the Midday Lessons
With the faithful you show yourself faithful, O God;* with the forthright you show yourself forthright.
With the pure you show yourself pure,* but with the crooked you are wily.
Psalm 18:26–27

A Reading
YAHWEH said to Abram, 'Leave your country, your kindred and your father's house for a country which I shall show you; and I shall make you a great nation, I shall bless you and make your name famous; you are to be a blessing! I shall bless those who bless you, and shall curse those who curse you, and all clans on earth will bless themselves by you.' So Abram went as YAHWEH told him, and Lot went with him. Abram was seventy-five years old when he left Haran.
Genesis 12:1–4

The Refrain
With the faithful you show yourself faithful, O God;* with the forthright you show yourself forthright.
With the pure you show yourself pure,* but with the crooked you are wily.

The Midday Psalm   *May His Name Remain For Ever*

May his Name remain for ever and be established as long as the sun endures;*
    may all the nations bless themselves in him and call him blessed.
Blessed be the Lord GOD, the God of Israel,* who alone does wondrous deeds!
And blessed be his glorious Name for ever!* and may all the earth be filled with
    his glory. Amen. Amen.

Psalm 72:17–19

The Refrain

With the faithful you show yourself faithful, O God;* with the forthright you show
    yourself forthright.
With the pure you show yourself pure,* but with the crooked you are wily.

The Cry of the Church

O God, come to my assistance! O Lord, make haste to help me!

The Lord's Prayer

The Prayer Appointed for the Week

O God, who wonderfully created, and yet more wonderfully restored, the dignity
    of human nature: Grant that we may share the divine life of him who humbled
    himself to share our humanity, your Son Jesus Christ; who lives and reigns
    with you, in the unity of the Holy Spirit, one God, for ever and ever. *Amen.*

The Concluding Prayer of the Church

O Lord, my God, accept the fervent prayers of all of us your people; in the multi-
    tude of your mercies, look with compassion upon all of us who turn to you for
    help; for you are gracious, O lover of souls, and to you we give glory, Father,
    Son, and Holy Spirit, now and forever. *Amen.*†

The Vespers Office   **To Be Observed on the Hour or Half Hour**
Between 5 and 8 p.m.

The Call to Prayer

Come, let us bow down, and bend the knee,* and kneel before the LORD our
    Maker.
For he is our God,* and we are the people of his pasture and the sheep of his hand.

Psalm 95:6–7

The Request for Presence

O LORD, watch over us* and save us from this generation for ever.
The wicked prowl on every side,* and that which is worthless is highly prized by
    everyone.

Psalm 12:7–8

The Greeting

How glorious you are!* more splendid than the everlasting mountains!

Psalm 76:4

The Hymn

Blow now the trumpet, blow!
The gladly solemn sound
Let all the nations know,
To earth's remotest bound:
The year of jubilee is come!
The year of jubilee is come!
Return, you ransomed sinners, home.

Jesus, our great high priest,
Has full atonement made;
You weary spirits, rest;
You mournful souls, be glad:
The year of jubilee is come!
The year of jubilee is come!
Return, you ransomed sinners, home.

You who have sold for naught
Your heritage above
Shall have it back unbought,
The gift of Jesus' love:
The year of jubilee is come!
The year of jubilee is come!
Return, you ransomed sinners, home.

The gospel trumpet hear,
The news of heavenly grace;
And saved from earth appear
Before our Savior's face:
The year of jubilee is come!
The year of jubilee is come!
Return to your eternal home.

Charles Wesley

The Refrain for the Vespers Lessons

Tell it out among the nations: "The LORD is King!"

Psalm 96:10

The Vespers Psalm   God Will Ransom My Life

Hear this, all you peoples; hearken, all you who dwell in the world,* you of high
    degree and low, rich and poor together.
My mouth shall speak of wisdom,* and my heart shall meditate on
    understanding.
I will incline my ear to a proverb* and set forth my riddle upon the harp.
Why should I be afraid in evil days,* when the wickedness of those at my heels
    surrounds me,
The wickedness of those who put their trust in their goods,* and boast of their
    great riches?
We can never ransom ourselves,* or deliver to God the price of our life;
For the ransom of our life is so great,* that we should never have enough to pay it,
In order to live for ever and ever,* and never see the grave.
But God will ransom my life;* he will snatch me from the grasp of death.

Psalm 49:1–8, 15

The Refrain

Tell it out among the nations: "The LORD is King!"

The Gloria

The Lord's Prayer

The Prayer Appointed for the Week

O God, who wonderfully created, and yet more wonderfully restored, the dignity
    of human nature: Grant that we may share the divine life of him who humbled

himself to share our humanity, your Son Jesus Christ; who lives and reigns
with you, in the unity of the Holy Spirit, one God, for ever and ever. *Amen.*

The Concluding Prayer of the Church
Blessed be God, who has not rejected my prayer,* nor withheld his love from me.

Psalm 66:18

The Morning Office

**To Be Observed on the Hour or Half Hour
Between 6 and 9 a.m.**

The Call to Prayer
But I will call upon God,* and the LORD will deliver me.
In the evening, in the morning, and at noonday,* I will complain and lament,
He will bring me safely back . . . * God, who is enthroned of old, will hear me . . .

Psalm 55:17ff

The Request for Presence
Save me, O God, by your Name;* in your might, defend my cause.
Hear my prayer, O God;* give ear to the words of my mouth.

Psalm 54:1–2

The Greeting
I will offer you the sacrifice of thanksgiving* and call upon the Name of the LORD.

Psalm 116:15

The Refrain for the Morning Lessons
Let all flesh bless his holy Name for ever and ever.

Psalm 145:22

A Reading
Jesus taught the people, saying: "I tell you most solemnly everyone who commits
sin is a slave. Now a slave has no permanent standing in the household, but a
son belongs to it for ever. So if the Son sets you free, you will indeed be free."

John 8:34–36

The Refrain
Let all flesh bless his holy Name for ever and ever.

The Morning Psalm   *Ascribe to the LORD Glory and Strength*
Ascribe to the LORD, you gods,* ascribe to the LORD glory and strength.
Ascribe to the LORD the glory due his Name;* worship the LORD in the beauty of
holiness.
The voice of the LORD is upon the waters; the God of glory thunders;* the LORD is
upon the mighty waters.
The voice of the LORD is a powerful voice;* the voice of the LORD is a voice of
splendor.
The voice of the LORD breaks the cedar trees;* the LORD breaks the cedars of
Lebanon;

He makes Lebanon skip like a calf,* and Mount Hermon like a young wild ox.
The voice of the LORD splits the flames of fire; the voice of the LORD shakes the
    wilderness;* the LORD shakes the wilderness of Kadesh.
The voice of the LORD makes the oak trees writhe* and strips the forests bare.
And in the temple of the LORD* all are crying, "Glory!"
The LORD sits enthroned above the flood;* the LORD sits enthroned as King for
    evermore.
The LORD shall give strength to his people;* the LORD shall give his people the
    blessing of peace.

Psalm 29

The Refrain
Let all flesh bless his holy Name for ever and ever.

The Cry of the Church
O Lord, hear my prayer and let my cry come unto you. Thanks be to God.

THE SHORT BREVIARY

The Lord's Prayer

The Prayer Appointed for the Week
O God, who wonderfully created, and yet more wonderfully restored, the dignity
    of human nature: Grant that we may share the divine life of him who humbled
    himself to share our humanity, your Son Jesus Christ; who lives and reigns
    with you, in the unity of the Holy Spirit, one God, for ever and ever. *Amen.*

The Concluding Prayer of the Church
Lord God, almighty and everlasting Father, you have brought me in safety to this
    new day: Preserve me with your mighty power, that I may not fall into sin, nor
    be overcome by adversity; and in all I do direct me to the fulfilling of your pur-
    pose; through Jesus Christ my Lord. *Amen.*†

The Midday Office   **To Be Observed on the Hour or Half Hour**
                                          Between 11 a.m. and 2 p.m.

The Call to Prayer
Open my lips, O Lord,* and my mouth shall proclaim your praise.
Had you desired it, I would have offered sacrifice,* but you take no delight in
    burnt-offerings.
The sacrifice of God is a troubled spirit;* a broken and contrite heart, O God, you
    will not despise.

Psalm 51:16–18

The Request for Presence
Let your ways be known upon earth,* your saving health among all nations.

Psalm 67:2

The Greeting
I hate those who have a divided heart,* but your law do I love.

Psalm 119:113

The Refrain for the Midday Lessons
I will listen to what the LORD God is saying,* for he is speaking peace to his faithful
people and to those who turn their hearts to him.

Psalm 85:8

A Reading
To sum up the whole matter: fear God and keep his commandments, for that is the
duty of everyone.

Ecclesiates 12:13

The Refrain
I will listen to what the LORD God is saying,* for he is speaking peace to his faithful
people and to those who turn their hearts to him.

The Midday Psalm   *You Who Fear the Lord, Bless the LORD*
O LORD, your Name is everlasting;* your renown, O LORD, endures from age to
   age.
For the LORD gives his people justice* and shows compassion to his servants.
The idols of the heathen are silver and gold,* the work of human hands.
They have mouths, but they cannot speak;* eyes have they, but they cannot see.
They have ears, but they cannot hear;* neither is there any breath in their mouth.
Those who make them are like them,* and so are all who put their trust in them.
Bless the LORD, O house of Israel;* O house of Aaron, bless the LORD.
Bless the LORD, O house of Levi;* you who fear the LORD, bless the LORD.
Blessed be the LORD out of Zion,* who dwells in Jerusalem. Hallelujah!

Psalm 135:13–21

The Refrain
I will listen to what the LORD God is saying,* for he is speaking peace to his faithful
people and to those who turn their hearts to him.

The Cry of the Church
Lord, have mercy on us. Christ, have mercy on us. Lord, have mercy on us.

The Lord's Prayer

The Prayer Appointed for the Week
O God, who wonderfully created, and yet more wonderfully restored, the dignity
   of human nature: Grant that we may share the divine life of him who humbled
   himself to share our humanity, your Son Jesus Christ; who lives and reigns
   with you, in the unity of the Holy Spirit, one God, for ever and ever. *Amen.*

The Concluding Prayer of the Church
Heavenly Father, in you I live and move and have my being: I humbly pray you so
   to guide and govern me by your Holy Spirit, that in all the cares and occupa-

tions of my life I may not forget you, but may remember that I am ever walking in your sight; through Jesus Christ my Lord. *Amen.†*

The Vespers Office   **To Be Observed on the Hour or Half Hour**
Between 5 and 8 p.m.

The Call to Prayer
Bless the LORD, you angels of his, you mighty ones who do his bidding,* and hearken to the voice of his word.
Bless the LORD, all you his hosts,* you ministers of his who do his will.
Bless the LORD, all you works of his,* in all places of his dominion;

Psalm 103:20–22

The Request for Presence
LORD God of hosts, hear my prayer;* hearken, O God of Jacob.

Psalm 84:7

The Greeting
Show me your ways, O LORD,* and teach me your paths.
Lead me in your truth and teach me,* for you are the God of my salvation; in you have I trusted all the day long.

Psalm 25:3–4

The Hymn
    Songs of thankfulness and praise, Jesus, Lord, to you we raise,
    Manifested by the star to the sages from afar;
    Branch of royal David's stem in your birth at Bethlehem;
    Anthems be to you addressed, God in man made manifest.

    Manifest at Jordan's stream, Prophet, Priest, and King supreme;
    And at Cana, wedding guest, in your Godhead manifest;
    Manifest in power divine, changing water into wine;
    Anthems be to you addressed, God in man made manifest.

    Manifest in making whole palsied limbs and fainting souls;
    Manifest in valiant fight, quelling all the devil's might;
    Manifest in gracious will, ever bringing good from ill;
    Anthems be to you addressed, God in man made manifest.

Christopher Wordsworth

The Refrain for the Vespers Lessons
But it is good for me to be near God;* I have made the Lord GOD my refuge.

Psalm 73:28

The Vespers Psalm   *O Mighty King, You Have Executed Righteousness in Jacob*
The LORD is King; let the people tremble;* he is enthroned upon the cherubim; let the earth shake.
The LORD is great in Zion;* he is high above all peoples.

Let them confess his Name, which is great and awesome;* he is the Holy One.
"O mighty King, lover of justice, you have established equity;* you have executed
justice and righteousness in Jacob."

Psalm 99:1–4

The Refrain

But it is good for me to be near God;* I have made the Lord GOD my refuge.

The Small Verse

Keep me, Lord, as the apple of your eye and carry me under the shadow of your
wings.

Traditional

The Lord's Prayer

The Prayer Appointed for the Week

O God, who wonderfully created, and yet more wonderfully restored, the dignity
of human nature: Grant that we may share the divine life of him who humbled
himself to share our humanity, your Son Jesus Christ; who lives and reigns
with you, in the unity of the Holy Spirit, one God, for ever and ever. *Amen.*

The Concluding Prayer of the Church

Protect us, Lord, as we stay awake; watch over us as we sleep, that awake we may
watch with Christ, and asleep, rest in his peace. *Amen.*

The Morning Office

**To Be Observed on the Hour or Half Hour
Between 6 and 9 a.m.**

The Call to Prayer

Sing to the LORD and bless his Name;* proclaim the good news of his salvation
from day to day.
Declare his glory among the nations* and his wonders among all peoples.
For great is the LORD and greatly to be praised;* he is more to be feared than all
gods.

Psalm 96:2–4

The Request for Presence

Save me, O God,* for the waters have risen up to my neck.

Psalm 69:1

The Greeting

The LORD lives! Blessed is my Rock!* Exalted is the God of my salvation!

Psalm 18:46

The Refrain for the Morning Lessons

He looks at the earth and it trembles;* he touches the mountains and they smoke.

Psalm 104:33

A Reading   *The Feast of the Epiphany celebrates the manifestation or revealing of our Lord to the gentiles. In the contemporary Church this means an emphasis on the coming of the Magi to Bethlehem with slightly less emphasis on the baptism of Jesus by John and on His first miracle, the wedding at Cana.*

After Jesus had been born at Bethlehem in Judea during the reign of Herod, suddenly some wise men came to Jerusalem from the east asking, 'Where is the infant king of the Jews? We saw his star as it rose and have come to do him homage.' When King Herod heard this he was perturbed, and so was the whole of Jerusalem. He called together all the chief priests and the scribes of the people, and inquired of them where the Christ was to be born. They told him, 'At Bethlehem in Judea, for this is what the prophet wrote: *And you Bethlehem*, in the land of Judah, you are by no means the *least among the leaders of Judah* for *from you will come a leader* who will *shepherd* my people Israel.' Then Herod summoned the wise men to see him privately. He asked them the exact date on which the star had appeared and sent them on to Bethlehem with the words, 'Go and find out all about the child, and when you have found him, let me know, so that I too may do him homage.' Having listened to what the king had to say, they set out. And suddenly the star they had seen rising went forward and halted over the place where the child was. The sight of the star filled them with delight, and going into the house they saw the child with his mother Mary, and falling to their knees they did him homage. Then opening their treasures they offered him gifts of gold and frankincense and myrrh. But they were given warning in a dream not to go back to Herod, and returned to their own country by a different way.

Matthew 2:1–12

The Refrain
He looks at the earth and it trembles;* he touches the mountains and they smoke.

The Morning Psalm   *The Rulers of the Earth Belong to God*
Clap your hands, all you peoples;* shout to God with a cry of joy.
For the LORD Most High is to be feared;* he is the great King over all the earth.
He subdues the peoples under us,* and the nations under our feet.
He chooses our inheritance for us,* the pride of Jacob whom he loves.
God has gone up with a shout,* the LORD with the sound of the ram's-horn.
Sing praises to God, sing praises;* sing praises to our King, sing praises.
For God is King of all the earth;* sing praises with all your skill.
God reigns over the nations;* God sits upon his holy throne.
The nobles of the peoples have gathered together* with the people of the God of Abraham.
The rulers of the earth belong to God,* and he is highly exalted.

Psalm 47

The Refrain
He looks at the earth and it trembles;* he touches the mountains and they smoke.

The Cry of the Church
O God, come to my assistance! O Lord, make haste to help me!

The Lord's Prayer

The Prayer Appointed for the Week
O God, who wonderfully created, and yet more wonderfully restored, the dignity
    of human nature: Grant that we may share the divine life of him who humbled
    himself to share our humanity, your Son Jesus Christ; who lives and reigns
    with you, in the unity of the Holy Spirit, one God, for ever and ever. *Amen.*

The Concluding Prayer of the Church
Lord God, almighty and everlasting Father, you have brought me in safety to this
    new day: Preserve me with your mighty power, that I may not fall into sin, nor
    be overcome by adversity; and in all I do direct me to the fulfilling of your pur-
    pose; through Jesus Christ my Lord. *Amen.*†

The Midday Office   **To Be Observed on the Hour or Half Hour**
                                         Between 11 a.m. and 2 p.m.

The Call to Prayer
God has gone up with a shout,* the LORD with the sound of the ram's-horn.
Sing praises to God, sing praises;* sing praises to our King, sing praises.
For God is King of all the earth;* sing praises with all your skill.
God reigns over the nations;* God sits upon his holy throne.

Psalm 47:5–8

The Request for Presence
Answer me when I call, O God, defender of my cause;* you set me free when I am
    hard-pressed; have mercy on me and hear my prayer.

Psalm 4:1

The Greeting
Deliver me, my God, from the hand of the wicked,* from the clutches of the evil-
    doer and the oppressor.
For you are my hope, O Lord GOD,* my confidence since I was young.
I have been sustained by you ever since I was born;* from my mother's womb you
    have been my strength; my praise shall be always of you.

Psalm 71:4–6

The Refrain for the Midday Lessons
Your love, O LORD, for ever will I sing;* from age to age my mouth will proclaim
    your faithfulness.

Psalm 89:1

A Reading
Arise, shine out, for your light has come, and the glory of YAHWEH has risen on
    you. Look! Though night still covers the earth and darkness the peoples, on

you YAHWEH is rising and over you his glory can be seen. The nations will come to your light and kings to your dawning brightness. Lift up your eyes and look around: all are assembling and coming towards you, your sons coming from far away and your daughters being carried on the hip. At this sight you will grow radiant, your heart will throb and dilate, since the riches of the sea will flow to you, the wealth of the nations will come to you; camels in throngs will fill your streets, the young camels of Midian and Ephah; everyone in Saba will come, bringing gold and incense and proclaiming YAHWEH's praises. Why, the coasts and islands put their hope in me and the vessels of Tarshish take the lead in bringing your children from far away, and their silver and gold with them, for the sake of the name of YAHWEH your God, of the holy one of Israel who has made you glorious.

Isaiah 60:1–6, 9

The Refrain
Your love, O LORD, for ever will I sing;* from age to age my mouth will proclaim your faithfulness.

The Midday Psalm   The LORD Has Chosen Israel for His Own
Hallelujah! Praise the Name of the LORD;* give praise, you servants of the LORD.
You who stand in the house of the LORD,* in the courts of the house of our God.
Praise the LORD, for the LORD is good;* sing praises to his Name, for it is lovely.
For the LORD has chosen Jacob for himself* and Israel for his own possession.
For I know that the LORD is great,* and that our Lord is above all gods.

Psalm 135:1–5

The Refrain
Your love, O LORD, for ever will I sing;* from age to age my mouth will proclaim your faithfulness.

The Gloria

The Lord's Prayer

The Prayer Appointed for the Week
O God, who wonderfully created, and yet more wonderfully restored, the dignity of human nature: Grant that we may share the divine life of him who humbled himself to share our humanity, your Son Jesus Christ; who lives and reigns with you, in the unity of the Holy Spirit, one God, for ever and ever. *Amen.*

The Concluding Prayer of the Church
In truth God has heard me; he has attended the voice of my prayer. Thanks be to God. *Amen.*

based on Psalm 66:17

The Vespers Office   **To Be Observed on the Hour or Half Hour**
                                          Between 5 and 8 p.m.

The Call to Prayer
Bless God in the congregation;* bless the LORD, you that are of the fountain of
Israel.

Psalm 68:26

The Request for Presence
O LORD, watch over us* and save us from this generation for ever.
The wicked prowl on every side,* and that which is worthless is highly prized by
everyone.

Psalm 12:7–8

The Greeting
One generation shall praise your works to another* and shall declare your power.

Psalm 145:4

The Hymn
We three kings of Orient are, bearing gifts we traverse afar,
Field and fountain, moor and mountain, following yonder star.
O star of wonder, star of night, star with royal beauty bright;
Westward leading still proceeding, guide us to your perfect light.

Born a king on Bethlehem's plain, gold I bring to crown him again
King for ever, ceasing never over us all to reign.
O star of wonder, star of night, star with royal beauty bright;
Westward leading still proceeding, guide us to your perfect light.

Frankincense to offer have I: incense owns a Deity nigh;
Prayer and praising, gladly raising, worship him God Most High.
O star of wonder, star of night, star with royal beauty bright;
Westward leading still proceeding, guide us to your perfect light.

Myrrh is mine; its bitter perfume breathes a life of gathering gloom;
Sorrowing, sighing, bleeding, dying, sealed in the stone cold tomb.
O star of wonder, star of night, star with royal beauty bright;
Westward leading still proceeding, guide us to your perfect light.

Glorious now, behold him arise, King and God and Sacrifice;
Heaven sings alleluia: alleluia the earth replies.
O star of wonder, star of night, star with royal beauty bright;
Westward leading still proceeding, guide us to your perfect light.

John H. Hopkins, Jr.

The Refrain for the Vespers Lessons
The heaven of heavens is the LORD's,* but he entrusted the earth to its peoples.

Psalm 115:16

The Vespers Psalm   *All Kings Shall Bow Down Before Him*

In his time shall the righteous flourish;* there shall be abundance of peace till the
  moon shall be no more.

He shall rule from sea to sea,* and from the River to the ends of the earth.

His foes shall bow down before him,* and his enemies lick the dust.

The kings of Tarshish and of the isles shall pay tribute,* and the kings of Arabia
  and Saba offer gifts.

All kings shall bow down before him,* and all the nations do him service.

For he shall deliver the poor who cries out in distress,* and the oppressed who has
  no helper.

He shall have pity on the lowly and poor;* he shall preserve the lives of the needy.

He shall redeem their lives from oppression and violence,* and dear shall their
  blood be in his sight.

Long may he live! and may there be given to him gold from Arabia;* may prayer
  be made for him always, and may they bless him all the day long.

May there be abundance of grain on the earth, growing thick even on the hilltops;*
  may its fruit flourish like Lebanon, and its grain like grass upon the earth.

                                                                    Psalm 72:6–15

The Refrain
The heaven of heavens is the LORD's,* but he entrusted the earth to its peoples.

The Cry of the Church
Even so, come, Lord Jesus!

The Lord's Prayer

The Prayer Appointed for the Week
O God, who wonderfully created, and yet more wonderfully restored, the dignity
  of human nature: Grant that we may share the divine life of him who humbled
  himself to share our humanity, your Son Jesus Christ; who lives and reigns
  with you, in the unity of the Holy Spirit, one God, for ever and ever. *Amen.*

The Concluding Prayer of the Church
Grant me, I beseech thee, O merciful God, prudently to study, rightly to understand and perfectly to fulfill that which is pleasing to thee, to the praise and
  glory of thy name. Amen.

                                                                    St. Thomas Aquinas

The Morning Office   **To Be Observed on the Hour or Half Hour**
                                          Between 6 and 9 a.m.

The Call to Prayer
Search for the LORD and his strength;* continually seek his face.

                                                                    Psalm 105:4

The Request for Presence
Hearken to my voice, O LORD, when I call;* have mercy on me and answer me.
You speak in my heart and say, "Seek my face."* Your face, LORD, will I seek.
Hide not your face from me,* nor turn away your servant in displeasure.

Psalm 27:10–12

The Greeting
What terror you inspire!* who can stand before you when you are angry?

Psalm 76:7

The Refrain for the Morning Lessons
I sought the LORD, and he answered me* and delivered me out of all my terror.

Psalm 34:4

A Reading
Every year his parents used to go to Jerusalem for the feast of Passover. When he
was twelve years old, they went up to the feast as usual. When the days of the
feast were over and they set off home, the boy Jesus stayed behind in Jerusalem
without his parents knowing it. They assumed he was somewhere in the party,
and it was only after a day's journey that they went to look for him among
their relations and acquaintances. When they failed to find him they went back
to Jerusalem looking for him everywhere. It happened that, three days later,
they found him at the Temple, sitting among the teachers, listening to them,
and asking them questions; and all those who heard him were astounded at his
intelligence and his replies. They were overcome when they saw him, and his
mother said to him, 'My child, why have you done this to us? See how worried
your father and I have been, looking for you.' He replied, 'Why were you looking for me? Did you not know that I must be in my Father's house?' But they
did not understand what he meant. He went down with them then and came
to Nazareth and lived under their authority. His mother stored up all these
things in her heart. And Jesus increased in wisdom, in stature, and in favor
with God and with people.

Luke 2:41–52

The Refrain
I sought the LORD, and he answered me* and delivered me out of all my terror.

The Morning Psalm   *They Shall Sing of Your Righteous Deeds*
I will exalt you, O God my King,* and bless your Name for ever and ever.
Every day will I bless you* and praise your Name for ever and ever.
Great is the LORD and greatly to be praised;* there is no end to his greatness.
One generation shall praise your works to another* and shall declare your power.
I will ponder the glorious splendor of your majesty* and all your marvelous works.
They shall speak of the might of your wondrous acts,* and I will tell of your greatness.
They shall publish the remembrance of your great goodness;* they shall sing of
    your righteous deeds.

Psalm 145:1–7

The Refrain
I sought the LORD, and he answered me* and delivered me out of all my terror.

The Cry of the Church
Lord, have mercy on us. Christ, have mercy on us. Lord, have mercy on us.

The Lord's Prayer

The Prayer Appointed for the Week
O God, who wonderfully created, and yet more wonderfully restored, the dignity
of human nature: Grant that we may share the divine life of him who humbled
himself to share our humanity, your Son Jesus Christ; who lives and reigns
with you, in the unity of the Holy Spirit, one God, for ever and ever. *Amen.*

The Concluding Prayer of the Church
Lord God, almighty and everlasting Father, you have brought me in safety to this
new day: Preserve me with your mighty power, that I may not fall into sin, nor
be overcome by adversity; and in all I do direct me to the fulfilling of your purpose; through Jesus Christ my Lord. *Amen.*†

The Midday Office   **To Be Observed on the Hour or Half Hour
Between 11 a.m. and 2 p.m.**

The Call to Prayer
Let us bless the LORD, from this time forth for evermore. Hallelujah!
based on Psalm 115:18

The Request for Presence
Send forth your strength, O God;* establish, O God, what you have wrought
for us.
Psalm 68:28

The Greeting
I will thank you, O LORD my God, with all my heart,* and glorify your Name for
evermore.
Psalm 86:12

The Refrain for the Midday Lessons
This is the LORD's doing,* and it is marvelous in our eyes.
Psalm 118:23

A Reading
Let us examine our path, let us ponder it and return to YAHWEH. Let us raise our
hearts and hands to God in heaven. We are the ones who have sinned . . .
Lamentations 3:40–42

The Refrain
This is the LORD's doing,* and it is marvelous in our eyes.

The Midday Psalm   **God Has Spoken**

There is a river whose streams make glad the city of God,* the holy habitation of
    the Most High.

God is in the midst of her; she shall not be overthrown;* God shall help her at the
    break of day.

The nations make much ado, and the kingdoms are shaken;* God has spoken, and
    the earth shall melt away.

The LORD of hosts is with us;* the God of Jacob is our stronghold.

Psalm 46:5–8

The Refrain

This is the LORD's doing,* and it is marvelous in our eyes.

The Cry of the Church

O Lord, hear my prayer and let my cry come unto you. Thanks be to God.

THE SHORT BREVIARY

The Lord's Prayer

The Prayer Appointed for the Week

O God, who wonderfully created, and yet more wonderfully restored, the dignity
    of human nature: Grant that we may share the divine life of him who humbled
    himself to share our humanity, your Son Jesus Christ; who lives and reigns
    with you, in the unity of the Holy Spirit, one God, for ever and ever. *Amen.*

The Concluding Prayer of the Church

Lord Jesus Christ, by your death you took away the sting of death: Grant me to so
    follow in faith where you have led the way, that I may at length fall asleep
    peacefully in you and wake in your likeness; for your tender mercies' sake.
    Amen.†

The Vespers Office   **To Be Observed on the Hour or Half Hour**
                                              Between 5 and 8 p.m.

The Call to Prayer

Glory in his holy Name;* let the hearts of those who seek the LORD rejoice.

Psalm 105:3

The Request for Presence

Send forth your strength, O God;* establish, O God, what you have wrought for us.

Psalm 68:28

The Greeting

The LORD is my strength and my song,* and he has become my salvation.

Psalm 118:14

The Hymn

Fairest Lord Jesus, Ruler of all nature,
O you of God and man the Son,
You will I cherish, you will I honor,
You, my soul's glory, joy, and crown.

Fair are the meadows, fairer still the woodlands,
Robed in the blooming garb of spring:
Jesus is fairer, Jesus is purer,
Who makes the woeful heart to sing.

Fair is the sunshine, fairer still the moonlight,
And all the twinkling, starry host:
Jesus shines brighter, Jesus shines purer,
Than all the angels heaven can boast.

German

The Refrain for the Vespers Lessons

Keep watch over my life, for I am faithful;* save your servant whose trust is in you.

based on Psalm 86:2

The Vespers Psalm   *He Put a New Song in My Mouth*

I waited patiently upon the LORD;* he stooped to me and heard my cry.
He lifted me out of the desolate pit, out of the mire and clay;* he set my feet upon a
    high cliff and made my footing sure.
He put a new song in my mouth, a song of praise to our God;* many shall see, and
    stand in awe, and put their trust in the LORD.
Happy are they who trust in the LORD!

Psalm 40:1–4

The Refrain

Keep watch over my life, for I am faithful;* save your servant whose trust is in you.

The Small Verse

My help is in the Name of the Lord who made the heavens and the earth. What
    then shall I fear, of what shall I be afraid?

Traditional

The Lord's Prayer

The Prayer Appointed for the Week

O God, who wonderfully created, and yet more wonderfully restored, the dignity
    of human nature: Grant that we may share the divine life of him who humbled
    himself to share our humanity, your Son Jesus Christ; who lives and reigns
    with you, in the unity of the Holy Spirit, one God, for ever and ever. *Amen.*

Concluding Prayers of the Church

Almighty God, who has promised to hear the petitions of those who ask in your
    Son's Name: I beseech you mercifully to incline your ear to me who have made

my prayers and supplications to you; and grant that those things which I have faithfully asked according to your will, I may effectually obtain, to the relief of my necessity, and to the setting forth of your glory; through Jesus Christ my Lord. *Amen.*

May the souls of the faithful departed, through the mercy of God, rest in eternal peace. *Amen.*

The Morning Office

To Be Observed on the Hour or Half Hour Between 6 and 9 a.m.

The Call to Prayer

Sing to the LORD a new song;* sing to the LORD, all the whole earth.

Psalm 96:1

The Request for Presence

I call with my whole heart;* answer me, O LORD, that I may keep your statutes.

Psalm 119:145

The Greeting

Te Deum

Glory to you, Lord God of our fathers; you are worthy of praise; glory to you. Glory to you for the radiance of your holy Name; we will praise you and highly exalt you for ever. Glory to you in the splendor of your temple; on the throne of your majesty, glory to you. Glory to you, seated between the Cherubim; we will praise you and highly exalt you for ever. Glory to you, beholding the depths; in the high vault of heaven, glory to you. Glory to you, Father, Son, and Holy Spirit; we will praise you and highly exalt you for ever.

The Refrain for the Morning Lessons

Righteousness shall go before him,* and peace shall be a pathway for his feet.

Psalm 85:13

A Reading

Jesus answered them: "In all truth I tell you, it was not Moses who gave you bread from heaven, it is my Father who gives you bread from heaven, the true bread; for the bread of God is the bread which comes down from heaven and gives life to the world. I am the living bread which has come down from heaven. Anyone who eats this bread will live for ever; and the bread that I shall give is my flesh, for the life of the world."

John 6:32–33, 51

The Refrain

Righteousness shall go before him,* and peace shall be a pathway for his feet.

The Morning Psalm

He Has Shown Me the Wonders of His Love

How great is your goodness, O LORD! which you have laid up for those who fear you;* which you have done in the sight of all for those who put their trust in you.

You hide them in the covert of your presence from those who slander them;* you
keep them in your shelter from the strife of tongues.
Blessed be the LORD!* for he has shown me the wonders of his love in a besieged city.

Psalm 31:19–21

The Refrain
Righteousness shall go before him,* and peace shall be a pathway for his feet.

The Gloria

The Lord's Prayer

The Prayer Appointed for the Week
O God, who wonderfully created, and yet more wonderfully restored, the dignity
of human nature: Grant that we may share the divine life of him who humbled
himself to share our humanity, your Son Jesus Christ; who lives and reigns
with you, in the unity of the Holy Spirit, one God, for ever and ever. *Amen.*

The Concluding Prayer of the Church
Lord God, almighty and everlasting Father, you have brought me in safety to this
new day: Preserve me with your mighty power, that I may not fall into sin, nor
be overcome by adversity; and in all I do direct me to the fulfilling of your purpose; through Jesus Christ my Lord. *Amen.*†

The Midday Office   **To Be Observed on the Hour or Half Hour**
Between 11 a.m. and 2 p.m.

The Call to Prayer
Bless our God, you peoples;* make the voice of his praise to be heard;
Who holds our souls in life,* and will not allow our feet to slip.

Psalm 66:7–8

The Request for Presence
Let your ways be known upon earth,* your saving health among all nations.

Psalm 67:2

The Greeting
How great is your goodness, O LORD! which you have laid up for those who fear
you;* which you have done in the sight of all for those who put their trust in you.

Psalm 31:19

The Refrain for the Midday Lessons
Your love, O LORD, reaches to the heavens,* and your faithfulness to the clouds.

Psalm 36:5

A Reading
I am coming to gather every nation and every language. They will come to witness
my glory. I shall give them a sign and send some of their survivors to the nations:
to Tarshish, Put, Lud, Meshech, Tubal and Javan, to the distant coasts and islands

that have never heard of me or seen my glory. They will proclaim my glory to the nations, and from all the nations they will bring all your brothers as an offering to YAHWEH, on horses, in chariots, in litters, on mules and on camels, to my holy mountain, Jerusalem, YAHWEH says, like Israelites bringing offerings in clean vessels to YAHWEH's house. And some of them I shall make into priests and Levites, YAHWEH says. For as the new heavens and the new earth I am making will endure before me, declares YAHWEH, so will your race and your name endure.

Isaiah 66:18–23

The Refrain
Your love, O LORD, reaches to the heavens,* and your faithfulness to the clouds.

The Midday Psalm   The Word of the LORD Is Sure
Rejoice in the LORD, you righteous;* it is good for the just to sing praises.
Praise the LORD with the harp;* play to him upon the psaltery and lyre.
Sing for him a new song;* sound a fanfare with all your skill upon the trumpet.
For the word of the LORD is right,* and all his works are sure.
He loves righteousness and justice;* the loving-kindness of the LORD fills the
    whole earth.

Psalm 33:1–5

The Refrain
Your love, O LORD, reaches to the heavens,* and your faithfulness to the clouds.

The Small Verse
My help is in the name of the Lord who made heaven and earth and all that is in
    them. Thanks be to God.

Traditional

The Lord's Prayer

The Prayer Appointed for the Week
O God, who wonderfully created, and yet more wonderfully restored, the dignity
    of human nature: Grant that we may share the divine life of him who humbled
    himself to share our humanity, your Son Jesus Christ; who lives and reigns
    with you, in the unity of the Holy Spirit, one God, for ever and ever. *Amen.*

The Concluding Prayer of the Church
O God, the source of eternal light: Shed forth your unending day upon all of us
    who watch for you, that our lips may praise you, our lives may bless you, and
    our worship may give you glory; through Jesus Christ our Lord. *Amen.*†

The Vespers Office   To Be Observed on the Hour or Half Hour
                                                    Between 5 and 8 p.m.

The Call to Prayer
Behold now, bless the LORD, all you servants of the LORD,* you that stand by night
    in the house of the LORD.

Psalm 134:1

The Request for Presence
My soul waits for the LORD, more than watchmen for the morning,* more than
 watchmen for the morning.

Psalm 130:5

The Greeting
You, O LORD, are my lamp;* my God, you make my darkness bright.
With you I will break down an enclosure;* with the help of my God I will scale any
 wall.

Psalm 18:29–30

The Hymn
We would see Jesus, lo! His star is shining
Above the stable while the angels sing;
There in a manger on the hay reclining;
Haste, let us lay our gifts before the King.

We would see Jesus, Mary's son most holy,
Light of the village life from day to day;
Shining revealed through every task most lowly,
The Christ of God, the life, the truth, the way.

We would see Jesus, on the mountain teaching,
With all the listening people gathered round;
While birds and flowers and sky above are preaching
The blessedness which simple trust has found.

We would see Jesus, in his work of healing,
At eventide before the sun was set;
Divine and human, in his deep revealing
Of God made flesh, in loving service met.

We would see Jesus, in the early morning,
Still as his fold he calls, "Follow me!"
Let us arise, all meaner service scorning,
Lord, we are yours, and give ourselves to Thee.

J. Edgar Park

The Refrain for the Vespers Lessons
I lie down and go to sleep;* I wake again, because the LORD sustains me.

Psalm 3:5

The Vespers Psalm   For God Alone My Soul in Silence Waits
For God alone my soul in silence waits;* truly, my hope is in him.
He alone is my rock and my salvation,* my stronghold, so that I shall not be
 shaken.
In God is my safety and my honor;* God is my strong rock and my refuge.
Put your trust in him always, O people,* pour out your hearts before him, for God
 is our refuge.

Psalm 62:6–9

The Refrain
I lie down and go to sleep;* I wake again, because the Lord sustains me.

The Cry of the Church
O Lamb of God, that takes away the sins of the world, have mercy upon me.
O Lamb of God, that takes away the sins of the world, have mercy upon me.
O Lamb of God, that takes away the sins of the world, grant me your peace.

The Lord's Prayer

The Prayer Appointed for the Week
O God, who wonderfully created, and yet more wonderfully restored, the dignity
of human nature: Grant that we may share the divine life of him who humbled
himself to share our humanity, your Son Jesus Christ; who lives and reigns
with you, in the unity of the Holy Spirit, one God, for ever and ever. *Amen.*

The Concluding Prayer of the Church
Almighty God, who after the creation of the world rested from all your works and
sanctified a day of rest for all your creatures: Grant that I, putting away all
earthly anxieties, may be duly prepared for the service of public worship, and
grant as well that my Sabbath upon earth may be a preparation for the eternal
rest promised to your people in heaven; through Jesus Christ our Lord. *Amen.*†

January Compline

Sunday
The Night Office   **To Be Observed Before Retiring**

The Call to Prayer
May the Lord Almighty grant me and those I love a peaceful night and a perfect
    end. *Amen.*†

The Request for Presence
Our help is in the Name of the Lord; the maker of heaven and earth.

The Greeting
Almighty God, my heavenly Father: I have sinned against you, through my own
    fault, in thought, and word, and deed, in what I have done and what I have left
    undone. For the sake of your Son our Lord Jesus Christ, forgive me all my
    offenses; and grant that I may serve you in newness of life, to the glory of your
    Name. *Amen.*†

The Reading
So you are no longer aliens or foreign visitors; you are fellow citizens with the
    holy people of God and part of God's household. You are built upon the foun-
    dations of the apostles and prophets, and Christ Jesus himself is the corner-
    stone. Every structure knit together in him grows into a holy temple in the
    Lord; and you too, in him, are being built up into a dwelling-place of God in
    the Spirit.

Ephesians 2:19–22

The Gloria

The Psalm   *Tell It Out Among the Nations*
Oh, the majesty and magnificence of his presence!* Oh, the power and the
    splendor of his sanctuary!
Ascribe to the LORD, you families of the peoples;* ascribe to the LORD honor and
    power.
Ascribe to the LORD the honor due his Name;* bring offerings and come into his
    courts.
Worship the LORD in the beauty of holiness;* let the whole earth tremble before
    him.
Tell it out among the nations: "The LORD is King!* he has made the world so firm
    that it cannot be moved; he will judge the peoples with equity."

Psalm 96:6–10

The Gloria

The Small Verse
Into your hands, O Lord, I commend my spirit; for you have redeemed me, O
    Lord, O God of truth. Keep me, O Lord, as the apple of your eye; hide me
    under the shadow of your wings.†

The Lord's Prayer

The Petition

Watch, O Lord, with those who wake, or watch, or weep tonight, and give Your
angels and saints charge over those who sleep. Tend Your sick ones, O Lord
Christ. Rest Your weary ones. Bless Your dying ones. Soothe Your suffering
ones. Shield Your joyous ones, and all for Your love's sake. *Amen.*§

The Final Thanksgiving

Lord, you now have set your servant free to go in peace as you have promised; for
these eyes of mine have seen the Savior, whom you have prepared for all the
world to see: a Light to enlighten the nations, and the glory of your people
Israel. Glory to the Father, and to the Son, and to the Holy Spirit: as it was in the
beginning, is now, and will be for ever. *Amen.*

Monday
The Night Office   To Be Observed Before Retiring

The Call to Prayer

May the Lord Almighty grant me and those I love a peaceful night and a perfect
end. *Amen.*†

The Request for Presence

Our help is in the Name of the Lord; the maker of heaven and earth.

The Greeting

Almighty God, my heavenly Father: I have sinned against you, through my own
fault, in thought, and word, and deed, in what I have done and what I have left
undone. For the sake of your Son our Lord Jesus Christ, forgive me all my
offenses; and grant that I may serve you in newness of life, to the glory of your
Name. *Amen.*†

The Reading

He comes to us as One unknown, without a name, as of old, by the lakeside, He
came to those men who knew Him not. He speaks to us the same word:
"Follow thou me!" and sets us the tasks which he has to fulfill for our time. He
commands. And to those who obey Him, whether they be wise or simple, He
will reveal Himself in the toils, the conflicts, the sufferings which they will pass
through in his fellowship, and, as an ineffable mystery, they shall learn in their
own experience Who He is.

Albert Schweitzer

The Gloria

The Psalm   *Serve the Lord with Gladness*

Be joyful in the Lord, all you lands;* serve the Lord with gladness and come
before his presence with a song.
Know this: The Lord himself is God;* he himself has made us, and we are his; we
are his people and the sheep of his pasture.

Enter his gates with thanksgiving; go into his courts with praise;* give thanks to
  him and call upon his Name.
For the LORD is good; his mercy is everlasting;* and his faithfulness endures from
  age to age.

Psalm 100

The Gloria

The Small Verse
Into your hands, O Lord, I commend my spirit; for you have redeemed me, O
  Lord, O God of truth. Keep me, O Lord, as the apple of your eye; hide me
  under the shadow of your wings.†

The Lord's Prayer

The Petition
Watch, O Lord, with those who wake, or watch, or weep tonight, and give Your
  angels and saints charge over those who sleep. Tend Your sick ones, O Lord
  Christ. Rest Your weary ones. Bless Your dying ones. Soothe Your suffering
  ones. Shield Your joyous ones, and all for Your love's sake. *Amen.*§

The Final Thanksgiving
Lord, you now have set your servant free to go in peace as you have promised; for
  these eyes of mine have seen the Savior, whom you have prepared for all the
  world to see: a Light to enlighten the nations, and the glory of your people
  Israel. Glory to the Father, and to the Son, and to the Holy Spirit: as it was in the
  beginning, is now, and will be for ever. *Amen.*

Tuesday
The Night Office   To Be Observed Before Retiring

The Call to Prayer
May the Lord Almighty grant me and those I love a peaceful night and a perfect
  end. *Amen.*†

The Request for Presence
Our help is in the Name of the Lord; the maker of heaven and earth.

The Greeting
Almighty God, my heavenly Father: I have sinned against you, through my own
  fault, in thought, and word, and deed, in what I have done and what I have left
  undone. For the sake of your Son our Lord Jesus Christ, forgive me all my
  offenses; and grant that I may serve you in newness of life, to the glory of your
  Name. *Amen.*†

The Reading   *Pied Beauty*
  Glory be to God for dappled things—
  For skies of couple-colour as a brindled cow;

For rose-moles all in stipple upon trout that swim;
Fresh-firecoal chestnut-falls; finches' wings;
Landscape plotted and pieced-fold, fallow and plough;
And all trades, their gear and tackle and trim.
All things counter, original, spare, strange;
Whatever is fickle, freckled (who knows how?)
With swift, slow; sweet, sour; adazzle dim;
He fathers-forth whose beauty is past change:
Praise him.

Gerard M. Hopkins

The Gloria

The Psalm   *Your Paths Overflow with Plenty*
Those who dwell at the ends of the earth will tremble at your marvelous signs;*
   you make the dawn and the dusk to sing for joy.
You visit the earth and water it abundantly; you make it very plenteous;* the river
   of God is full of water.
You prepare the grain,* for so you provide for the earth.
You drench the furrows and smooth out the ridges;* with heavy rain you soften
   the ground and bless its increase.
You crown the year with your goodness,* and your paths overflow with plenty.
May the fields of the wilderness be rich for grazing,* and the hills be clothed with joy.
May the meadows cover themselves with flocks, and the valleys cloak themselves
   with grain;* let them shout for joy and sing.

Psalm 65:8–14

The Gloria

The Small Verse
Into your hands, O Lord, I commend my spirit; for you have redeemed me, O
   Lord, O God of truth. Keep me, O Lord, as the apple of your eye; hide me
   under the shadow of your wings.†

The Lord's Prayer

The Petition
Watch, O Lord, with those who wake, or watch, or weep tonight, and give Your
   angels and saints charge over those who sleep. Tend Your sick ones, O Lord
   Christ. Rest Your weary ones. Bless Your dying ones. Soothe Your suffering
   ones. Shield Your joyous ones, and all for Your love's sake. *Amen.*§

The Final Thanksgiving
Lord, you now have set your servant free to go in peace as you have promised; for
   these eyes of mine have seen the Savior, whom you have prepared for all the
   world to see: a Light to enlighten the nations, and the glory of your people
   Israel. Glory to the Father, and to the Son, and to the Holy Spirit: as it was in the
   beginning, is now, and will be for ever. *Amen.*

Wednesday
The Night Office   **To Be Observed Before Retiring**

The Call to Prayer
May the Lord Almighty grant me and those I love a peaceful night and a perfect
    end. *Amen.*†

The Request for Presence
Our help is in the Name of the Lord; the maker of heaven and earth.

The Greeting
Almighty God, my heavenly Father: I have sinned against you, through my own
    fault, in thought, and word, and deed, in what I have done and what I have left
    undone. For the sake of your Son our Lord Jesus Christ, forgive me all my
    offenses; and grant that I may serve you in newness of life, to the glory of your
    Name. *Amen.*†

The Reading
There is no greater proof in the world of our spiritual danger than the reluctance
    which most people always have and all people sometimes have to pray; so
    weary of their length, so glad when they are done, so clever to excuse and
    neglect their opportunity. Yet prayer is nothing but desiring God to give us the
    greatest and best things we can have and that can make us happy. It is a work
    so easy, so honorable, and to so great a purpose, that (except in the incarnation
    of His Son) God has never given us a greater argument of His willingness to
    have us saved and our unwillingness to accept it, of His goodness and our
    gracelessness, of His infinite condescension and our folly, than by rewarding so
    easy a duty with such great blessings.

Jeremy Taylor

The Gloria

The Psalm
O Lord, you are my shepherd;
I shall not want.
You make me lie down
In green pastures;
You lead me beside still waters.
You restore my soul;
You lead me in paths of righteousness
For your name's sake.
Even though I walk
Through the darkest valley,
I will fear no evil;
For you are with me;
Your rod and your staff—
They comfort me.
You prepare a table before me

In the presence of my enemies;
You anoint my head with oil;
My cup overflows.
Surely, goodness and mercy
Shall follow me
All the days of my life,
And I shall dwell in your house, O Lord,
My whole life long.❖

The Gloria

The Small Verse
Into your hands, O Lord, I commend my spirit; for you have redeemed me, O
   Lord, O God of truth. Keep me, O Lord, as the apple of your eye; hide me
   under the shadow of your wings.†

The Lord's Prayer

The Petition
Watch, O Lord, with those who wake, or watch, or weep tonight, and give Your
   angels and saints charge over those who sleep. Tend Your sick ones, O Lord
   Christ. Rest Your weary ones. Bless Your dying ones. Soothe Your suffering
   ones. Shield Your joyous ones, and all for Your love's sake. *Amen.*§

The Final Thanksgiving
Lord, you now have set your servant free to go in peace as you have promised; for
   these eyes of mine have seen the Savior, whom you have prepared for all the
   world to see: a Light to enlighten the nations, and the glory of your people
   Israel. Glory to the Father, and to the Son, and to the Holy Spirit: as it was in the
   beginning, is now, and will be for ever. *Amen.*

Thursday
The Night Office   **To Be Observed Before Retiring**

The Call to Prayer
May the Lord Almighty grant me and those I love a peaceful night and a perfect
   end. *Amen.*†

The Request for Presence
Our help is in the Name of the Lord; the maker of heaven and earth.

The Greeting
Almighty God, my heavenly Father: I have sinned against you, through my own
   fault, in thought, and word, and deed, in what I have done and what I have left
   undone. For the sake of your Son our Lord Jesus Christ, forgive me all my
   offenses; and grant that I may serve you in newness of life, to the glory of your
   Name. *Amen.*†

The Reading   *Two Went Up into the Temple to Pray*

Two went up to pray? or rather say
One went to brag, th' other to pray;

One stands up close and treads on high,
Where th' other dares not send his eye.

One nearer to God's altar trod,
The other to the altar's God.

Richard Crashaw

The Gloria

The Psalm   *Eagerly I Seek You*

O God, you are my God; eagerly I seek you;* my soul thirsts for you, my flesh
   faints for you, as in a barren and dry land where there is no water.
Therefore I have gazed upon you in your holy place,* that I might behold your
   power and your glory.
For your loving-kindness is better than life itself;* my lips shall give you praise.
So will I bless you as long as I live* and lift up my hands in your Name.
My soul is content, as with marrow and fatness,* and my mouth praises you with
   joyful lips,
When I remember you upon my bed,* and meditate on you in the night watches.
For you have been my helper,* and under the shadow of your wings I will rejoice.
My soul clings to you;* your right hand holds me fast.

Psalm 63:1–8

The Gloria

The Small Verse

Into your hands, O Lord, I commend my spirit; for you have redeemed me, O
   Lord, O God of truth. Keep me, O Lord, as the apple of your eye; hide me
   under the shadow of your wings.†

The Lord's Prayer

The Petition

Watch, O Lord, with those who wake, or watch, or weep tonight, and give Your
   angels and saints charge over those who sleep. Tend Your sick ones, O Lord
   Christ. Rest Your weary ones. Bless Your dying ones. Soothe Your suffering
   ones. Shield Your joyous ones, and all for Your love's sake. *Amen.*§

The Final Thanksgiving

Lord, you now have set your servant free to go in peace as you have promised; for
   these eyes of mine have seen the Savior, whom you have prepared for all the
   world to see: a Light to enlighten the nations, and the glory of your people
   Israel. Glory to the Father, and to the Son, and to the Holy Spirit: as it was in the
   beginning, is now, and will be for ever. *Amen.*

Friday
The Night Office   To Be Observed Before Retiring

The Call to Prayer
May the Lord Almighty grant me and those I love a peaceful night and a perfect
    end. *Amen.*†

The Request for Presence
Our help is in the Name of the Lord; the maker of heaven and earth.

The Greeting
Almighty God, my heavenly Father: I have sinned against you, through my own
    fault, in thought, and word, and deed, in what I have done and what I have left
    undone. For the sake of your Son our Lord Jesus Christ, forgive me all my
    offenses; and grant that I may serve you in newness of life, to the glory of your
    Name. *Amen.*†

The Reading   *Litany of Penitence*
Most holy and merciful Father:
I confess to you and to the whole communion of saints in heaven and on earth.
I have not loved you with my whole heart, and mind, and strength. I have not
    loved my neighbors as myself. I have not forgiven others, as I have been for-
    given.
Have mercy on me, Lord.
I have been deaf to your call to serve, as Christ served us. I have not been true to
    the mind of Christ. I have grieved your Holy Spirit.
Have mercy on me, Lord.
I confess to you, Lord, all my past unfaithfulness: the pride, hypocrisy, and impa-
    tience of my life,
I confess to you, Lord.
My self-indulgent appetites and ways, and my exploitation of other people,
I confess to you, Lord.
My anger at my own frustration, and my envy of those more fortunate than I,
I confess to you, Lord.
My intemperate love of worldly goods and comforts, and my dishonesty in daily
    life and work,
I confess to you, Lord.
My negligence in prayer and worship, and my failure to commend the faith that is
    in me,
I confess to you, Lord.
Accept my repentance, Lord, for the wrongs I have done: for my blindness to
    human need and suffering, and my indifference to injustice and cruelty,
Accept my repentance, Lord.
For all false judgments, for uncharitable thoughts toward my neighbors, and for
    my prejudice and contempt toward those who differ from me,

Accept my repentance, Lord.

For my waste and pollution of your creation, and my lack of concern for those
  who come after us,

Accept my repentance, Lord.

Restore me, good Lord, and let your anger depart from me,

Favorably hear me for your mercy is great.

Accomplish in me and all of your church the work of your salvation,

That I may show forth your glory in the world.

By the cross and passion of your Son our Lord,

Bring me with all your saints to the joy of his resurrection.†

The Gloria

The Psalm   *Teach Us to Number Our Days*

Our iniquities you have set before you,* and our secret sins in the light of your
  countenance.

When you are angry, all our days are gone;* we bring our years to an end like a
  sigh.

The span of our life is seventy years, perhaps in strength even eighty;* yet the sum
  of them is but labor and sorrow, for they pass away quickly and we are gone.

Who regards the power of your wrath?* who rightly fears your indignation?

So teach us to number our days* that we may apply our hearts to wisdom.

Psalm 90:8–12

The Gloria

The Small Verse

Into your hands, O Lord, I commend my spirit; for you have redeemed me, O
  Lord, O God of truth. Keep me, O Lord, as the apple of your eye; hide me
  under the shadow of your wings.†

The Lord's Prayer

The Petition

Watch, O Lord, with those who wake, or watch, or weep tonight, and give Your
  angels and saints charge over those who sleep. Tend Your sick ones, O Lord
  Christ. Rest Your weary ones. Bless Your dying ones. Soothe Your suffering
  ones. Shield Your joyous ones, and all for Your love's sake. *Amen.*§

The Final Thanksgiving

Lord, you now have set your servant free to go in peace as you have promised; for
  these eyes of mine have seen the Savior, whom you have prepared for all the
  world to see: a Light to enlighten the nations, and the glory of your people
  Israel. Glory to the Father, and to the Son, and to the Holy Spirit: as it was in the
  beginning, is now, and will be for ever. *Amen.*

Saturday
The Night Office To Be Observed Before Retiring

The Call to Prayer
May the Lord Almighty grant me and those I love a peaceful night and a perfect
end. *Amen.*†

The Request for Presence
Our help is in the Name of the Lord; the maker of heaven and earth.

The Greeting
Almighty God, my heavenly Father: I have sinned against you, through my own
fault, in thought, and word, and deed, in what I have done and what I have left
undone. For the sake of your Son our Lord Jesus Christ, forgive me all my
offenses; and grant that I may serve you in newness of life, to the glory of your
Name. *Amen.*†

The Reading *The Apostles' Creed*
I believe in God, the Father almighty,
Maker of heaven and earth;
And in Jesus Christ his only Son our Lord;
Who was conceived by the Holy Ghost,
Born of the Virgin Mary,
Suffered under Pontius Pilate,
Was crucified, died and was buried.
He descended into hell.
On the third day he rose again from the dead.
He ascended into heaven,
And sits on the right hand of God the Father almighty.
From thence he shall come to judge the quick and the dead.
I believe in the Holy Ghost,
The holy catholic Church,
The communion of saints,
The forgiveness of sins,
The resurrection of the body,
And the life everlasting. *Amen.*†

The Gloria

The Psalm *What Our Forefathers Have Told Us*
We Will Not Hide from Their Children
Hear my teaching, O my people;* incline your ears to the words of my mouth.
I will open my mouth in a parable,* I will declare the mysteries of ancient times.
That which we have heard and known, and what our forefathers have told us,* we
will not hide from their children.
We will recount to generations to come the praiseworthy deeds and the power of
the LORD,* and the wonderful works he has done.

He gave his decrees to Jacob and established a law for Israel,* which he
    commanded them to teach their children;
That the generations to come might know, and the children yet unborn;* that they
    in their turn might tell it to their children;
So that they might put their trust in God,* and not forget the deeds of God, but
    keep his commandments;
And not be like their forefathers, a stubborn and rebellious generation,* a
    generation whose heart was not steadfast, and whose spirit was not faithful to
    God.

Psalm 78:1–8

The Gloria

The Small Verse
Into your hands, O Lord, I commend my spirit; for you have redeemed me, O
    Lord, O God of truth. Keep me, O Lord, as the apple of your eye; hide me
    under the shadow of your wings.†

The Lord's Prayer

The Petition
Watch, O Lord, with those who wake, or watch, or weep tonight, and give Your
    angels and saints charge over those who sleep. Tend Your sick ones, O Lord
    Christ. Rest Your weary ones. Bless Your dying ones. Soothe Your suffering
    ones. Shield Your joyous ones, and all for Your love's sake. *Amen.*§

The Final Thanksgiving
Lord, you now have set your servant free to go in peace as you have promised; for
    these eyes of mine have seen the Savior, whom you have prepared for all the
    world to see: a Light to enlighten the nations, and the glory of your people
    Israel. Glory to the Father, and to the Son, and to the Holy Spirit: as it was in the
    beginning, is now, and will be for ever. *Amen.*

Acknowledgments

"The Angels Will Deliver Us" from *An African Prayer Book* by Desmond Tutu. Copyright 1997 by Doubleday. Used by permission.

"God, You Have Prepared in Peace the Path" from *An African Prayer Book* by Desmond Tutu. Copyright 1997 by Doubleday. Used by permission.

"He Comes as One Unknown" by Albert Schweitzer from *Gospel: the Life of Jesus as Told by the World's Greatest Writers*, compiled by Constance & Daniel Pollock. Copyright 1998 by Word Publishing. Used by permission.

"Help Each One of Us, Gracious Father/Prayer from China" from *Another Day: Prayers of the Human Family*, compiled by John Carden. Copyright 1986 by Church Missionary Society.

"Late Have I Loved Thee" from *An African Prayer Book* by Desmond Tutu. Copyright 1997 by Doubleday. Used by permission.

"A Mind to Know You" from *Speaking to God* by Nancy Benvenga. Copyright 1993 by Ave Maria Press. Used by Permission.

"O Lord, You Are My Shepherd" from *Awake My Heart* by Fred Bassett. Copyright 1998 by Paraclete Press. Used by permission.

"The Privilege Is Ours to Share in the Loving" from *An African Prayer Book* by Desmond Tutu. Copyright 1997 by Doubleday. Used by permission.

"Two Went Up into the Temple to Pray" by Richard Crashaw from *Gospel: The Life of Jesus as Told by the World's Greatest Writers* compiled by Constance & Daniel Pollock. Copyright 1998 by Word Publishing. Used by permission.

Excerpts from *Creative Prayer* by Brigid Herman. Copyright 1998 by Paraclete Press. Used by permission.

Excerpts from *The Doubleday Christian Quotation Collection* selected and arranged by Hannah Ward and Jennifer Wild. Copyright 1997 by Doubleday. Used by permission.

Excerpts from *The Doubleday Prayer Collection* selected and arranged by Mary Batchelor. Copyright 1997 by Doubleday. Used by permission.

Excerpts from *Holy Living* by Jeremy Taylor. Copyright 1988 by Paraclete Press. Used by permission.

Excerpts from *The Hours of the Divine Office in English and Latin* prepared by the staff of Liturgical Press. Copyright 1963 by The Liturgical Press. Used by permission.

Excerpts from *Imitation of Christ* (Thomas à Kempis) edited by Hal M. Helms. Copyright 1982 by Paraclete Press. Used by permission.

Excerpts from *The Joy of Full Surrender* (Jean-Pierre de Caussade) edited by Hal M. Helms. Copyright 1986 by Paraclete Press. Used by permission.

Excerpts from *Liturgy of the Hours, Vol. III* by International Commission on English in the Liturgy. Copyright 1974 by International Commission on English in the Liturgy. Used by permission.

Excerpts from *New Companion to the Breviary*. Copyright 1988 by the Carmelites of Indianapolis, Indiana. Used by permission.

Excerpts from *The Oxford Book of Prayer* edited by George Appleton. Copyright 1985 by Oxford University Press. Used by permission.

Excerpts from *Praying with Mary* by Janice Connell. Copyright 1997 by HarperCollins Publishers. Used by permission.

Excerpts from *Sacred Poems and Prayers of Love* edited by Mary Ford-Grabowsky. Copyright 1998 by Doubleday. Used by permission.

Excerpts from *A Short Breviary* edited by The Monks of St. John's Abbey. Copyright 1949 by St. John's Abbey. Used by permission of The Liturgical Press.

All verses, other than Psalms, are excerpted from *The New Jerusalem Bible* unless otherwise noted.

All verses from Psalms are excerpted from *The Book of Common Prayer* unless otherwise noted.

KJV refers to verses excerpted from the King James Version of the Bible.

Notes

Notes

_____
_____
_____
_____
_____
_____
_____
_____
_____
_____
_____
_____
_____
_____
_____
_____
_____
_____
_____
_____
_____
_____

Notes

Notes

Notes

Notes

Notes

© Peter Murphy

PHYLLIS TICKLE is Contributing Editor in Religion for *Publishers Weekly*. One of America's most respected authorities on religion, she is frequently interviewed for both print and electronic media and is a regular guest on PBS's *Religion & Ethics NewsWeekly*. The author of more than two dozen books, including the recently published *The Divine Hours*, she lives in Lucy, Tennessee.